TEN YEARS AT HITLER'S SIDE

THE TESTIMONY OF WILHELM KEITEL

TEN YEARS AT HITLER'S SIDE

THE TESTIMONY OF WILHELM KEITEL

EDITED AND INTRODUCED
BY BOB CARRUTHERS

Pen & Sword
MILITARY

This edition published in 2018 by

Pen & Sword Military
An imprint of
Pen & Sword Books Ltd
47 Church Street
Barnsley
South Yorkshire
S70 2AS

Copyright © Coda Books Ltd. 2018.
Published under licence by Pen & Sword Books Ltd.

ISBN: 9781473868922

A CIP catalogue record for this book is available from the British Library.

All rights reserved. No part of this book may be reproduced or transmitted in any form or by any means, electronic or mechanical including photocopying, recording or by any information storage and retrieval system, without permission from the Publisher in writing.

Printed and bound in England
By CPI Group (UK) Ltd, Croydon, CR0 4YY

Pen & Sword Books Ltd incorporates the imprints of Pen & Sword Aviation, Pen & Sword Family History, Pen & Sword Maritime, Pen & Sword Military, Pen & Sword Discovery, Pen & Sword Politics, Pen & Sword Atlas, Pen & Sword Archaeology, Wharncliffe Local History, Wharncliffe True Crime, Wharncliffe Transport, Pen & Sword Select, Pen & Sword Military Classics, Leo Cooper, The Praetorian Press, Claymore Press, Remember When, Seaforth Publishing and Frontline Publishing

For a complete list of Pen & Sword titles please contact
PEN & SWORD BOOKS LIMITED
47 Church Street, Barnsley, South Yorkshire, S70 2AS, England
E-mail: enquiries@pen-and-sword.co.uk
Website: www.pen-and-sword.co.uk

CONTENTS

INTRODUCTION 9

NUREMBERG TRIAL PROCEEDINGS

WEDNESDAY, 3 APRIL 1946
    MORNING SESSION 11
    AFTERNOON SESSION 27

THURSDAY, 4 APRIL 1946
    MORNING SESSION 65
    AFTERNOON SESSION 103

FRIDAY, 5 APRIL 1946
    MORNING SESSION 132
    AFTERNOON SESSION 169

SATURDAY, 6 APRIL 1946
    MORNING SESSION 220

INTRODUCTION

'I began my term as prisoner of war on 13 May 1945, at Mondorf. I was transferred to a prison cell at Nuremberg on the 13 August, and am awaiting my execution on 13 October 1946. I never dreamed that such a Via Dolorosa lay ahead of me, with this tragic end at Nuremberg.

How often I have found myself seriously confronted with suicide as a possible way out, only to reject it because, as suicides have always demonstrated, nothing is changed and nothing bettered by such action. Quite the contrary, the armed forces, whose counsellor and mediator I had so often been, would have labelled me a deserter and branded me a coward.

Hitler himself chose death rather than accept responsibility for the actions of the OKW, of Colonel-General Jodl and myself. I do not doubt that he would have done us justice and identified himself wholly with my utterances. But for him, as I learned only later, to have committed suicide when he knew he was defeated, shunning thereby his own ultimate personal responsibility, upon which he had always laid such great stress, and which he had unreservedly taken upon himself alone, instead of giving himself up to the enemy, and to have left it to a subordinate to account for his autocratic and arbitrary actions, these two shortcomings will remain forever incomprehensible to me. They are my final disillusion.'

Those were the last written words of Field Marshal Wilhelm Keitel, Chief of Staff to the *Führer* and Chief of the OKW, *Oberkommando der Wehrmacht*. How different they were from the heady days of late June 1940, when the jubilant crowds that flocked the streets of Berlin and Munich to celebrate the surrender of France hailed Adolf Hitler as a great German hero. The crowds ecstatically proclaimed Hitler as the architect of the most stunning victory the world had ever seen and the man who was then *Generaloberst* Wilhelm Keitel, who dubbed Hitler 'the greatest general of all time', elevated the febrile atmosphere further. With his enthusiastic endorsement of Hitler, General Keitel was feeding the Nazi propaganda machine. In the hands of Dr. Goebbels the full force of a modern media was harnessed to constantly bolster and reinforce the party line. The Nazi propaganda effort depicted Hitler as a bold front-line trench warrior, and the rightful leader of the *Nationalsocializter Deutscher Frontkämpferbund*. Hitler was keen to embrace this hardened military image, as he felt it would bring him closer to achieving acceptance into the ranks of the *Frontgemeinschaft* (the brotherhood of front-line fighters), a privilege his experience as a trench messenger had not afforded him.

Ultimately, Hitler was to be thwarted and acceptance into the *Kameradschaft* would never be his to enjoy. Just five years after his triumphal visit to France he would die a coward's death by his own hand, leaving the front-line fighters of the Wehrmacht to soldier on; fighting a war that he had brought about yet had no intention of seeing through. In 1945, many of the soldiers whose acceptance Hitler so valued were left with no option but to face the long march into captivity in Russia, where they would be forced into slave labour for ten years or more. That was the true nature of comradeship as practised by Adolf Hitler. Ironically, Field Marshal Keitel exhibited the genuine spirit of *Kameradschaft*. His sense of honour and duty compelled him to answer for his crimes and lead him to Nuremberg where, in October 1946, he would face the hangman's noose.

There is no notable evidence to suggest that Wilhelm Keitel did not tell the plain and unvarnished truth at Nuremberg. This is his sworn testimony.

Bob Carruthers

NUREMBERG TRIAL PROCEEDINGS
NINETY-EIGHTH DAY
WEDNESDAY, 3 APRIL 1946

MORNING SESSION

[The Defendant Keitel took the stand.]

THE PRESIDENT: Will you state your full name?

WILHELM KEITEL (Defendant): Wilhelm Keitel.

THE PRESIDENT: Will you repeat this oath after me:
I swear by God – the Almighty and Omniscient – that I will speak the pure truth – and will withhold and add nothing.

[The defendant repeated the oath in German.]

THE PRESIDENT: You may sit down if you wish.

DR. NELTE: Please describe your military career briefly.

KEITEL: In the year 1901, in the beginning of March, I became an officer candidate in an artillery regiment of the Prussian Army. At the beginning of the first World War, in 1914, I was the regimental adjutant of my regiment. I was wounded in September 1914, and in the beginning of November I became chief of a battery of my regiment. Since the spring of 1915 I served in various general staff capacities, first with higher commands of the field army, later as a general staff officer of a division. Towards the end I was the first general staff officer of the Naval Corps in Flanders. Then I joined the *Reichswehr* as a volunteer. Beginning with the year 1929 I was Division Head (*Abteilungsleiter*) of the Army Organizational Division in the *Reichswehrministerium*. After an interruption from 1933 to 1935 I became, on 1 October 1935, Chief of the Wehrmacht Department (*Wehrmachtsamt*) of the *Reichskriegsminister*, that is Chief of Staff with the Minister of War. While on active service I became *Generalmajor*. At that time I was chief of an infantry brigade. On 4 February 1938 to my surprise I was appointed Chief of Staff of the *Führer*, or Chief of the OKW – *Oberkommando der Wehrmacht*. On 1 October 1939, I became General of the Infantry and after the campaign in the West in 1940 I became Field Marshal.

DR. NELTE: Were you a member of the National Socialist German Labour Party?

KEITEL: No, I was not a member. According to military law I could not be or become a member.

DR. NELTE: But you received the Golden Party Badge. For what reason?

KEITEL: That is correct. Hitler presented this Golden Badge of the Party to me in April 1939, at the same time that the Commander-in-Chief of the Army, General Von Brauchitsch, received it. The *Führer* said it was to be in commemoration of the march into Czechoslovakia. The Golden Badge had "16 and 17 March" engraved on it.

DR. NELTE: In the year 1944 the Military Service Law was changed so that active soldiers could also become members of the Party. What did you do at that time?

KEITEL: That is correct. In the late summer or autumn of 1944 the Military Service Law was changed so that active soldiers could also be Party members. At that time I was invited to submit personal data for the Party in order to be listed as a member of the Party. At the same time I was asked to send in a donation of money to the Party. I submitted personal data to Party headquarters and also sent in a donation, but as far as I know I never became a member. I never received a membership card.

DR. NELTE: To what extent did you participate at Party functions?

KEITEL: Owing to my position and to the fact that I accompanied the *Führer* constantly, I participated at public functions of the Party several times, for example, at the Party rallies in Nuremberg, also each year when the Winter Relief Work campaign was launched. Finally, according to orders, each year on 9 November, I had to attend, together with a representative of the Party a memorial service at the graves of the victims of 9 November 1923. It took place symbolically in memory of the fight on 9 November, between the Party and the Wehrmacht. I never participated in internal conferences or meetings of the Party directorate. The *Führer* had let me know that he did not want this. Thus, for example, every year on 9 November I was in Munich, but never participated in the gatherings of the so-called *Hoheitsträger* (bearers of power) of the Party.

DR. NELTE: What decorations did you receive during the war?

KEITEL: During the war – it must have been in the winter of 1939-1940 – I received the Knight's Cross of the Iron Cross. I did not receive any other German war decorations.

DR. NELTE: Do you have any sons?

KEITEL: I had three sons, all of whom served at the front as officers during this war. The youngest one died in battle in Russia in 1941. The second was a major in Russia and has been missing in action, and the eldest son, who was a major, is a prisoner of war.

DR. NELTE: Field Marshal Keitel, beginning with essential matters,

I would like to put the following basic questions to you: What basic attitude did you, as a soldier, an officer, and a general, have toward the problems with which you had to deal in your profession?

KEITEL: I can say that I was a soldier by inclination and conviction. For more than 44 years without interruption I served my country and my people as a soldier, and I tried to do my best in the service of my profession. I believed that I should do this as a matter of duty, labouring unceasingly and giving myself completely to those tasks which fell to me in my many and diverse positions. I did this with the same devotion under the Kaiser, under President Ebert, under Field Marshal Von Hindenburg, and under the *Führer*, Adolf Hitler.

DR. NELTE: What is your attitude today?

KEITEL: As a German officer, I naturally consider it my duty to answer for what I have done, even if it should have been wrong. I am grateful that I am being given the opportunity to give an account here and before the German people of what I was and my participation in the events which have taken place. It will not always be possible to separate clearly guilt and entanglement in the threads of destiny. But I do consider one thing impossible, that the men in the front lines and the leaders and the subleaders at the front should be charged with the guilt, while the highest leaders reject responsibility. That, in my opinion, is wrong, and I consider it unworthy. I am convinced that the large mass of our brave soldiers were really decent, and that wherever they overstepped the bounds of acceptable behaviour, our soldiers acted in good faith, believing in military necessity, and the orders which they received.

DR. NELTE: The Prosecution, in presenting evidence regarding violations of the laws of war, Crimes against Humanity, repeatedly point to letters, orders, *et cetera*, which bear your name. Many so-called Keitel orders and Keitel decrees, have been submitted here. Now we have to examine whether and to what degree you and your actions are guilty of and responsible for the results of these orders. What do you wish to say to this general accusation?

KEITEL: It is correct that there are a large number of orders, instructions, and directives with which my name is connected, and it must also be admitted that such orders often contain deviations from existing international law. On the other hand, there are a group of directives and orders based not on military inspiration but on an ideological foundation and point of view. In this connection I am thinking of the group of directives which were issued before the campaign against the Soviet Union and also which were issued subsequently.

DR. NELTE: What can you say in your defence in regard to those orders?

KEITEL: I can say only that fundamentally I bear that responsibility which arises from my position for all those things which resulted from these orders and which are connected with my name and my signature. Further, I bear the responsibility, insofar as it is based on legal and moral principles, for those offices and divisions of the OKW which were subordinate to me.

DR. NELTE: From what may your official position and the scope of your legal responsibility be inferred?

KEITEL: That is contained in the *Führer*'s decree of 4 February 1938 which has been frequently cited.

DR. NELTE: I am submitting this decree to you so that you can have the text before you. In this *Führer* decree, Paragraph 1, you will find:
"From now on I will directly and personally take over the Supreme Command of the entire Wehrmacht."
What did that mean compared with the conditions that had existed until then?

KEITEL: Until that time we had a Commander-in-Chief of the Wehrmacht, Field Marshal Von Blomberg. In addition there was the Supreme Commander of the Wehrmacht who, according to the constitution, was the head of the State – in this case, Hitler. With the resignation of the Commander-in-Chief of the Wehrmacht, Von Blomberg, there was only one Supreme Commander and that was Hitler himself. And from that time on he himself exercised command of all three arms of the Wehrmacht: the Army, Navy, and Air Force. It also says "from now on directly". That should establish unequivocally that any intermediary position with authority to issue orders was no longer to exist, but that Hitler's orders as Supreme Commander were issued directly to the three arms of the Wehrmacht and their Commanders. It also says here "directly" and "personally". That, too, had its meaning, for the word "personally" was to express the fact that there was and would be no, I would say, "deputizing" of this authority.

DR. NELTE: I assume therefore that you never signed your orders "acting for"?

KEITEL: No, I do not remember a single instance in which I signed "acting for". According to our military principles, if the question had arisen to appoint a deputy, it could have been only one person, the Commander-in-Chief of the three arms of the Wehrmacht, namely the one highest in rank.

DR. NELTE: In Paragraph 2 of the decree of 4 February 1939 it says:
"… the former Wehrmacht office in the Ministry of War, with its functions is placed directly under my command as OKW and as my military staff."
What does this signify in regard to the staff which was thereby formed?

KEITEL: The Commander-in-Chief of the Wehrmacht had his

military staff in the *Wehrmachtsamt*, that is to say, the *Wehrmachtsamt* in the Ministry of War. Hitler, as Supreme Commander, took over the *Wehrmachtsamt* as his military staff. Thus, this staff was to be his personal working staff. At the same time that the post of Supreme Commander of the Wehrmacht was eliminated, that of Reich Minister of War was also removed. There was no War Ministry and no Minister of War as heretofore. Thus one could clearly see what Hitler wanted, namely, that between him and the Wehrmacht divisions there was to be no one holding office with any authority either in command channels or in ministerial functions.

DR. NELTE: When this decree was issued you were installed as holder of a new office with the title of "Chief OKW". Will you please clarify whether this term "Chief OKW" is correct; that is, whether it really was what the title seems to indicate.

KEITEL: I must add that I realize only now that this term in its abbreviated form is not quite apt. To be exact one should have said, "Chief of Staff of the High Command of the Wehrmacht", and not the abbreviation, "Chief OKW". From the case presented by the Prosecution I gathered that the idea of "Chief" was interpreted as if that were a commander, chief of an office, with authority to issue orders. And that, of course, is an erroneous conclusion. It was neither a position of a chief in the sense of a commander, nor, as might have been assumed or has been assumed, was it a position as chief of a general staff. That too, is incorrect. I was never Chief of the General Staff of the Wehrmacht. It was Hitler's unmistakable wish to concentrate in his own person all the authority, all the power of command. That is not merely a retrospective statement. He clearly expressed this desire to me on several occasions, partly in connection with the fact that he told me repeatedly, "I could never put this through with Blomberg".

DR. NELTE: I have here a statement made by Field Marshal Von Brauchitsch and submitted by the Prosecution.

KEITEL: Perhaps I might add something further. I was discussing the fact that it was not a position of Chief of the General Staff, since it was Hitler's basic view that commanders-in-chief of the Wehrmacht branches each had his own general staff, or operations staff, and that he did not want the High Command of the Wehrmacht, including the Wehrmacht Operations Staff, to take over the functions of a general staff. Therefore, in practice the work was done by the general staffs of the Wehrmacht branches, while the Wehrmacht Operations Staff of the OKW, which was purposely kept small, was a working staff for Hitler, a staff for strategic planning and for special missions.

DR. NELTE: Then Field Marshal Von Brauchitsch's statement in his affidavit, of which I have already spoken, is correct? It says here:

"When Hitler had decided to use military pressure or military power in attaining his political aims, the Commander-in-Chief of the Army, if he participated, received his instructions first orally, as a rule, or by an appropriate order. Thereupon the OKW worked out the operation and deployment plans. When they had been submitted to Hitler and were approved by him, a written order from the OKW to the branches of the Wehrmacht followed".
Is that correct?

KEITEL: Yes, in principle it is correct insofar as the final formulation of the order to the Commander-in-Chief of the Army took the form of a directive, as we called it, based on the general plans which had already been submitted and approved. This work was done by the Wehrmacht Operational Staff (*Wehrmachtführungsstab*); thus the Wehrmacht Operational Staff was not an office which became independently active and did not handle matters concerning the issuing of orders independently; rather the Wehrmacht Operational Staff and I took part in the basic determination or approval of these proposals and formulated them in the manner in which they were then carried out by Hitler as Commander-in-Chief. To speak technically we then passed these orders on.

DR. NELTE: Then I have an affidavit by *Generaloberst* Halder which deals with the same subject. You know this affidavit Number 1. I believe I can dispense with the reading of it and as evidence refer only to Halder's affidavit Number 1, which has been submitted by the Prosecution (Document Number 3702-PS).

In addition the Prosecution submitted another treatise without a special number. The title of the treatise is "Basis for the Organization of the German Wehrmacht".

THE PRESIDENT: Is this the document which you say the Prosecution offered in evidence but did not give a number to?

DR. NELTE: Mr. President, this document was given to us by the Prosecution, I believe by the American Prosecution, on 26 November 1945. I do not know…

THE PRESIDENT: You mean it never was deposited in evidence by the Prosecution?

DR. NELTE: I do not believe I can decide that. I assume that a document which has been submitted to the Defence Counsel was submitted to the High Tribunal at the same time, if not as evidence, then at least for judicial notice.

THE PRESIDENT: What is the document? Is it an affidavit or not?

DR. NELTE: It is not an affidavit; it is really a study by the American Prosecution. And, I assume, it is a basis for the indictment of the organization OKW, and so forth.

THE PRESIDENT: Have you got it in your document book or not?

DR. NELTE: No, I do not have it in the document book, because I assumed that was also at the disposal of the High Tribunal. Besides, Mr. President, it is a short document.

THE PRESIDENT: Perhaps, Mr. Dodd can tell us what it is.

MR. DODD: If I could see it I might be able to be helpful. I am not familiar with it. It is probably one of the documents which we submitted to the Defence but which we did not actually introduce in evidence, and that happened more than once, I think, in the early days of the Trial.

THE PRESIDENT: Yes.

DR. NELTE: I refer to a single short paragraph of this study which I would like to read. Perhaps we can thus obviate submitting the document.

THE PRESIDENT: Are you offering in evidence the whole of the affidavit? I do not mean at this moment, but are you proposing to offer it?

DR. NELTE: I assume that the Prosecution have already submitted it. I am only referring to it.

THE PRESIDENT: The whole affidavit? What is the number of it, if it has been submitted?

DR. NELTE: This affidavit also does not have a number. The Prosecution…

THE PRESIDENT: It has not been submitted if it has not a number on it then.
It suggested to me that possibly the Halder affidavit was offered and then rejected.

DR. NELTE: No. At that time a series of affidavits was submitted: By Brauchitsch, Halder, Heusinger, and many other generals who are in Nuremberg. None of these affidavits had an exhibit number.

MR. DODD: This affidavit was put in by the United States as an exhibit. I do not have the number handy, but I think it was submitted at the time Colonel Telford Taylor submitted the case on behalf of the Prosecution against the High Command and the OKW. This Halder "affidavit", the first document which Doctor Nelte referred to, is not an affidavit. It was a paper submitted to the Tribunal and to the Defence by Colonel Taylor. It set out some of the basic principles of the organization of the High Command and the OKW wholly before he presented his part of the case. It is really just the work of our own staff here in Nuremberg.

THE PRESIDENT: Doctor Nelte, as the document you are referring to, not the Halder affidavit, appears to be a mere compilation, the Tribunal thinks it should not go in as an exhibit, but you can put a question to the witness upon it.

DR. NELTE: *[Turning to the defendant.]* In the essay which you have before you, the Prosecution asserted the following: After 1938 there were four divisions: The OKW (High Command of the Wehrmacht); the OKH (High Command of the Army); the OKL (High Command of the Air Force); the OKM (High Command of the Navy); and each had its own general staff. What can you tell us about that?

KEITEL: I can say only that this is not correct, and also contradicts the description which I have already given of the functions of the High Commands of the Wehrmacht branches and of the OKW. There were not four such departments. There were only three: The High Command of the Army, the High Command of the Navy, and the High Command of the Air Force.

As I have just stated, the High Command of the Wehrmacht as a

21

personal, direct working staff, was in no way an independent authority in that sense. The commanders-in-chief of the Wehrmacht branches were commanders, had the authority to issue orders and exercised this power over troops which were subordinate to them. The OKW had neither the power to issue orders, nor subordinate troops to which orders could have been issued. It is also not correct, if I recall the speeches of the Prosecution, to use the expression "Keitel was Commander-in-Chief of the Wehrmacht". I am mentioning it only to emphasize this point. Further, I would like, briefly, to call attention to the diagram on the last page of the document which has been shown to me.

DR. NELTE: This sketch is the diagram which is called "The Wehrmacht". It is an exposition, a diagrammatic exposition of the entire Wehrmacht and its branches.

KEITEL: I believe I should point briefly to the fact that it is this diagram which was the basis for this erroneous conception, because in it the High Command of the Wehrmacht is designated as a special office or office of command, and that is incorrect.

DR. NELTE: What tasks had you in this military sector as the Chief of the OKW?

KEITEL: First of all, it was an essential task to secure for the *Führer* with and through the Wehrmacht Operational Staff, all the documents and all the numerous informations and reports which he desired. I dare say that the Wehrmacht Operational Staff had, in this connection, the function to, one might say, arrange and establish direct and close communication between Hitler and the general staffs of the branches of the Wehrmacht. In addition to securing a countless number of such documents which were demanded daily, there was a second function, namely to be regularly present at all conferences in which the commanders-in-chief of the Wehrmacht branches and the chiefs of their staffs participated as well as the Chief of the Wehrmacht Operational

Staff. On those occasions as soon as a series of oral orders was given, these orders, in compliance with military principles, naturally had later to be confirmed in writing. Only in this way could we prevent mistakes or misunderstandings from arising, that is, by confirming these orders to those who had already received them orally the orders were made clear. That is the purpose and meaning of the order.

DR. NELTE: How did you sign the orders and documents which you drew up?

KEITEL: It is correct that this form of orders and directives were almost exclusively signed by me. They were actually orders which had already been given and which had already long since been transmitted through military channels. As can be seen from the bulk of the documents submitted here, this gave rise to the form which I made a habit of using in which I always wrote at the beginning or after a few preliminary words, "The *Führer* has therefore ordered…"

In the large majority of cases this order was no longer a surprise to the office which received it. It was nothing new but it was only a confirmation. In a similar way I naturally had also a considerable number of organizational and other directives and orders also in not purely operational fields worked out under my supervision and passed on. In this respect I should like to point out particularly that in no case did I send out orders without having shown them again to my supreme commander when making the daily reports, in order to be certain that I had not misunderstood him in any form or manner or that I was not issuing anything which – and this I would like to emphasize – did not have his approval to the letter.

DR. NELTE: There was another category of orders and directives…

KEITEL: May I perhaps add a few words?

DR. NELTE: Please do.

KEITEL: In order to clarify this: Among the documents submitted here are those which Hitler personally signed and released under the heading "The *Führer* and Supreme Commander of the Wehrmacht". There are some exceptions in which such directives were signed by me "by order of", I would like to explain this matter also. In this case it is also true that if these directives, which for the most part had been corrected several times by Hitler personally, had to be issued urgently and the Supreme Commander was prevented from signing himself, it was necessary for me to let the signature go out in this form, never as "deputy" but always as "by order of". Otherwise, orders were issued as I have already stated, in the form of directives which were signed by me.

At the same time I should like to mention that even if we have a series of documents here headed "Chief, Supreme Commander of the Wehrmacht" or – some of them are different: "High Command of the Wehrmacht" – if they are signed, "by order, Jodl", I can say that it can be proved almost automatically that I did not happen to be there at the time; otherwise I would have signed it myself, knowing that I was Chief of Staff who, in accordance with military regulations, had to sign such documents.

DR. NELTE: The memorandum which you have before you contains the following sentence:
> "The OKW united in itself the activity of a staff and of a ministry; the matters involved, which had previously been taken care of by the Reich War Ministry, have probably also been turned over to the OKW".

Please clarify the ministerial function of the OKW.

KEITEL: Yes, this formulation as set down in this document is not exactly incorrect, but it is on important points at least, open to misunderstanding, for it was not at all true that all functions which had been previously carried out by the War Minister were turned over to the OKW. There were many functions and rights which the War Minister, in his capacity as minister, and thus the person responsible for them, could and did decide even for the branches of the Wehrmacht and their commanders, which were never transmitted to the Chief of the OKW, that is, to me.

The following things happened at that time: Everything in this connection involving authority to issue orders or exercise supreme command, and which the *Führer* did not wish to take over personally, was transferred to the commanders-in-chief of the branches of the Wehrmacht as far as supreme authority and authority to make decisions were concerned. To touch on the subject briefly, I should like to mention a few essential facts which I remember. For example, the officers' personnel records, decisions on complaints, documentary material on budget questions, court jurisdiction and court authority, which formerly belonged to the Minister of War, were transferred to the commander-in-chief, as well as all questions concerning officials and all questions of the rights of officials. I could mention still more, but I merely wished to point out that even in cases where decisions had to be made, as for example, removing an official or dismissing an employee, the chief of the OKW did not decide. These powers were delegated to the commanders-in-chief in addition to the powers they held previously and which were transferred from the War Minister's jurisdiction. There were only certain reservations which the *Führer* made for himself. Similarly some of the other fields of the OKW were limited in their assignments in the course of the following years through the dissolution of the Economic Armament Office. The position of Armament Minister was created because of the dissolution of the *Arnt Ausland Abwehr*, that is, the Counterintelligence Service, of which only the branch self-protection of the troops was left with the Wehrmacht; everything else was transferred, and so forth.

My authority included the following: It was my duty in all cases to get Hitler's decision on all basic questions with which this ministerial section was concerned. I was free from the necessity of doing this only in current matters or if there was complete agreement between the persons involved in a ministerial or administrative question and the branches of the Wehrmacht in my department. In such a case a decision by Hitler was not necessary. I must emphasize again, in summary, that the OKW had no authority of its own, and that one can say only that Hitler actually functioned as Supreme Commander of the Wehrmacht, just as the functions of the War Minister were combined in his person so as to, to repeat that, to eliminate an intermediary official at all costs. That is, there was to be no intermediary between him and the commanders-in-chief of the Wehrmacht branches.

THE PRESIDENT: We will adjourn now until 2 o'clock.

[The Tribunal recessed until 1400 hours.]

AFTERNOON SESSION

THE PRESIDENT: Dr. Nelte, although the Tribunal did say that they would hear Dr. Horn at 2 o'clock, they would not wish to interrupt the examination of the Defendant Keitel if you prefer to go on with that now. It is .a matter for you to consider whichever you like.

DR. NELTE: Dr. Horn agrees that I continue the interrogation of Keitel now.

THE PRESIDENT: Very well.

MR. DODD: If it please the Tribunal, for the assistance of the Tribunal I have ascertained that the first Halder affidavit, referred to this morning by Dr. Nelte, was introduced as Exhibit USA-531 (Document Number 3702-PS) on 4 January, by Colonel Taylor; and the second Halder affidavit referred to by Dr. Nelte was introduced as Exhibit USA-533 (Document Number 3707-PS) on 5 January, by Colonel Taylor.

THE PRESIDENT: Thank you.

DR. NELTE: Mr. President, Mr. Dodd was kind enough to put at my disposal a number of copies of the pamphlet, "Principles of Organization of the German Armed Forces" so that I can submit them to the Tribunal. I do so now.

[Turning to the defendant.] You last explained that on 4 February 1938, part of the authority of the War Ministry was transferred to branches of the Armed Forces, and part to the High Command of the Wehrmacht. In the decree which has been mentioned it says, concerning this matter:

"The OKW at the same time is taking care of the affairs of the Reich War Ministry. The Chief of the OKW, on my orders will exercise the authority which the Reich Minister of War had heretofore".

Tell me briefly to which fields this applied. I myself will submit to the Tribunal a diagram which has already been sent to the Translation Division for translation. I do not know, however, if the Tribunal already has the translation.

KEITEL: The ministerial functions actually transferred to the OKW were executed by a number of offices. I shall name the most important now, indicating their functions:

First of all, a few words about the Wehrmacht Operations Staff (*Wehrmachtführungsstab*) which, being an office of the OKW, was subordinated to it in the same way as the other offices of the OKW were, but which was on a higher level than the other offices. As the name implies, the Wehrmacht Operations Staff was an organ of the *Führer*'s High Command with which he frequently – I might say, mostly – collaborated personally. It had no ministerial powers.

Then there was the General Armed Forces Office (*Allgemeines Wehrmachtsamt*) which took care mainly of ministerial and administrative questions. One could almost call it a war ministry on a small scale.

Then the office of Counterintelligence Service (*Amt Ausland Abwehr*), which was to a large extent ministerial but to some degree an aid in operational questions.

Then the Economic Armament Office, in regard to which I must point out that in the year 1940 this office was dissolved and only a small Defence Economy Office (*Wehrwirtschaftsamt*) remained, which was mainly concerned with questions of supply of all consumer goods needed by the Armed Forces, such as fuel, coal, gasoline, *et cetera*, and which I need not mention further.

Then an important field of activity: Replacements Administration for the entire Armed Forces, or abbreviated, Recruiting, a central office which was designed mostly to take care of personnel questions within the OKW.

Then the Legal Administration, the Budget Department, and a number of other offices which it is not necessary to enumerate.

In these offices the ministerial functions of the OKW were carried out. I would like...

THE PRESIDENT: Dr. Nelte, I think the Tribunal has followed the distinction which the defendant has made between the General Staff for the High Commands and the position of the OKW; but is it necessary for the Tribunal to go into all these details?

DR. NELTE: I had finished dealing with this section.

THE PRESIDENT: Very well.

DR. NELTE: I want to put just one more...

THE PRESIDENT: Before you pass from this document that you have just put before the Tribunal, this diagram, are you desiring to make an exhibit of that?

DR. NELTE: I would like to submit it in evidence. You will also be given a translation.

THE PRESIDENT: If so, what number will you give it? You must number all your exhibits.

DR. NELTE: Please number it, Keitel-1(a).

THE PRESIDENT: Who prepared it?

DR. NELTE: We prepared it and the technical division of the Prosecution has reproduced it. The Prosecution also are in possession of the diagram.

THE PRESIDENT: Have you asked the defendant to confirm that it is correct?

DR. NELTE: Field Marshal, would you please look at this diagram and confirm whether it is correct?

KEITEL: Yes, I recognize the diagram…

GEN. RUDENKO: Mr. President, the Prosecution have not received this diagram. Therefore, the Prosecution would like, before making conclusions, to acquaint themselves with this diagram.

THE PRESIDENT: Have you got any more copies of it, Dr. Nelte?

DR. NELTE: They can be obtained and distributed right away. Then I would like the Tribunal to reserve its decision until the diagrams have been submitted in sufficient numbers.

KEITEL: I recognize this diagram as correct. It does not contain the minor changes which occurred from the time of the creation of the OKW up to the time which I have mentioned, changes brought about by the reorganization of the armament ministries, *et cetera*, but it shows the manner in which it actually worked during the last years.

THE PRESIDENT: Go on, Dr. Nelte.

DR. NELTE: In order to terminate this group of questions I would like to say the following: Is it correct that according to this, all the Keitel orders, Keitel decrees, which have been submitted by the Prosecution, were in reality *Führer* orders, that is to say, orders which were the expression of Hitler's will, based on his instructions and commands?

KEITEL: Yes, that is the correct definition of the summary of the testimony I have given. I would like to state again in summarizing that, as I have stated from the beginning, I assume and have assumed responsibility for these orders insofar as they are connected with my name, for the position was this: I, of course, knew the contents of these orders which I executed. I recognize my signature, of course, in the documents which have been submitted to me and therefore I accept the documents as authentic. I may add that insofar as I had military or other objections to the orders, I naturally expressed them very forcibly and that I endeavoured to prevent orders being given which I considered controversial. But I must state in all truth that if the decision had been finally made by Hitler, I then issued these orders and transmitted them, I might almost say, without checking them in any way.

DR. NELTE: Mr. President, before I enter upon the next phase of my questions I should like to state the following:

The Prosecution have deduced Keitel's participation in the many crimes which have been described here from various facts, facts which cannot always be connected with each other and made to agree. The Prosecution have stated that he was a powerful and important staff officer. That is set out in the Indictment. Then the Prosecution stated that he was a tool without a will of his mand, that the relation between himself and Hitler was an intimate one.

You will understand that if the defendant wants to clarify or to protest against these things he must explain the relation between himself and Hitler.

THE PRESIDENT: Dr. Nelte, that is what the defendant has been doing. He has been explaining his relationship to Hitler, and if you want to elucidate it further you must ask him further questions.

DR. NELTE: I only wanted to let him speak about the private relation to Hitler. So far we have been concerned only with the official relation.

[Turning to the defendant.] Would you please tell us something about the cooperation between you and Hitler? I ask you to be as brief as possible and tell us only the most necessary facts, but at the same time give us a correct picture.

KEITEL: The cooperation can be characterized only as one between a high military superior and his subordinate. In other words, the same relations as I have always had in my military career with the senior officers of whose staff I was a member. The relation between Hitler and myself never departed from this strictly military and soldierly relationship. Of course, it was my right and my duty to express my opinions. How difficult that was can be judged only by someone who knows that Hitler, after a few words, was wont to take over the entire discussion and to exhaust the subject entirely from his point of view. It was then very difficult, of course, to come back to the subject again. I may say that due to my various positions in high staff offices I was quite used to dealing with the superior commanders, if I may use that expression. However, I was quite unaccustomed to the conditions which I encountered here. They surprised me, and not infrequently they reduced me to a state of real uncertainty. That can be understood if one knows that Hitler, in soldiering or military questions, if I were to express myself very cautiously, was a man with far-reaching plans for reform with which I, with my 37 years of service as a soldier of the old school, was confronted.

DR. NELTE: Was it .the same during the war or do you refer to the time before the war?

KEITEL: During the war these controversies were moderated by the events, so that actuality was strongly influenced by the urgency of the situation. Therefore, these things did not appear in that form. On the other hand, the position then was that Hitler in his discussions about the situation had a comparatively large circle of about twenty people assembled around him, and speaking in military terms, unsparingly made his accusations – objections and criticism – directed, as a rule, at people who were not present. I took the part of the absent person as a matter of principle, because he could not defend himself. The result was that the accusations and criticism were then aimed at me, and my training as a soldier finally forced me to control myself, because it is unseemly to answer back or to oppose or to attempt to contradict a superior before very young subordinates, such as those who were present. Opposition to a superior or to personalities, no matter what their rank, was unbearable to the *Führer*. One could then attempt to speak to him about these things only in private.

DR. NELTE: Had you the feeling that you had Hitler's confidence?

KEITEL: I could not say yes. I must frankly admit that Hitler's confidence in me was not without reservations, and today I know only too well that there were many things concerning which he had never spoken frankly to me and about which he never took me into his confidence. It was a fact that Hitler was very suspicious of the old or elderly generals. For him they were products of an old and antiquated school and in this sense he was to us old soldiers a man who brought new revolutionary ideas into .the Wehrmacht and wished to incorporate then; into Wehrmacht training. This frequently led to serious crises. I believe I do not have to elaborate on that. The real evil, however, was that this lack of confidence led him to believe that I was in conspiracy with the Army generals behind his back and that I supported them against him. Perhaps that was a result of my habit of defending them because they could not defend themselves. At various instances that led to extremely acute and serious crises.

DR. NELTE: Much will depend upon stating how your cooperation with Hitler has to be valued, particularly to what extent you could be considered his collaborator or adviser. Will you tell me whether Hitler discussed his plans with you in the manner which is customary in close collaboration?

KEITEL: In general I must deny that. It was not in any way in keeping with Hitler's peculiar disposition and personality to have advisers of that kind, that is, if you call an adviser someone who gives advice in the sense of presenting, let us say, a great number of military elements from long experience as an officer, but not in the sense of an adviser to help to formulate a decision, such far-reaching decisions which are doubtlessly meant here. On principle, such a decision was preceded by weeks or months of careful consideration. During that time one had to assist by procuring documents, but concerning the main point, the decision itself, he did not brook any influence. Therefore, strange as it may sound, the final answer always was: "This is my decision and it is unalterable". That was the announcement of his decision.

DR. NELTE: But if various departments were competent for these decisions, were there no general conferences?

KEITEL: No. I cannot recall that any one of the really important decisions after the year 1938 had ever been formulated as the result of joint counsel for instance between the politicians, the soldiers or other ministers, because it was Adolf Hitler's own way to speak, privately as a rule, to each department and each department chief, to learn from him what he wanted to know, and then to find out some element that could be used in the elaboration of his plans. Things were not at all as would appear from the documents here of minutes of conferences of generals, of meetings and similar things with a list of those present. Never did such a meeting have the character of a deliberation. There could be no question of that. Rather, the *Führer* had a certain idea, and if for various reasons he thought that we opposed that idea even inwardly, he used that as a reason to clarify his thoughts before a large circle without any discussion. In other words, in these assemblies, which the documents here speak of as conferences, there was never any deliberation. I must add that even the external form which these things took was such that, following the military example, the senior commander convened a certain number of generals, everyone was seated, the *Führer* arrived, spoke and went out. No one in such a situation could have found an opening to say anything. To use just one word for it, and I certainly do not exaggerate, it was the issuing of an order but not a conference.

DR. NELTE: To come to a different subject, the Prosecution have asserted that you had been a member of the Reich Government. What do you have to say about that?

KEITEL: I never belonged to the Reich Government and I was also never a member of the Cabinet. I must also state that I never became a minister, but as is stated in the decree of 1938, "he has the rank of a Reich minister", not "he is Reich minister". The expression "minister" is, of course, simply intended to indicate the rank of minister and there was a good reason for that. I need point out only what I said this morning: It was not intended that there should be anyone holding an office with the authority of a minister between Hitler and the Wehrmacht, and the branches of the Wehrmacht. I must clarify the question which has been frequently raised by the Prosecution that "He had the rank of a minister", by saying that, before the decree was issued, I asked whether I was to deal with the State secretaries or with the ministers, and Hitler said, "If on my orders you deal with other ministers of the Reich, then, of course, you can do so only with the rank of a minister, not on the level of a state secretary".

That is the explanation of the expression in the decree "He has the rank of a Reich minister".

DR. NELTE: Did you, in the headquarters have any conferences with other important and competent personalities, such as Ribbentrop, Rosenberg, Speer, Sauckel, *et cetera*?

KEITEL: Ministers or special plenipotentiaries visited headquarters according to a plan which very seldom led to the simultaneous presence of several of them. Generally, it was carefully arranged so that a special time was set aside for each one. As a rule, I was of course informed that "the Foreign Minister is here" or "Minister Speer is here" or the "Plenipotentiary General for Allocation of Labour Sauckel is here". However, I was called in only in regard to purely military questions which the *Führer* discussed with these gentlemen in private and I could give instances of this. However, as has already been mentioned recently, during the interrogation of State Secretary Steengracht, it would be false to believe that these gentlemen who came to headquarters formed a small or select cabinet. Hitler dealt with each of these officials and functionaries separately, gave him his orders, and dismissed him. It sometimes happened that on the way home, these gentlemen visited me, mostly to ask me about small questions and small favours which I could do for them or with instructions to inform me about a decision or with the order to forward a decision to those military offices which had to be notified.

DR. NELTE: In concluding, I would like to know whether the expression "intimate" which is contained in the Indictment, is correct in order to describe the relations between you and Hitler, privately or officially?

KEITEL: I found the word "intimate" in the Indictment and I asked myself the question, "Where does this conception originate?" To be quite frank, I have but one answer for it, that is that no one ever heard a single word from me about the actual and constant difficulties that I had. I deliberately kept quiet about them. Intimate relations are, according to my definition of "intimate" – I do not know if in the English translation "intimate" expresses the same thing which we call *"intim"* – relations where there is confidence and frank discussion and these did not exist. I have already characterized it. Intimacy was not Hitler's attitude towards the generals, to whose senior generation I also belonged. Apart from the very formal intercourse which sometimes lasted for weeks and in which even the external forms were hardly observed – I do not want to discuss this in detail here – the relation never reached a point where it could be classified as that of a close adviser or a close collaborator as I conceived it in my Army staff positions. I must say that for my part I have been faithful and loyal and I always fulfilled my duties in that manner. However, I must also say that a sincere and personal relation based upon mutual understanding and confidence never existed. It has always been correct, but it was military and official, and never went beyond that.

DR. NELTE: By the decree of 4 February 1938 a Secret Cabinet Council was established. According to the contents of that decree, you are supposed to have been a member of the Cabinet Council. In order to save time, I merely wish to ask you: Do you confirm from your own knowledge the statement made by *Reichsmarschall* Göring, that the Secret Cabinet Council was established only for appearances and that a Secret Cabinet Council was never constituted and that it never had a session?

KEITEL: I can answer only, "Yes, never".

DR. NELTE: I come now to the question of the Reich Defence Council (*Reichsverteidigungsrat*). In the session of 23 November, the prosecutor submitted in evidence, as proof of the rearmament and the active participation of the Wehrmacht in the planning of war of aggression, among others:

Document EC-177, which was designated as "Meeting of the Reich Defence Council of 22 May 1933". I must say that I have taken the translation from the minutes and I am not sure whether the expression *"Reichsverteidigungsrat"* was translated correctly. In the minutes it states that it is a meeting of the working committee. For your information may I say that the *Reichsverteidigungsrat* was supposed to be a sort of ministerial body and that in addition, there was a working committee.

A second document, EC-405, was submitted concerning a meeting of the same body on 7 March 1934; and a third document, 2261-PS, dealing with the Reich Defence Law of 1935 and the simultaneous appointment of Dr. Schacht as Plenipotentiary General for War Economy.

Beyond doubt, you have been active in questions of national defence. These documents are also submitted as evidence against you. I ask you, therefore, to state whether these meetings in which you participated and which you conducted, were concerned with preparations for war and rearmament.

KEITEL: From the very beginning, as long as we were working on these things and by means of a committee of experts from which everything else evolved, I personally participated in these matters, and I may call myself the founder of that committee of ministerial experts which was set up to cooperate with the War Ministry. As Chief of the Organizational Department of the Army, in the winter of 1929 and 1930, that is, 3 years before Hitler came to power, I formed and personally assembled that committee after the Chancellor – I believe it was Brüning – and the Prussian and Reich Minister of the Interior Severing had consented to it. I would like to add that a representative of Minister Severing was always present to make sure that nothing took place which would have been in violation of the Treaty of Versailles. This work was very difficult, because no Reich minister and no department head was officially obliged to carry out the wishes of the National Ministry of Defence, this was purely voluntary. Consequently, the work went along haltingly and slowly. In this committee of experts which met perhaps two or three times a year, we dealt with, if I may put it briefly, what assistance the Civilian Department could render, in order to set free the small army of 100,000 soldiers for purely military tasks, naturally limiting ourselves to the defence of our frontiers, as stated in the Treaty of Versailles: "The Defence of the Frontiers"; I could perhaps still repeat our discussion from memory, since, with the exception of the period from 1933 to 1935, I conducted every one of these meetings myself, that is as leader of the discussion, not as chairman. I can, however, refer you now to the *Mobilization Handbook for Civil Authorities*, which was the outcome of this work and about which I shall speak later. It may be possible to submit it here. We were concerned only with questions of defence, such as the protection of our frontiers, and, in order to make myself clear, I should like to mention some of them. The Wehrmacht was to be free to protect railway property, post office property, repeater stations, radio stations, and to man the frontiers with security units for which the Customs Services were to be responsible. Cable and sea communications with East Prussia were also to be improved.

I will not bore you with all this. They were all defensive measures with a view to freeing the few soldiers for purely military functions, because for purposes of actual military operations I need not tell you what we could have done with an army of only 100,000 men. Any questions which went beyond this were never dealt with in that committee. The manner in which we worked was this: I asked the experts to submit their wishes to the heads of departments or state secretaries and then to try to persuade the heads of departments to take over the tasks from us, so that we could say that was being done by others and we need not bother about it. I can guarantee that operational questions, strategic questions, armament questions, questions of supply of war equipment, were never discussed in this committee. They were only organizational questions of the taking over of functions which generally should be performed by a soldier, but which we wanted to transfer to the civil authorities.

Now, as to the meeting of 22 May 1933, which has been discussed several times, it was already stated in the heading of the minutes which we have before us: "Competency – heretofore the *Reichswehrminister*, now the Reich Defence Council" – I have just explained that. Hitherto *Reichswehrminister*, over the committee, voluntary participation of the ministers of other departments, now obligatory activity of the heads of departments, that is, the group of ministers who received the title of "Defence Council". I will express that even more clearly, so that it cannot be misunderstood. Every member of the committee represented a ministry. The minister to whom the committee member was responsible, along with his colleagues, formed the Reich Defence Council, as envisaged by us then. They were the Council and we were the Committee. Therefore, "heretofore the *Reichswehrminister*" – now, one could say, as I have just expressed it, the other ministers were obliged to do that.

In Paragraph 3 the working plans were particularly mentioned. These working plans, in a word, are the forerunner of the *Mobilization Book*, which is the final stage; whereas the working plans of about 1933 were the intermediary stage. Then as regards the concluding words at the meeting of 22 May 1933, which have been given special prominence here by the Prosecution, and which deal with the need for secrecy – the passage where I said, according to the minutes, that nothing which could lead to objections at the Disarmament Conference should be left lying in the desks of the ministries – that is correct. I did say that, and I have said it because the experts told me that, with the exception of a small wooden box or a drawer in a desk which could not be locked, they had no place in which to keep anything, and because Von Blomberg, Reich War Minister at that time, who had been in Geneva at the Disarmament Conference for almost two years, gave me the definite order before this meeting, to point out these things, because in Geneva one was surrounded by an extremely large number of agents who were only waiting to be able to present proof that, in spite of the disarmament negotiations, there were things going on which could be interpreted as violations of the Versailles Treaty. That is what I had to say about the document.

DR. NELTE: I have given to you now the *Mobilization Book for the Civil Administration*. It is Document 1639-PS. It has been submitted in order to prove that aggressive wars were being planned. Would you explain to us the purpose of this book?

KEITEL: I have already stated that at an earlier stage, that is, during the years 1932-33, the individual ministries had so-called working plans, indicating what they were to do if something happened which necessitated their participation in defending the country. In the course of years, naturally, a number of new tasks were added and that finally led to this *Mobilization Book* for the civil authorities and civil administration, the study of which would certainly show nothing which might have anything to do with strategic, operational, or other preparations for war. On the other hand, I am not in a position to prove that everything contained in this book could never have been useful in military operations which could develop from an aggressive war plan. Many measures, one could almost say most measures, in the event of mobilization would not indicate on the surface whether it is a measure for defence or a measure which is necessary or indispensable for aggressive action. That cannot be determined. But I believe I can say, because I, myself, than in have any other, been engaged that there so was deeply no in reason this at work, all to perhaps burden more the civilian experts – they were high government counsellors – with strategic or operational planning. I do not believe that it is necessary to prove that such work is not within their scope. I have looked through and studied this mobilization book here. I do not wish to bore you by citing points which are of a purely defensive nature. I could name them: barriers, reinforcement of the frontier defences, demolitions, cutting of railroads and similar things, all this is in the book. One of the most important chapters, which, if I remember correctly, we discussed during four or five of these sessions, was the question of evacuation, that is, evacuating territories close to the border of valuable war material and personnel, so that, in case of war with the neighbour, they should not fall into the hands of the enemy. This problem of evacuation was one of the most difficult, because the extent to which one can evacuate, that is, what things can be evacuated, is perhaps one of the most difficult decisions to make.

I would like to say one more thing about the Reich Defence Committee, supplementing the ideas which I expressed before. Until the year 1938, no meeting or session of the Reich Defence Council was ever held, that is, the ministers who were the superiors of the committee members never met, not even once. I would have known about it, although at the cabinet meeting, I believe as early as March 1933, we passed a resolution to make these ministers responsible for a Reich Defence Council which should deal with these tasks, and to oblige them to take over these tasks as their necessary contribution to the defence of the Reich, and, of course, to finance them. That was the main purpose, otherwise the Reich Defence Council never met.

DR. NELTE: Actually, the minutes which have been presented, for the period of '33 to '38, are of the meetings of the working committee. But you know that about eight days ago two documents were submitted which appeared to be the minutes of the meetings of the Reich Defence Council. One session or assembly is supposed to have taken place in November 1938, and the second one in March 1939. Unfortunately these documents have not been submitted to me, but I have looked at them and you have also seen them. Can you explain to us how these minutes, that is, these meetings came about and what they mean?

KEITEL: I merely wish to add a few supplementary words to the statement which *Reichsmarschall* Göring has already made. In December 1938, there was passed the Reich Defence Law, which had been drawn up in 1935, a shelved law, that is, a law which had not been made public and which required modification, the reason being that the Reich Defence Law of '35 was devised by the Reich War Minister, Commander-in-Chief Von Blomberg, who no longer held office. I was with *Reichsmarschall* Göring at that time to discuss this with him and to find a new basis for this law, which until then had not been published. This law of the autumn of 1938 had a number of supplementary clauses as compared to the old one, and perhaps I will be able to give details later. Among other things, according to this law also, *Reichsmarschall* Göring was the delegate of the *Führer*, a function formerly held by the Reich War Minister and which I could not exercise.

This conference in November 1938, to recall it briefly, had been convened by *Reichsmarschall* Göring in order to present this law which had not been published, and which was not to be published, to a large circle of members of the ministries. There were about seventy or more persons present to whom the *Reichsmarschall* explained the purpose and the essence of this law in the form of a speech. There was no discussion, apart from that speech, and there was certainly no question of a meeting of the Reich Defence Council at that time.

You also recently showed me the second document of a meeting of the Reich Defence Council as it is called and as also appears in the heading of the minutes of the summer 1939.

DR. NELTE: No, March 1939.

KEITEL: That has been mentioned here, and I believe it was the second meeting of the Reich Defence Council. I can explain that. This is how it was: I called a meeting of the committee and, of course, furnished *Reichsmarschall* Göring with the agenda and the names of the people who were to be present. *Reichsmarschall* Göring informed me that he would come himself and that since he wished to discuss other questions, he would accordingly enlarge the attendance. This conference, therefore, had an agenda which I had planned for the committee, and concrete questions were also brought up for debate. It is, however, remarkable that according to the list of those present, that is, according to the numbers, the members of the Reich Defence Council were represented by only a very small number, almost not at all, although there were about forty or fifty people present. The Reich Defence Council itself was a body of 12 people, and it needs no further explanation that, from the form in which these two conferences took place, one could not say that this was a plenary session of the Reich Defence Council based upon a clearly defined agenda, but rather that there were two meetings, the motive and extent of which I have described here.

[A recess was taken.]

THE PRESIDENT: Dr. Nelte, the Tribunal think that you might get on a little more quickly with the defendant. The Tribunal recall that you asked a few days ago that you might submit an affidavit of the defendant's evidence, and there is in your document book an affidavit. You have been over all those matters in the affidavit at very much greater length than you would have gone into them if you read the affidavit, and we hope that you will be able to deal more shortly with the evidence in future.

DR. NELTE: Mr. President, I made every effort to be as brief and concise as possible in my questions, but testimony is, of course, always subjective. The defendant is unfortunately the one who is mentioned most frequently in this Trial and naturally he is interested in clarifying those matters which he considers essential in order to present his case clearly.

THE PRESIDENT: Well, Dr. Nelte, I do not think it is necessary to discuss the matter further; but the Tribunal have expressed their wish.

DR. NELTE: As far as I am able, I shall comply with your request, Mr. President.
[Turning to the defendant.] Field Marshal Keitel, you have just given us an explanation of the Reich Defence Council and the Reich Defence Committee. You probably realize that we are not and should not be so much concerned with whether decisions are made by a Reich Defence Council or a Reich Defence Committee. We are interested in what actually took place and whether or not these things justify the imputations of the Prosecution. In this respect I ask you to tell me if those things which you discussed and planned on the Reich Defence Committee justify the suspicion that you were considering aggressive war?

KEITEL: I realize fully that we are not concerned with the formality of whether it was the Council or the Committee, since the Council was a board of ministers while the Committee was a board of minor experts. We are concerned with what actually did take place and what was done. With the exception that in the year 1934 and until the autumn of 1935 I was not present at these discussions, and therefore cannot vouch for every word which was spoken at that time, I must state that nothing about the planning of wars, the preparing for wars, the operational, strategical, or armed preparedness for war, was ever discussed.

DR. NELTE: The Prosecution has labelled you as a member of the Three Man College, from which they have deduced that you had special powers to act within the German Reich Government. I am submitting to you Document 2194-PS. In this document in the Reich Defence Law of 1938, Paragraph 5, Subsection 4, you will find the source of this term which in itself is not official.

KEITEL: The Reich Defence Law of 1938 provided for a plenipotentiary general for administration in order to restrict the size of the body. The Reich Minister of the Interior was to have this office and further, according to Paragraph 5, Subsection 4, the Supreme Command of the Army was to have priority influence in regard to the State Railways and the State Postal Services, for in the event of mobilization, transports must run and the services for the transmission of news must be available, as is the case in all countries.

The Three Man College is a concept which I have never heard of until just now. It probably refers to the Plenipotentiary General for Administration, the Plenipotentiary General for Economy and the Chief of the OKW. It referred to these three. There is no doubt about it, because, in line with the Reich Defence Law, they were already supposed to have a number of decrees ready in the drawers which were to be published when this law was made public, and each one of the three had to make the necessary preparations in his own sphere. From the right to assume these functions by reason of these authorities the Three Man College concept originated.

DR. NELTE: The Prosecution then contended that according to Document 2852-PS you were a member of the Council of Ministers for Defence of the Reich. Did you become a minister through this membership in the Reich Defence Council?

KEITEL: I might perhaps say a few words to begin with about the Council of Ministers, insofar as the Reich Defence Law, the Reich Defence Committee and the Reich Defence Council, disappeared as a result of the law regarding the Council of Ministers for Defence of the Reich, that is, they were never made public and never put into effect. The Council of Ministers for Defence of the Reich was newly created on

1 September 1939 and this made all these preparations on paper in the Reich Defence Council, Reich Defence Committee and the law null and void and put in its place a new thing, an institution. This institution, the Council of Ministers for Defence of the Reich, was now the small war cabinet, which, if I may say so, should previously have been the Reich Defence Council with their limited number of members. Thus, a new basis was established, and new decrees which were necessary were put into effect by the Council of Ministers for Defence of the Reich, after it had been created and officially confirmed.

I was called into this Council of Ministers or rather I received a chair in this Council of Ministers. I prefer not to give the reasons, because they were entirely private. It was a compensation for opposition against these things – I never became active in this Council of Ministers for Defence of the Reich, but I was a member; it was not necessary to be active since in the purely military sphere, that is, things with which the Wehrmacht immediately was concerned, the *Führer* personally, without the Council of Ministers, issued the necessary decrees with his own signature and the detour via the Council of Ministers in Berlin was not necessary; and in my opinion I must deny that I became a minister by this appointment. The authority to exercise the functions of a minister was in no way given. I was only the representative of the Wehrmacht in this Council of Ministers.

DR. NELTE: However, your name is indisputably at the bottom of many laws and decrees which were issued. How do you explain the signature on these laws?

KEITEL: Yes, I did sign a series of decrees issued by the Council of Ministers because they were submitted to me by the Secretariat, that is, the Chief of the Reich Chancellery, Minister Lammers, with a request for my signature. When I questioned the necessity for doing this, I received a formal answer from Lammers to the effect that other Reich departments might see that the Wehrmacht was not excluded from these decrees or laws. That is why my signature is included. It means that the

Wehrmacht must also obey these decrees and laws. That is why I had no misgivings in signing my name.

DR. NELTE: The Prosecution further accuse you of having been a political general. Undoubtedly you appeared at various special functions. Will you please answer this accusation and tell us how it came about?

KEITEL: I can readily understand the fact that functions of a ministerial nature which necessarily brought me frequently into contact with ministers of the Reich – in the course of a war everything is tied up with the Wehrmacht in some way or other – would seem to indicate that I had exercised a political function in these matters. The same conclusion can be drawn from other events. That is, my presence at State visits and similar functions as indicated by many documents might suggest that I was exercising political functions or in some way had been called to exercise such functions. Neither is true; neither in regard to internal German ministerial functions nor in regard to matters connected with foreign policy. There were naturally a great many things to be settled with the ministries, the technical ministries. The Wehrmacht had to participate and had a voice in almost all the decrees which were issued by the civilian ministries. This work was naturally done in Berlin. The fact that I had to remain with the *Führer* at his headquarters kept me away; and this meant that my offices, the offices of the OKW, had to settle these questions with the Reich departments and their experts rather independently on the whole. Thus it happened, naturally, that decrees of this kind were drawn up requiring my comments and the *Führer*'s consent, which was obtained through me and that in this connection I was the person who coordinated the various wishes and views of the High Commanders of the Wehrmacht branches and reduced them to a common Wehrmacht denominator, so to speak. Through these activities I was naturally drawn into the general apparatus of this work, but I do not believe that this would justify the application of the term "political general" to the *Führer*'s Military Chief of Staff.

DR. NELTE: What can you tell us with regard to foreign policy and the meetings at which foreign policy was discussed?

KEITEL: Concerning the sphere of foreign policy, I would merely like to emphasize what the former Reich Foreign Minister has already said about collaboration with the leaders of the Wehrmacht. If at all, two of the leading partners marched their own roads, then it was the foreign policy on one side and the Wehrmacht on the other, especially under the influence of the *Führer* himself, who did not desire collaboration and opposed the mutual exchange of ideas. He kept us in avowedly separate camps, and wished to work with each one separately. I must emphasize that most strongly. To conclude, this applied to all other departments who came to headquarters, that is, everything was discussed with them alone, and they also left the headquarters alone.

There were contacts with the Foreign Office, as State Secretary Von Steengracht has stated, with regard to all questions of international law or, in connection therewith, with questions affecting the prisoners of war, questions of communication with the protecting powers, and questions which Von Steengracht may have had in mind when he said, "With the Wehrmacht the whole field of an attaché's work", since all reports sent by military attachés in neutral and friendly countries to the Commanders-in-Chief of the Wehrmacht branches went through Foreign Office channels. They all arrived there and we received them from there. It was quite natural that during the war any news of special interest might call for special contacts in that we often had to complain that the reports did not reach us in time from the Foreign Office, and that our Ministry wanted to have them sent direct and not by a roundabout way. Otherwise, however, I must emphasize that there was no collaboration in any other field nor, I might say, any community of work in the field of strategics with the Foreign Office.

DR. NELTE: About ten days ago Document D-665 was submitted by the Prosecution. This document is headed "The *Führer's* Ideas

Regarding the Waffen-SS" dated 6 August 1940. In this document there is a passage by the OKW which states the following:

"The Chief of the OKW has decided in this connection that it can be only desirable for the ideas of the *Führer* to be given the utmost publicity."

Do you know this document?

KEITEL: Yes, I read this document at the time it was submitted, and I remembered it. To explain the origin of this document I must say briefly: After the war in France Hitler planned to give an independent status to the SS units, the Waffen-SS units, or form them into complete military bodies of troops. Until that time they had been parts of infantry troops attached to different Army formations. Now these groups were to be made into independent and fully-equipped units and would thus become independent formations. This created extreme unrest in the Army, and caused acute dissatisfaction among the generals. It was said to denote competition to the Army and the breaking of the promise made to the army that "there is only one bearer of arms in Germany, and that is the Wehrmacht". They asked: "Where would this lead to?"

At that time the Commander-in-Chief of the Army asked Hitler's chief adjutant for information about this revolting affair and General Schmundt, with Hitler's approval, then wrote the passage mentioned in this document.

I went to the *Führer* personally about this question to tell him plainly that the Army considered it an insult. He decided to handle the matter through his chief adjutant, as it had nothing to do with the High Command of the Wehrmacht. This announcement was then made by the Army itself in order to calm the excited minds. My personal comment that there was no objection to the widest publicity in this case either was given to satisfy General Von Brauchitsch, who expressly requested to be allowed to distribute it to every unit, in order to reassure the Army that the troops in question were police troops who under all circumstances had to have experience of active service, as otherwise they would be denied any recognition at home as troops. That is how that came about, and if I am asked today about my views on this matter I may say briefly: I also thought at the time that there ought to be a limit to these things; I believe 10 per cent was the figure mentioned. With the development of events in connection with the setting up of new formations after 1942, these troops lost their original character of an elite selected on physical and racial grounds. There was no mistaking the fact that considerable pressure was exercised; and I myself was very much afraid that some day this instrument of the Waffen-SS, which had swelled to a force more than 20 divisions strong, would grow into a new Army with a different ideology. We had very grave misgivings in this respect, especially as what we now saw before us was no longer an elite in any sense of the term, and since we even saw commissioned and noncommissioned officers and men transferred from these troops to the Wehrmacht. It was no longer the pick of volunteers. I do not think there is anything further to add.

DR. NELTE: The Prosecution have submitted Document L-211 to me. It is headed "War Operations as an Organizational Problem", and contains the comments of the OKW on the memorandum of the Commander-in-Chief of the Army regarding the organization of the leadership of the Wehrmacht. This document was submitted to prove that the OKW and you, as Chief of the High Command of the Wehrmacht, held views which favoured aggression and had expressed them in this study.

I assume that you remember this study. What have you to say about the accusation which is based on this study?

KEITEL: This study was submitted to me during my preliminary interrogation and thus I was reminded of its existence. In this connection I must also give a brief description of the background. It is not an exaggeration to say that in the early twenties, that is, shortly after the end of World War I, there was a great deal of literature produced, I believe, in all countries which had taken part in the war, on the most efficient organization and coordination at the highest level in the Armed Forces

(*Kriegsspitzengliederung*). I myself wrote on the subject and I know the opinions held in the United States, England, and France. At that time everybody was occupied with the question of that organization, and Von Blomberg said he was in favour of the eighth solution – seven had already been discarded.

In this connection a struggle developed, led by the High Command of the Army and the General Staff of the Army, who constantly opposed the idea of a combined supreme operational command of the Wehrmacht, and demanded that the supreme authority should be in the hands of the Army General Staff, as it was before.

When the High Command of the Wehrmacht was created and Blomberg had gone, the Army thought the moment opportune to return with renewed vigour to the attack. The result was a memorandum from the Commander-in-Chief of the Army, written by General Beck, and the answer to this is the study mentioned here. As I collaborated in the drafting of this answer, I can vouch for the two men responsible for it, namely, *Generaloberst* Jodl and myself, who were the only two who worked on it. I can state that at that time we were not motivated by any acute problem or by any preliminary general staff work in preparation for war, but only by the fact, as I might put it, that of all the many memoranda and investigations into the most expedient method, the one drawn up by us appeared to be the most practical.

THE PRESIDENT: Dr. Nelte, does not the document speak for itself? He says he collaborated in it, but that it was not concerned with war, so that is all that needs to be said. The document speaks for itself then.

DR. NELTE: But surely he may clarify some of the ideas contained in this document. Moreover, Mr. President, in regard to this question I took the liberty of submitting the affidavit in Document Book Number 2: "High Command of the Wehrmacht and General Staff" which is signed by the Defendant Keitel as well as by Herr Jodl. It has been submitted to you as Number 2 of Document Book 2.

THE PRESIDENT: Is that the affidavit of 8 March?

DR. NELTE: 29 March, Mr. President.

THE PRESIDENT: The first one in the book, or where is it?

DR. NELTE: No, in the second part.

THE PRESIDENT: But what page?

DR. NELTE: The pages have not been numbered consecutively, it has a table of contents, and under that you will find it as Number 2.

THE PRESIDENT: Are you quoting them from L-211 now? Are you finished with that?

DR. NELTE: This affidavit belongs to L-211.

THE PRESIDENT: I thought the witness said he had collaborated in the study, which is L-211, and that it was not concerned with war. You might leave it at that.

DR. NELTE: I believe, Mr. President, in this Trial it matters to hear what the defendants have to say about those documents which allegedly accuse them. The explanation of Document L-211 which the Defendant Keitel wishes to make is contained in the affidavit which I submitted in Document Book Number 2.

THE PRESIDENT: If what he wishes to say was put down in the affidavit then he should not have been asked about it; the affidavit should have been read.

DR. NELTE: The difference between the length of his verbal statement and the length of the affidavit is indicated by the relation of 1 to 10. He gave only a brief summary of the answer he wished to make. The affidavit is longer, and therefore I thought I could dispense with reading the affidavit if he would give us a brief summary of the chief points with which we are concerned.

THE PRESIDENT: You and I have a different idea of the word summary.

DR. NELTE: May I continue, Mr. President?

THE PRESIDENT: Yes, go on.

DR. NELTE: I now come to the question of rearmament, and the various cases of Austria, Czechoslovakia, *et cetera*. I would like to ask you about the accusation of the Prosecution that you participated in the planning and preparation of wars of aggression. So that we can understand each other, and that you can give your answers correctly, we must be quite clear as to what is meant by war of aggression. Will you tell us your views on that subject?

KEITEL: As a soldier, I must say that the term "War of Aggression" as used here is meaningless as far as I am concerned; we learned how to conduct actions of attack, actions of defence, and actions of retreat. However, according to my own personal feelings as a military man, the concept "war of aggression" is a purely political concept and not a military one. I mean that if the Wehrmacht and the soldier are a tool of the politicians, they are not qualified in my opinion to decide or to judge whether these military operations did or did not constitute a war of aggression. I think I can summarize my views by saying that military offices should not have authority to decide this question and are not in a position to do so; and that these decisions are not the task of the soldier, but solely that of the statesman.

DR. NELTE: Then you mean to say, and this applies also to all commanders and offices involved, that the question of whether or not a war is a war of aggression, or whether it has to be conducted for the defence of a country, in other words, whether a war is a just war or not, was not in the field of your professional deliberations and decisions?

KEITEL: No; that is what I wish to express, since…

DR. NELTE: What you are giving is an explanation. But you are not only a soldier, you are also an individual with a life of your own. When facts brought to your notice in your professional capacity seemed to reveal that a projected operation was unjust, did you not give it consideration?

KEITEL: I believe I can truthfully say that throughout the whole of my military career I was brought up, so to speak, in the old traditional concept that one never discussed this question. Naturally, one has one's own opinion and a life of one's own, but in the exercise of one's professional functions as a soldier and an officer, one has given this life away, yielded it up. Therefore I could not say either at that time or later that I had misgivings about questions of a purely political discretion, for I took the stand that a soldier has a right to have confidence in his state leadership, and accordingly he is obliged to do his duty and to obey.

DR. NELTE: Now let us take up the questions individually. Did you know Hitler's plans first in regard to rearmament, and later in regard to any aggression, as the Prosecution calls it? I am thinking chiefly of the period from February 1933 to 1938.

KEITEL: It was clear to me that when Hitler became Chancellor, we soldiers would undoubtedly have a different position in the Reich under new leadership, and that the military factor would certainly be viewed differently from what had been the case before. Therefore we quite honestly and openly welcomed the fact that at the head of the Reich Government there was a man who was determined to bring about an era which would lead us out of the deplorable conditions then prevailing. This much I must confess, that I welcomed the plan and intention to rearm as far as was possible at that time, as well as the ideas which tended in that direction. In any event, as early as 1933, in the late summer, I resigned from my activities in the War Ministry. I spent two years on active service and returned only at the time when the military sovereignty had been won back and we were rearming openly. Therefore, during my absence I did not follow these matters. At any rate, in the period from 1935 to 1938, during which I was Chief under Blomberg, I naturally saw and witnessed everything that took place in connection with rearmament and everything that was done in this field by the War Ministry to help the Wehrmacht branches.

DR. NELTE: Did you know that the occupation of the Rhineland in the demilitarized zone, the re-establishment of military sovereignty, the introduction of conscription, the building up of the Air Force and the increase in the number of Wehrmacht contingents violated the Versailles Treaty?

KEITEL: The wording of the Versailles Treaty, as long as it was considered binding upon us, did not, of course, permit these things. The Treaty of Versailles, may I say, was studied very closely by us in order to find loopholes which allowed us, without violating the treaty, to take measures which would not make us guilty of breaking the treaty. That was the daily task of the Reich Defence Committee.

From 1935 on, conditions were entirely different, and after my return as Chief, under Blomberg, I must state frankly that I no longer had any misgivings as to whether the Treaty of Versailles was violated or not because what was done, was done openly. We announced that we would raise 36 divisions. Discussions were held quite openly, and I could see nothing in which we soldiers could, in any way, see a violation of the treaty. It was clear to all of us, and it was our will to do everything to free ourselves of the territorial and military fetters of the Treaty of Versailles. I must say honestly that any soldier or officer who did not feel similarly about these things would in my estimation have been worthless. It was taken as a matter of course if one was a soldier.

DR. NELTE: During this Trial, an order, C-194, which bears your signature, was submitted. It concerns aerial reconnaissance and movements of U-boats at the time of the occupation of the Rhineland. This order leads to the inference that you participated in the occupation of the Rhineland. In what capacity did you sign this order?

KEITEL: The order shows already the future introductory phrasing: "The Commander-in-Chief of the Wehrmacht, Minister Von Blomberg, upon report, has ordered…" I transmitted in this form an instruction which General Von Blomberg had given me, to the Commander-in-Chief of the Air Force and I recall that it concerned the introduction of control measures during the days when the three battalions were marching into the demilitarized zone.

DR. NELTE: Did you, up to the time of your appointment as Chief of the OKW, learn from Hitler himself or from other sources, that there were plans in existence which, contrary to Hitler's avowed peace assurances could be put into effect only by force, that is, through a war?

KEITEL: During this period of time until the first practical measures were taken in the case of Austria, I cannot remember having had any knowledge of a programme, or the establishment of a programme or far-reaching plan, or one covering a period of years. I must say also that we were so occupied with the reorganization of this small army of seven divisions into an expanded force of twice or three times its original size, apart from the creation of a large air force which had no equipment at all, that in those years a visit to our office would have shown that we were completely occupied with purely organizational problems, and from the way Hitler worked, as described by me today, it is quite obvious that we saw nothing of these things.

DR. NELTE: Did you have any personal connection with Hitler before 4 February 1938?

KEITEL: In the years from 1935 to 1938, as chief under Blomberg, I saw the *Führer* three times. He never spoke one word to me and so he did not know me. If he knew anything at all about me it could have been only through Herr Von Blomberg. I had absolutely no contact with the *Führer* either personally or through other people who were prominent in the Party or in politics. My first conversation with him was in the last days of January before I was appointed to this office.

DR. NELTE: Did you hear anything of the meeting or discussion with Hitler in November 1937? I am referring to a conference in which Hitler, as it is alleged, made public his last will.

KEITEL: I already stated under oath at the preliminary interrogation that I did not know about this, and that I saw a document or the minutes or a record of this meeting at this Trial for the first time. I believe it is the Hossbach document and I do not remember that Von Blomberg gave me any directions to take preparatory steps after this conference. That is not the case.

DR. NELTE: Did you know of any of Hitler's intentions regarding territorial questions?

KEITEL: Yes. I must answer that in the affirmative. I learned of them, and I also knew from public political discussions that he proposed to settle in some form, gradually, sooner or later, a series of territorial problems which were the result of the Treaty of Versailles. That is true.

DR. NELTE: And what did you think about the realization of these territorial aims, I mean the manner in which they were to be solved?

KEITEL: At that time I saw these things and judged them only according to what we were capable of in military terms. I can only say, when I left the troops in 1935, none of these 24 divisions which were to be established existed. I did not view all this from the standpoint of political aims, but with the sober consideration: Can we accomplish anything by attack and the conduct of war if we have no military means at our disposal? Consequently for me everything in this connection revolved around the programmes of rearmament, which were to be completed in 1943-1945, and for the Navy in 1945. Therefore, we had 10 years in which to build up a concentrated Wehrmacht. Hence, I did not consider these problems acute even when they came to my attention in a political way, for I thought it impossible to realize these plans except by negotiations.

DR. NELTE: How do you explain the general directives of June 1937 for preparation for mobilization?

KEITEL: This document is actually an instruction for mobilization kept in general terms and was in line with our traditional General Staff policy before the war and before the World War, the World War I, that on principle something of the kind must be prepared beforehand. In my opinion, this had nothing to do with any of Hitler's political plans, for at that time I was already Chief of Staff under Blomberg, and General Jodl was at that time the Chief of the National Defence Division. Perhaps it sounds somewhat arrogant for me to say that we were very much satisfied that we were at last beginning to tell the Wehrmacht each year what it had to do intellectually and theoretically. In the former General Staff training which I received before the World War, the chief aim of these instructions was that the General Staff tours for the purpose of study should afford an opportunity for the theoretical elaboration of all problems. Such was the former training of the Great General Staff. I no longer know whether in this connection Blomberg himself originally thought out these salient ideas of possible complications or possible military contingencies, or whether he was perhaps influenced by the *Führer*.

It is certain that Hitler never saw this. It was the inside work of the General Staff of the Wehrmacht.

DR. NELTE: But in it you find a reference to a "Case Otto", and you know that that was the affair with Austria.

KEITEL: Of course I remember the Case Otto, which indicated by its name that it concerns Otto von Hapsburg. There must have been – were of course – certain reports about an attempted restoration, and in that case an intervention, eventually an armed one, was to take place. The *Führer*, Adolf Hitler, wished to prevent a restoration of the monarchy in Austria. Later this came up again in connection with the *Anschluss*. I believe that I can omit that now and perhaps explain later. In any event, we believed that on the basis of the deliberations by the Army some sort of preparations were being made which would bring into being Case Otto, because the code word was "Case Otto comes into force".

DR. NELTE: You mean to say that no concrete orders were given in regard to Case Otto on the basis of this general directive?

KEITEL: You mean the *Anschluss* at the beginning of February?

DR. NELTE: I beg your pardon?

KEITEL: I can state here only what I experienced when Hitler sent me to the Army. I went into General Beck's office and said: "The *Führer* demands that you report to him immediately and inform him about the preparations which have already been made for a possible invasion of Austria", and General Beck then said, "We have prepared nothing; nothing has been done, nothing at all".

DR. NELTE: The Prosecution contends that you participated in planning the action against Austria as it was put into effect in March of 1938. I have here the directive regarding Case Otto, C-102.

Can you still affirm that the whole matter was improvised?

KEITEL: I remember that this order was not issued to the Commander-in-Chief of the Army and to the other Commanders-in-Chief until the whole project was under way. Nothing had been prepared. It was all improvised and this was to be the documentary registration of facts which were being put into practice. The commands were given verbally and individually regarding what was to be done and what actually was done on the morning of 12 March, when Austria was invaded.

DR. NELTE: I must now return to the events preceding the case of Austria. You know that in General Jodl's diary it is stated: "Schuschnigg signs under strongest political and military pressure." In what manner did you participate in this conference at the Obersalzberg which took place with Schuschnigg?

KEITEL: May I add to my previous answer that we can see from this that the invasion took place on the morning of 12 March and the order was issued late in the evening of 11 March. Therefore this document could not have had any real influence on this affair. Such an order cannot be worked out between 10 in the evening and 6 in the morning.

I can say the following in regard to my participation at Obersalzberg on 10 or 11 February:

It was the first official action in which I took part. In the evening of 4 February Hitler left Berlin. He summoned me to be at Obersalzberg on 10 February. There, on that day the meeting with the Austrian Federal Chancellor, Schuschnigg, which has been frequently discussed here, took place. Shortly after I arrived – I had no idea why I had been summoned – General Von Reichenau arrived from Munich, and General of the Air Force, Sperrle; so that we three Generals were present when at about 10:30 Herr Schuschnigg arrived with Herr Von Papen. Since I had never attended a conference or a political action or any meeting of that nature, I did not know what I was there for. I must tell you this frankly, otherwise you will not understand it. In the course of the day the reason for the presence of the three representatives of the Wehrmacht naturally became clear to me. In certain respects they represented a military, at least a military demonstration – I may safely call it that. In the preliminary interrogation and also in later discussions I was asked the significance of the fact that in the afternoon my name was suddenly called through the house and I was to visit the *Führer*. I went to him in his room. Perhaps it sounds strange for me to say that when I entered the room I thought that he would give me a directive but the words were "Nothing at all". He used the words, "Please sit down". Then he said, "Yes, the Federal Chancellor wishes to have a short conference with his Foreign Minister Schmidt; otherwise I have nothing at all". I can only assure you that not one word was said to me about a political action apart from the fact that Herr Schuschnigg did not leave until the evening and that further conferences took place.

We generals sat in the anteroom, and when in the evening, shortly before my departure, I received the direction to launch reports that we were taking certain measures for mobilization, of which you have been informed here through a document, then it became quite clear to me that this day had served to bring the discussions to a head by the introduction of military representatives, and the directive to spread reports was to keep up the pressure, as has been shown here.

Upon my return to my apartment in Berlin, in the presence of Goebbels and Canaris, we discussed the reports which were to be sent out and which Canaris then broadcast in Munich. Finally, in order to conclude this matter, it might be interesting to point out that the Chief of Intelligence in the Austrian Federal Ministry, Lahousen, who has been present here in court, told Jodl and me when later on he came into the service of the Wehrmacht: "We were not taken in by this bluff." And I indubitably gave Jodl a basis for his entry in the diary, even though it is somewhat drastically worded, for I was naturally impressed by this first experience.

DR. NELTE: What is your position on the measures against Austria?

KEITEL: Nothing further need be said concerning the further developments of the affair. It has already been presented here in detail. On the day of the invasion by the troops I flew with Hitler to the front. We drove along the highways through Braunau, Linz. We stayed overnight and proceeded to Vienna. And to put it modestly, it is true that in every village we were received most enthusiastically and the Austrian Federal Army marched side by side with the German soldiers through the streets over which we drove. Not a shot was fired. On the other side the only formation which had a certain military significance was an armoured unit on the road from Passau to Vienna which arrived in Vienna with very few vehicles. This division was on the spot for the parade the next day. That is a very sober picture of what I saw.

DR. NELTE: Now we come to the question of Czechoslovakia. When did Hitler for the first time discuss with you the question of Czechoslovakia and his intentions in that respect?

KEITEL: I believe 6 to 8 weeks after the march into Austria, that is, after the *Anschluss* toward the end of April. The *Anschluss* was about the middle of March and also took the form of a sudden summons, one evening, to the Reich Chancellery where the *Führer* then explained matters to me. This resulted in the well-known directive in the Case Green. The history of this case is well known by the Schmundt Files all of which I identified in the preliminary interrogation. At that time he gave me first directives in a rather hasty manner. It was not possible for me to ask any questions, as he wished to leave Berlin immediately. These were the bases for the questions regarding the conditions under which a warlike action against Czechoslovakia could or would arise.

DR. NELTE: Did you have the impression that Hitler wanted to attack Czechoslovakia?

KEITEL: In any event the instructions which he gave me that evening were to the effect that preparations for a military action with all the preliminary work, which was the responsibility of the General Staff, were to be made. He expressed himself very precisely although he explained explicitly that the date was quite open and said that for the time being it was not his intention. These were the words: "… for the time being it is not my intention."

DR. NELTE: In this connection was a difference made between the Sudetenland and the whole of Czechoslovakia?

KEITEL: I do not believe that we discussed it at all that evening during that short conference. The *Führer* did not discuss with me the political aspects; he merely assigned me to the consideration of the necessary military measures. He did not say whether he would be content with the Sudetenland or whether we were to break through the Czechoslovakian line of fortification. That was not the problem at that time. But in any event – if they had to be settled by going to war – then the war had to be prepared; if it came to a conflict with the Czech Army, that is, a real war it would have to be prepared.

DR. NELTE: You know that the record of the Hitler-General Keitel Conference on 21 April, of which there are two versions, speaks of a lightning action being necessary in case of an incident. In the first one after the word "incident" it reads: "for example, the assassination of the German Minister" following a demonstration hostile to Germany. In the second one, after the word "incident" it reads only "for example, action in case of an incident". Will you please explain to what this note, which is not a record in the proper sense of the word, can be attributed?

KEITEL: I saw the Schmundt notes for the first time here. We did not receive it at that time as a document to work with. It is not a record. These are notes made subsequently by an adjutant. I do not want to doubt their correctness or accuracy, for memory would not permit me to recall today the exact words which were used. However this question, which is considered significant here, the assassination of the German

Minister in Prague, is a situation which I have never heard of, if only for the reason that no one ever said such a thing. It was said it might happen that the Minister is assassinated whereupon I asked which minister, or something similar. Then, as I recall it, Hitler said that the war of 1914 also started with an assassination at Sarajevo, and that such incidents could happen. I did not in any way get the impression at that time that a war was to be created through a provocation.

DR. NELTE: You will have to tell me some more on that point.

THE PRESIDENT: Perhaps we had better adjourn now.

[The Tribunal adjourned until 4 April 1946 at 1000 hours.]

NUREMBERG TRIAL PROCEEDINGS
NINETY-NINTH DAY
THURSDAY, 4 APRIL 1946

MORNING SESSION

THE PRESIDENT: Go on, Dr. Nelte.

DR. NELTE: Yesterday we discussed last the meeting on 21 April of you, Hitler, and Adjutant Schmundt. I am again having Document 388-PS brought to you and ask you to answer when I ask you. Was this not a conference of the kind which you said yesterday in principle did not take place?

KEITEL: To a certain extent it is true that I was called in and to my complete surprise was presented with ideas concerning preparation for war against Czechoslovakia. This took place within a very short time, before one of Hitler's departures for Berchtesgaden. I do not recall saying one word during these short instructions, but I asked only one question, and then with these extremely surprising directives I went home.

DR. NELTE: What happened then, so far as you were concerned?

KEITEL: My reflections during the first hour after that were that this could not be carried out in view of the military strength which I knew we then possessed. I then comforted myself with the thought that the conversation premised that nothing had been planned within a measurable lapse of time. The following day I discussed the matter with the Chief of the Operations Staff, General Jodl. I never received any minutes of this discussion, nor any record. The outcome of our deliberations was "to leave things alone because there was plenty of time, and because any such action was out of the question for military reasons".

I also explained to Jodl that the introductory words had been: "It is not my intention to undertake military action against Czechoslovakia within a measurable lapse of time."

Then, in the next weeks, we started theoretical deliberations; this, however, without taking into consultation the branches of the Wehrmacht because I considered myself not authorized to do so. In the following period it is to be noted, as can be seen from the Schmundt File, that the adjutants, the military adjutants, continuously asked innumerable detailed questions regarding the strength of divisions, and so on. These questions were answered by the Wehrmacht Operations Staff to the best of their knowledge.

DR. NELTE: I believe we can shorten this considerably, Herr Marshal, however important your explanations are. The decisive point now is – if you would take the document in front of you and compare the draft which you finally made on pressure from Obersalzberg and tell me what happened after that.

KEITEL: Yes. About four weeks after I had been given this job, I sent to Obersalzberg a draft of a directive for the preparatory measures. In reply I was informed that Hitler himself would come to Berlin to speak with the commander-in-chief. He came to Berlin at the end of May, and I was present at the conference with *Generaloberst* Von Brauchitsch. In this conference the basic plan was changed altogether, namely, to the effect that Hitler expressed the intention to take military action against Czechoslovakia in the very near future. As reason why he changed his mind he gave the fact that Czechoslovakia – I believe it was on 20 or 21 May – had ordered general mobilization, and Hitler at that time declared this could have been directed only against us. Military preparations had not been made by Germany. This was the reason for the complete change of his intentions, which he communicated orally to the Commander-in-Chief of the Army and he ordered him to begin preparations at once. This explains the changes in the basic orders, that is to say, the directive which was now being issued had as its basic idea: "It is my irrevocable decision to take military action against Czechoslovakia in the near future."

DR. NELTE: War against Czechoslovakia was avoided as a result of the Munich Agreement. What was your opinion and that of the generals about this agreement?

KEITEL: We were extraordinarily happy that it had not come to a military operation, because throughout the time of preparation we had always been of the opinion that our means of attack against the frontier fortifications of Czechoslovakia were insufficient. From a purely military point of view we lacked the means for an attack which involved the piercing of the frontier fortifications. Consequently we were extremely satisfied that a peaceful political solution had been reached.

DR. NELTE: What effect did this agreement have on the generals regarding Hitler's prestige?

KEITEL: I believe I may say that as a result this greatly increased Hitler's prestige among the generals. We recognized that on the one hand military means and military preparations had not been neglected and on the other hand a solution had been found which we had not expected and for which we were extremely thankful.

DR. NELTE: Is it not amazing that 3 weeks after the Munich Agreement that had been so welcomed by everyone, including the generals, Hitler gave instructions for the occupation of the remainder of Czechoslovakia?

KEITEL: I believe that recently *Reichsmarschall* Göring enlarged on this question in the course of his examination. It was my impression, as I remember it, that Hitler told me at that time that he did not believe that Czechoslovakia would overcome the loss of the Sudeten-German territories with their strong fortifications; and, moreover, he was concerned about the close relations then existing between Czechoslovakia and the Soviet Union and thought that Czechoslovakia could and perhaps would become a military and strategic menace. These were the military reasons which were given to me.

DR. NELTE: Was it not pointed out to Hitler by anyone that a solution by force of the problem regarding the remainder of Czechoslovakia involved a great danger, namely, that the other powers, that is England, France would be offended?

KEITEL: I was not informed of the last conversation in Munich between the British Prime Minister Chamberlain and the *Führer*. However, I regarded this question as far as its further treatment was concerned as a political one, and consequently I did not raise any objections, if I may so express myself, especially as a considerable reduction in the military preparations decided on before the Munich meeting was ordered. Whenever the political question was raised, the *Führer* refused to discuss it.

DR. NELTE: In connection with this question of Czechoslovakia, I should like to mention Lieutenant Colonel Kochling, who was characterized by the Prosecution as the liaison man with Henlein. Was the Wehrmacht or the OKW engaged in this matter?

KEITEL: Kochling's job remained unknown to me; it was I who named Kochling. Hitler asked me if an officer was available for a special mission, and if so he should report to me. After I dispatched Lieutenant Colonel Kochling from Berlin I neither saw nor spoke to him again. I do know, however, that, as I heard later, he was with Henlein as a sort of military adviser.

DR. NELTE: The Prosecution has pointed out that you were present at the visit of Minister President Tiso in March 1939, as well as at the visit of President Hacha, and from this it was deduced that you participated in the political discussions which then took place. What role did you play on these occasions?

KEITEL: It is true, I believe in every case, that on the occasion of such state visits and visits of foreign statesmen I was present in the Reich Chancellery or at the reception. I never took part in the actual discussions of political questions. I was present at the reception and felt that I should be present to be introduced as a high-ranking representative of the Wehrmacht. But in each individual case that I can recall I was dismissed with thanks or waited in the antechamber in case I should be needed. I can positively say that I did not say one single word either to Tiso or to President Hacha on that night, nor did I take part in Hitler's direct discussions with these men. May I add that just on the night of President Hacha's visit I had to be present in the Reich Chancellery, because during that night the High Command of the Army had to be instructed as to how the entry which had been prepared was to take place.

DR. NELTE: In this connection I wish to establish only this since I assume that this question has been clarified by *Reichsmarschall* Göring's testimony. You never spoke to President Hacha of a possible bombing of Prague in the event that he should not be willing to sign?

KEITEL: No.

DR. NELTE: We come now to the case of Poland. Here too the Prosecution accuses you of having participated in the planning and preparation for military action against Poland and of having assisted in the execution of this action. Would you state in brief your basic attitude towards these Eastern problems?

KEITEL: The question concerning the problem of Danzig and the Corridor were known to me. I also knew that political discussions and negotiations with regard to these questions were pending. The case of the attack on Poland, which in the course of time had to be and was prepared, was, of course, closely connected with these problems.

Since I myself was not concerned with political matters, I personally was of the opinion that, as in the case of Munich and before Munich, military preparations, that is, military pressure if I may call it such, would play the same kind of role as in my opinion it had played at Munich. I did not believe that the matter would be brought to an end without military preparations.

DR. NELTE: Could not this question have been solved by direct preceding negotiations?

KEITEL: That is hard for me to say, although I know that several discussions took place concerning the Danzig question as well as concerning a solution of the Corridor problem. I recall a remark that impressed me at the time, when Hitler once said he deplored Marshal Pilsudski's death, because he believed he had reached or could have reached an agreement with this statesman. This statement was once made to me.

DR. NELTE: The Prosecution has stated that already in the autumn of 1938 Hitler was working on the question of a war against Poland. Did you participate in this in 1938?

KEITEL: No. This I cannot recall. I should like to believe that, to my recollection, at that time there were even signs that this was not the case. At that time I accompanied Hitler on an extensive tour of inspection of the eastern fortifications. We covered the entire front from Pomerania through the Oder-Warthe marshland as far as Breslau in order to inspect the various frontier fortifications against Poland. The question of fortifications in East Prussia was thoroughly discussed at that time. When I consider this in this connection today, I can only assume that for him these discussions were possibly connected with the Danzig and Corridor problem and he simply wanted to find out whether these eastern fortifications had sufficient defensive strength, should the Danzig and Corridor question eventually lead to war with Poland.

DR. NELTE: When were the preparations made for the occupation of Danzig?

KEITEL: I believe that as early as the late autumn of 1938 orders were issued that Danzig be occupied at a favourable moment by a *coup de main* from East Prussia. That is all I know about it.

DR. NELTE: Was the possibility of war against Poland discussed in this connection?

KEITEL: Yes, that was apparently connected with the examination of the possibilities to defend the border, but I do not recall any, nor was there any kind of preparation, any military preparations, at that time, apart from a surprise attack from East Prussia.

DR. NELTE: If I remember rightly you once told me, when we discussed this question, that Danzig was to be occupied only if this would not result in a war with Poland.

KEITEL: Yes, that is so. This statement was made time and again, that this occupation of, or the surprise attack on Danzig was to be carried out only if it was certain that it would not lead to war.

DR. NELTE: When did this view change?

KEITEL: I believe Poland's refusal to discuss any kind of solution of the Danzig question was apparently the reason for further deliberations and steps.

DR. NELTE: The Prosecution is in possession of the directive of 3 April 1939...

KEITEL: I might perhaps add that generally after Munich the situation also in regard to the Eastern problem was viewed differently, perhaps, or as I believe, from this point of view: The problem of Czechoslovakia has been solved satisfactorily without a shot. This will perhaps also be possible with regard to the other German problems in the East. I also believe I remember Hitler saying that he did not think the Western Powers, particularly England, would be interested in Germany's Eastern problem and would sooner act as mediators than raise any objection.

DR. NELTE: That is Document C-120, the *"Fall Weiss"*. According to this, the directive was issued on 3 April 1939.

KEITEL: Let us take the document first. In the first sentence it is already stated that this document was to replace the regular annual instructions of the Wehrmacht regarding possible preparations for mobilization, a further elaboration of subjects known to us from the instructions which had been issued in 1937-38 and which were issued every year. But in fact, at that time or shortly before, Hitler had, in my presence, directly instructed the Commander-in-Chief of the Army to make strategic and operative preparations for an attack on, for a war with Poland. I then issued these first considerations, as can be seen from this document, that is, the *Führer* had already ordered the following: Everything should be worked out by the OKH of the Army by 1 September 1939, and that after this a timetable should be drawn up. This document was signed by me at that time.

DR. NELTE: What was your attitude and that of the other generals towards this war?

KEITEL: I must say that at this time, as in the case of the preparations against Czechoslovakia, both the Commander-in-Chief of the Army and the generals to whom I spoke, and also I, myself, were opposed to the idea of waging a war against Poland. We did not want this war, but, of course, we immediately began to carry out the given orders, at least as far as the elaboration by the General Staff was concerned. Our reason was that to our knowledge the military means which were at our disposal at that time, that is to say, the divisions, their equipment, their armament, let alone their absolutely inadequate supply of munitions kept reminding us as soldiers that we were not ready to wage a war.

DR. NELTE: Do you mean to say that in your considerations only military viewpoints defined your attitude?

KEITEL: Yes. I must admit that. I did not concern myself with the political problems but only with the question: Can we or can we not?

DR. NELTE: I want to establish only this. Now, on 23 May 1939, there was a conference at which Hitler addressed the generals. You know this address? What was the reason for and the contents of this address?

KEITEL: I saw the minutes of it for the first time in the course of my interrogations here. It reminded me of the situation at that time. The purpose of this address was to show the generals that their misgivings were unfounded, to remove their misgivings, and finally to point out that the conditions were not yet given and that political negotiations about these matters still could and perhaps would change the situation. It was however simply to give encouragement.

DR. NELTE: Were you at that time of the opinion that war would actually break out?

KEITEL: No, at that time – and this was perhaps rather naive – I believed that war would not break out, that in view of the military preparations ordered, negotiations would take place again and a solution would be found. In our military considerations a strictly military point of view was always dominant. We generals believed that France – to a lesser extent England – in view of her mutual-assistance pact with

Poland would intervene and that we did not at all have the defensive means for this. For this very reason I personally was always convinced that there would be no war because we could not wage a war against Poland if France attacked us in the West.

DR. NELTE: Now then, what was your opinion of the situation after the speech of 22 August 1939?

KEITEL: This speech was made at the end of August and was addressed to the generals assembled at Obersalzberg, the commanders-in-chief of the troops preparing in the East. When Hitler, towards the end of this speech, declared that a pact had been concluded with the Soviet Union, I was firmly convinced that there would be no war because I believed that these conditions constituted a basis for negotiation and that Poland would not expose herself to it. I also believed that now a basis for negotiations had been found although Hitler said in this speech, a copy of which I read here for the first time from notes, that all preparations had been made, and that it was intended to put them into execution.

DR. NELTE: Did you know that England actually attempted to act as intermediary?

KEITEL: No, I knew nothing of these matters. The first thing which was very surprising to me was that on one of those days which have been discussed here repeatedly, namely on the 24th or 25th, only a few days after the conference at Obersalzberg, I was suddenly called to Hitler at the Reich Chancellery and he said to me only, "Stop everything at once, get Brauchitsch immediately. I need time for negotiations". I believe that after these few words I was dismissed.

DR. NELTE: What followed thereupon?

KEITEL: I at once rang up the Commander-in-Chief of the Army and passed on the order, and Brauchitsch was called to the *Führer*.

Everything was stopped and all decisions on possible military action were suspended, first without any time limit, on the following day for a certain limited period, I believe it was 5 days according to the calculations we can make today.

DR. NELTE: Did you know of the so-called minimum demands on Poland?

KEITEL: I believe that I saw them in the Reich Chancellery, that Hitler himself showed them to me, so that I knew about them.

DR. NELTE: As you saw them, I would like to ask whether you considered these demands to be serious?

KEITEL: At that time I was always only a few minutes in the Reich Chancellery and as a soldier I naturally believed that these were meant perfectly honestly.

DR. NELTE: Was there any talk at that time of border incidents?

KEITEL: No. This question of border incidents was also extensively discussed with me here in my interrogations. In this situation and in the few discussions we had at the Reich Chancellery in those days there was no talk at all on this question.

DR. NELTE: I am now having Document 795-PS brought to you, notes which deal with the Polish uniforms for Heydrich.

KEITEL: May I add…

DR. NELTE: Please do.

KEITEL: … namely, that on 30 August, I believe, the day for the attack, which took place on 1 September, was again postponed for

24 hours. For this reason Brauchitsch and I were again called to the Reich Chancellery and to my recollection the reason given was that a Polish Government plenipotentiary was expected. Everything was to be postponed for 24 hours. Then no further changes of the military instructions occurred.

This document deals with Polish uniforms for border incidents or for some sort of illegal actions. It has been shown to me, I know it; it is a subsequent note made by Admiral Canaris of a conversation he had with me. He told me at that time that he was to make available a few Polish uniforms. This had been communicated to him by the *Führer* through the adjutant. I asked: "For what purpose?" We both agreed that this was intended for some illegal action. If I remember rightly I told him at that time that I did not believe in such things at all and that he had better keep his hands off. We then had a short discussion about Dirschau which was also to be taken by a *coup de main* by the Wehrmacht. That is all I heard of it. I believe I told Canaris he could dodge the issue by saying that he had no Polish uniforms. He could simply say he had none and the matter would be settled.

DR. NELTE: You know, of course, that this matter was connected with the subsequent attack on the radio station at Gleiwitz. Do you know anything of this incident?

KEITEL: This incident, this action came to my knowledge for the first time here through the testimony of witnesses. I never found out who was charged to carry out such things and I knew nothing of the raid on the radio station at Gleiwitz until I heard the testimonies given here before the Tribunal. Neither do I recall having heard at that time that such an incident had occurred.

DR. NELTE: Did you know of the efforts of America and Italy after 1 September 1939 to end the war in one way or another?

KEITEL: I knew nothing at all of the political discussions that took place in those days from 24 to 30/31 August or the beginning of September 1939. I never knew anything about the visits of a Herr Dahlerus. I knew nothing of London's intervention. I remember only that, while in the Reich Chancellery for a short time, I met Hitler, who said to me: "Do not disturb me now, I am writing a letter to Daladier." This must have been in the first days of September. Neither I nor, to my knowledge, any of the other generals ever knew anything about the matters I have heard of here or about the steps that were still taken after 1 September. Nothing at all.

DR. NELTE: What did you say to Canaris and Lahousen in the *Führer's* train on 14 September, that is, shortly before the attack on Warsaw, with regard to the so-called political "house cleaning"?

KEITEL: I have been interrogated here about this point, but I did not recall this visit at all. But from Lahousen's testimony it appeared – he said, as I remember – that I had repeated what Hitler had said and had passed on these orders, as he put it. I know that the Commander-in-Chief of the Army who then directed the military operations in Poland had at the daily conferences already complained about interference by the police in occupied Polish territory. I can only say that I apparently repeated what had been said about these things in my presence between Hitler and Brauchitsch. I can make no statements regarding details.

I might add that to my recollection the Commander-in-Chief of the Army at that time complained several times that as long as he had the executive power in the occupied territories he would under no circumstances tolerate other agencies in this area and that at his request he was relieved of his responsibility for Poland in October. I therefore believe that the statements the witness made from memory or on the strength of notes are not quite correct.

DR. NELTE: We come now to the question of Norway. Did you know that in October 1939 Germany had given a declaration of neutrality to Denmark and Norway?

KEITEL: Yes, I knew that.

DR. NELTE: Were you and the OKW taken into consultation about declarations of neutrality in this or other cases?

KEITEL: No.

DR. NELTE: Were you informed of them?

KEITEL: No, we were not informed either. These were discussions referring to foreign policy, of which we soldiers were not informed.

DR. NELTE: You mean you were not informed officially. But you as a person who also reads newspapers knew of it?

KEITEL: Yes.

DR. NELTE: Good. Before our discussion about the problem of aggressive war I asked you a question which, in order to save time, I would not like to repeat. However, it seems to me that the question I put to you in order to get your opinion on aggressive war must be asked again in this connection because an attack on a neutral country, a country which had been given a guarantee was bound to cause particular scruples on the part of people who have to do with these things, with the waging of war.

Therefore, I put this question to you again in this case and ask you to describe what your attitude and the soldiers' attitude was to it.

KEITEL: In this connection, I must say we were already at war. There was a state of war with England and France. It would not be right for me to say that I interfered in the least with these matters, but I regarded them rather as political matters, and, as a soldier, I held the opinion that preparations for military actions against Norway and Denmark did not yet mean their outbreak and that these preparations would very obviously take months if such an action was executed at all and that in the meantime the situation could change. It was this train of thought which caused me not to take any steps in regard to the impossibility to consider and to prepare strategically this intervention in Norway and Denmark; therefore, I left these things, I must say, to those who were concerned with political matters. I cannot put it any other way.

DR. NELTE: When did the preparations for this action start?

KEITEL: I think the first deliberations took place already in October 1939; on the other hand, the first directives were issued only in January, that is to say, several months later. In connection with the discussions before this Tribunal and with the information given by *Reichsmarschall* Göring in his statements, I also remember that one day I was ordered to call Grand Admiral Raeder to the *Führer*. He wanted to discuss with him questions regarding sea warfare in the Bay of Helgoland and in the Atlantic Ocean and the dangers we would encounter in waging war in this area.

Then Hitler ordered me to call together a special staff which was to study all these problems from the viewpoint of sea, air, and land warfare. I remembered this also upon seeing the documents produced here. This special staff dispensed with my personal assistance. Hitler said at the time that he himself would furnish tasks for this staff. These were, I believe, the military considerations in the months from 1939 to the beginning of 1940.

DR. NELTE: In this connection I should only like to know further whether you had any conversation with Quisling at this stage of preliminary measures?

KEITEL: No, I saw Quisling neither before nor after the Norway campaign; I saw him for the first time approximately one or two years later. We had no contact, not even any kind of transmission of information. I already stated in a preliminary interrogation that by order of Hitler I sent an officer, I believe it was Colonel Pieckenbrock, to Copenhagen for conferences with Norwegians. I did not know Quisling.

DR. NELTE: As to the war in the West, there is once more in the foreground the question of violation of neutrality in the case of Luxembourg, Belgium, and Holland. Did you know that these three countries had been given assurances regarding the inviolability of their neutrality?

KEITEL: Yes, I knew and also was told that at that time.

DR. NELTE: I do not want to ask the same questions as in the case of Norway and Denmark, but, in this connection, however, I should like to ask: Did you consider these assurances by Hitler to be honest?

KEITEL: When I remember the situation as it was then, I did at that time believe, when I learned of these things, that there was no intention of bringing any other state into the war. At any rate, I had no reason, no justification, to assume the opposite, namely that this was intended as a deception.

DR. NELTE: After the conclusion of the Polish campaign did you still believe that there was any possibility of terminating or localizing the war?

KEITEL: Yes, I did believe this. My view was strengthened by the Reichstag speech after the Polish war, in which allusions were made which convinced me that political discussions about this question were going on, above all, with England, and because Hitler had told me time and again, whenever these questions were brought up, "The West is actually not interested in these Eastern problems of Germany". This was the phrase he always used to calm people, namely that the Western Powers were not interested in these problems.

Furthermore, seen from a purely military point of view, it must be added that we soldiers had, of course, always expected an attack by the Western Powers, that is to say, by France, during the Polish campaign, and were very surprised that in the West, apart from some skirmishes between the Maginot Line and the West Wall, nothing had actually happened, though we had – this I know for certain – along the whole Western Front from the Dutch border to Basel only five divisions, apart from the small forces manning the fortifications of the West Wall. Thus, from a purely military operative point of view, a French attack during the Polish campaign would have encountered only a German military screen not a real defence. Since nothing of this sort happened, we soldiers thought of course that the Western Powers had no serious intentions, because they did not take advantage of the extremely favourable situation for military operations and did not undertake anything, at least not anything serious, against us during the 3 to 4 weeks when all the German fighting formations were employed in the East. This also strengthened our views as to what the attitude of the Western Powers would probably be in the future.

DR. NELTE: What plans did Hitler have for the West?

KEITEL: During the last phase of the Polish campaign, he had already transferred all unnecessary forces to the West, in consideration of the fact that at any time something else might happen there. However, during the last days of the Polish campaign, he had already told me that he intended to throw his forces as swiftly as possible from the East to the West and if possible, attack in the West in the winter of 1939-1940.

DR. NELTE: Did these plans include attacks on and marching through Luxembourg, Belgium, and Holland?

KEITEL: Not in the beginning, but first, if we can express it from the military point of view, the deployment in the West was to be a protective measure, that is, a thorough strengthening of the frontiers, of course preferably to take place where there was nothing except border posts. Accordingly, already at the end of September and the beginning of October, a transportation of the army from the East to the West did take place, as a security measure without, however, any fixed centre of gravity.

DR. NELTE: What did the military leaders know about Belgium and Holland's attitude?

KEITEL: This naturally changed several times in the course of the winter. At that time, in the autumn of 1939 – I can speak only for myself, and there may be other opinions on this matter – I was convinced that Belgium wanted to remain out of the war under any circumstances and would do anything she could to preserve her neutrality. On the other hand, we received, through the close connections between the Belgian and Italian royal houses, a number of reports that sounded very threatening. I had no way of finding out whether they were true, but we learned of them, and they indicated that strong pressure was exerted on Belgium to give up her neutrality.

As for Holland, we knew at that time only that there were General Staff relations between her and England.

But then of course, in the months from October 1939 to May 1940 the situation changed considerably and the tension varied greatly. From the purely military point of view, we knew one thing: That all the French swift units, that is motorized units, were concentrated on the Belgian-French border, and from a military point of view, we interpreted this measure as meaning that at least preparations were being made for crossing through Belgium at any time with the swift units and advancing up to the borders of the Ruhr district.

I believe I should omit details here, because they are not important for the further developments, they are of a purely operative and strategic nature.

DR. NELTE: Were there differences of opinion between the generals and Hitler with reference to the attack in the West which had to take place through this neutral territory?

KEITEL: I believe I must say that this at that time was one of the most serious crises in the whole war, namely, the opinions held by a number of generals, including the Commander-in-Chief of the Army, Brauchitsch, and his Chief of General Staff, and I also personally belong to that group, which wanted at all costs to attempt to prevent an attack in the West which Hitler intended for that winter. There were various reasons for this: The difficulty of transporting the Eastern Army to the West; then the point of view – and this I must state – the fact that we believed at that time, perhaps more from the political point of view, that if we did not attack, the possibility of a peaceful solution might still exist and might still be realizable. Thus we considered it possible that between then and the spring many political changes could take place. Secondly, as soldiers, we were decidedly against the waging of a winter war, in view of the short days and long nights, which are always a great hindrance to all military operations. To Hitler's objection that the French swift forces might march through Belgium at any time and then stand before the Ruhr district, we answered that we were superior in such a situation in a war of movement, we were a match for it; that was our view. I may add that this situation led to a very serious crisis between Hitler and the Commander-in-Chief of the Army and also me, because I had this trend of thought which Hitler vigorously rejected because it was, as he declared, strategically wrong. In our talks he accused me in the sharpest manner of conspiring against him with the generals of the Army and strengthening them in their opposition to his views. I must state here that I then asked to be relieved immediately of my post and given another, because I felt that under these circumstances the confidence between Hitler and myself had been completely destroyed, and I was greatly offended. I may add that relations with the Commander-in-Chief of the Army also suffered greatly from this. But the idea of my discharge or employment elsewhere was sharply rejected, I would not be entitled to it. It has already been discussed here; I need not go into it any further. But this breach of confidence was not to be mended, not even in the future. In the case of Norway, there had already been a similar conflict because I had left the house. General Jodl's diary refers to it as a "serious crisis". I shall not go into this in detail.

DR. NELTE: What was the reason for Hitler's speech to the Commanders-in-Chief on 23 November 1939, in the Reich Chancellery?

KEITEL: I can say that this was very closely connected with the crisis between Hitler and the generals. He called a meeting of the generals at that time to present and substantiate his views, and we knew it was his intention to bring about a change of attitude on the part of the generals. In the notes on this speech, we see that individual persons were more than once directly and sharply rebuked. The reasons given by those who had spoken against this attack in the West were repeated. Moreover, he now wanted to make an irrevocable statement of his will to carry out this attack in the West that very winter, because this, in his view, was the only strategic solution, as every delay was to the enemy's advantage. In other words, at that time, he no longer counted on any other solution than resort to force of arms.

DR. NELTE: When, then, was the decision made to advance through Belgium and Holland?

KEITEL: The preparations for such a march through and attack on Belgium and Holland had already been made, but Hitler withheld the decision as to whether such a big attack or violation of the neutrality of these countries was actually to be carried out, and kept it open until the spring of 1940, obviously for all sorts of political reasons, and perhaps also with the idea that the problem would automatically be solved if the enemy invaded Belgium or if the mobile French troops entered, or something like that. I can only state that the decision for the carrying out of this plan was withheld until the very last moment and the order was given only immediately before it was to be executed. I believe that there was also one other factor in this, which I have already mentioned, namely the relationship between the royal houses of Italy and Belgium. Hitler always surrounded his decisions with secrecy for he was obviously afraid that they might become known through this relationship.

[A recess was taken.]

THE PRESIDENT: Dr. Nelte, the Tribunal will be glad if when you refer to Czechoslovakia or any other state you will refer to it by its proper name, you, and the defendants, and other witnesses.

DR. NELTE: Mr. President, the Defendant Keitel wishes to make a slight correction in the statement which he made earlier upon my question regarding the occupation in the West during the Polish campaign.

THE PRESIDENT: Very well.

KEITEL: I said earlier that in the West during the war against Poland, there were five divisions. I must rectify that statement. I had confused that with the year 1938. In 1939 there were approximately 20 divisions, including the reserves in the Rhineland and in the West district behind the lines. Therefore, the statement I made was made inadvertently and was a mistake.

DR. NELTE: Now we come to the Balkan wars. The Prosecution, with reference also to the war against Greece and Yugoslavia, have accused you of having cooperated in the preparation, planning, and above all in the carrying out of those wars. What is your attitude toward this?

KEITEL: We were drawn into the war against Greece and against Yugoslavia in the spring of 1941 to our complete surprise and without having made any plans. Let me take Greece first: I accompanied Hitler during his journey through France for the meetings with Marshal Petain and with Franco on the Spanish border, and during that journey we received our first news regarding the intention of Italy to attack Greece. The journey to Florence was immediately decided upon, and upon arrival in Florence, we received Mussolini's communication, which has already been mentioned by *Reichsmarschall* Göring, namely, that the attack against Greece had already begun.

I can only say from my own personal knowledge that Hitler was extremely angry about this development and the dragging of the Balkans into the war and that only the fact that Italy was an ally prevented a break with Mussolini. I never knew of any intentions to wage war against Greece.

DR. NELTE: Was there any necessity for Germany to enter into that war or how did that come about?

KEITEL: At first the necessity did not exist, but during the first months, October-November, of that campaign of the Italians, it already became clear that the Italian position in this war had become extremely precarious. Therefore, as early as November or December, there were calls on the part of Mussolini for help, calls to assist him in some form or other.

Moreover, seen from the military point of view, it was clear of course that for the entire military position in the war, a defeat of Italy in the Balkans would have had considerable and very serious consequences. Therefore, by improvised means, assistance was rendered. I think a mountain division was to be brought in, but it was technically impossible, since there were no transportation facilities. Then another solution was attempted by means of air transport and the like.

DR. NELTE: At the time when improvisations ceased, we come, however, to the plan presented by the Prosecution and called "Marita". When was that?

KEITEL: The war in Greece and Albania had begun to reach a certain standstill because of winter conditions. During that time, plans were conceived in order to avoid a catastrophe for Italy, to bring in against Greece certain forces from the North for an attack to relieve pressure, for such I must call it. That would, and did of course, take several months.

May I just explain that at that time the idea of a march through Yugoslavia, or even the suggestion that forces should be brought in through Yugoslavia was definitely turned down by Hitler, although the Army particularly had proposed that possibility as the most suitable way of bringing in troops.

Regarding the "Operation Marita", perhaps not much more can be said than to mention the march through Bulgaria, which had been prepared and discussed diplomatically with Bulgaria.

DR. NELTE: I would like to ask just one more question on that subject. The Prosecution have stated that even before the overthrow of the Yugoslav Government, that is to say, at the end of March 1941, negotiations were conducted with Hungary for the eventuality of an attack on Yugoslavia. Were you or the OKW informed of this, or were you consulted?

KEITEL: No. I have no recollection at all of any military discussion on the part of the OKW with Hungary regarding the eventuality of a military action in the case of Yugoslavia. That is completely unknown to me. On the contrary, everything that happened later on – a few words about Yugoslavia will have to be said later – was completely improvised. Nothing had been prepared, at any rate not with the knowledge of the OKW.

DR. NELTE: But it is known to you, is it not, that military discussions with Hungary had taken place during that period? I assume that you merely want to say that they did not refer to Yugoslavia.

KEITEL: Of course, it was known to me that several discussions had taken place with the Hungarian General Staff.

DR. NELTE: You said you wanted to say something else about the case of Yugoslavia. *Reichsmarschall* Göring has made statements upon that subject here. Can you add anything new? Otherwise, I have no further questions with regard to that subject.

KEITEL: I should merely like to confirm once more that the decision to proceed against Yugoslavia with military means meant completely upsetting any military advances and arrangements made up to that time. Marita had to be completely readjusted. Also new forces had to be brought through Hungary from the North. All that was completely improvised.

DR. NELTE: We come now to *Fall* Barbarossa. The Soviet Prosecution, particularly, have stressed that the Supreme Command of the Armed Forces and you as Chief of Staff, as early as the summer of 1940, had dealt with the plan of an attack against the Soviet Union. When did Hitler for the first time talk to you about the possibility of a conflict, of an armed conflict with the Soviet Union?

KEITEL: As far as I recollect, that was at the beginning of August 1940, on the occasion of a discussion of the situation at Berchtesgaden, or rather at his house, the Berghof. That was the first time that the possibility of an armed conflict with the Soviet Union was discussed.

DR. NELTE: What were the reasons which Hitler gave at that time which might possibly lead to a war?

KEITEL: I think I can refer to what *Reichsmarschall* Göring has said on this subject.
According to our notions, there were considerable troop concentrations in Bessarabia and Bukovina. The Foreign Minister,

too, had mentioned figures which I cannot recall, and there was the anxiety which had been repeatedly voiced by Hitler at that time that developments might result in the Romanian theatre which would endanger our source of petroleum, the fuel supply for the conduct of the war, which for the most part came from Romania. Apart from that, I think he talked about strong or manifest troop concentrations in the Baltic provinces.

DR. NELTE: Were any directives given by you at that time or by those branches of the Wehrmacht which were affected?

KEITEL: No. As far as I can recollect this was confined firstly to increased activities of the intelligence or espionage service against Russia and, secondly, to certain investigations regarding the possibility of transferring troops from the West, from France, as quickly as possible to the Southeast areas or to East Prussia. Certain return transports of troops from the Eastern military districts had already taken place at the end of July. Apart from that no instructions were given at that time.

DR. NELTE: How was the line of demarcation occupied?

KEITEL: There were continual reports from that border or demarcation line on frontier incidents, shootings, and particularly about frequent crossings of that line by aircraft of the Soviet Union, which led to the due exchange of notes. But at any rate there were continual small frontier fights and shootings, particularly in the South, and we received information through our frontier troops that continual or at certain times new Russian troop units appeared opposite them. I think that was all.

DR. NELTE: Do you know how many divisions of the German Wehrmacht were stationed there at the time?

KEITEL: During the Western campaign there were – I do not think I am wrong this time – seven divisions, seven divisions from East Prussia to the Carpathians, two of which, during the Western campaign, had even been transported to the West but later on were transported back again.

DR. NELTE: The Prosecution submitted that at the end of July 1940 *Generaloberst* Jodl had given general instructions at Reichenhall to several officers of the Wehrmacht Operations Staff to study the Russian problems and particularly to examine the railway transport problems. Since you said a little earlier that not until August did you hear for the first time from Hitler what the situation was, I am now asking you whether you were informed about these conferences of *Generaloberst* Jodl.

KEITEL: No. I did not hear until I came here, that such a conference took place in Berchtesgaden at the end of July or beginning of August. This was due to the fact that I was absent from Berchtesgaden. I did not know of this conference, and I think General Jodl probably forgot to tell me about it at the time. I did not know about it.

DR. NELTE: What were your personal views at that time regarding the problem which arose out of the conference with Hitler?

KEITEL: When I became conscious of the fact that the matter had been given really serious thought I was very surprised, and I considered it most unfortunate. I seriously considered what could be done to influence Hitler by using military considerations. At that time, as has been briefly discussed here by the Foreign Minister, I wrote a personal memorandum containing my thoughts on the subject, I should like to say, independently of the experts working in the General Staff and the Wehrmacht Operations Staff and wanted to present this memorandum to Hitler. I decided on that method because, as a rule, one could never get beyond the second sentence of a discussion with Hitler. He took the word out of one's mouth and afterwards one never was able to say what one wanted to say. And in this connection I should like to say right now that I had the idea – it was the first and only time – of visiting the

Foreign Minister personally, in order to ask him to support me from the political angle regarding that question. That is the visit to Fuschl, which has already been discussed here and which the Foreign Minister Von Ribbentrop confirmed during his examination the other day.

DR. NELTE: Then you confirm what Herr Von Ribbentrop has said, so that there is no need for me to repeat it?

KEITEL: I confirm that I went to Fuschl. I had the memorandum with me. It had been written by hand, since I did not want anybody else to get hold of it. And I left Fuschl conscious of the fact that he wanted to try to exercise influence on Hitler to the same end. He promised me that.

DR. NELTE: Did you give that memorandum to Hitler?

KEITEL: Yes. Some time later at the Berghof, after a report of the situation had been given, I handed him that memorandum when we were alone. I think he told me at the time that he was going to study it. He took it, and did not give me a chance to make any explanations.

DR. NELTE: Considering its importance did you later on find an opportunity to refer to it again?

KEITEL: Yes. At first nothing at all happened, so that after some time I reminded him of it and asked him to discuss the problem with me. This he did, and the matter was dealt with very briefly by his saying that the military and strategic considerations put forward by me were in no way convincing. He, Hitler, considered these ideas erroneous, and turned them down. In that connection I can perhaps mention very briefly that I was again very much upset and there was another crisis when I asked to be relieved of my post, and that another man be put in my office and that I be sent to the front. That once more led to a sharp controversy as has already been described by the *Reichsmarschall* when he said that Hitler took the attitude that he would not tolerate that a general whose views he did not agree with should ask to be relieved of his post because of this disagreement. I think he said that he had every right to turn down such suggestions and ideas if he considered them wrong. I had not the right to take any action.

DR. NELTE: Did he return that memorandum to you?

KEITEL: No, I do not think I got it back. I have always assumed that it was found among the captured Schmundt files, which apparently is not the case. I did not get it back; he kept it.

DR. NELTE: I do not wish to occupy the time of the Tribunal in this connection any further. I will leave it to you as to whether you wish to disclose the contents of that memorandum. I am not so much concerned with the military presentation – one can imagine what it was – but the question is: Did you refer to the Non-Aggression Pact of 1939 in that memorandum?

KEITEL: Yes, but I must say that the main part of my memorandum was devoted to military studies, military studies regarding the amount of forces, the requirements of effectives, and the dispersal of forces in France and Norway at the time, and the Luftwaffe in Italy, and our being tied down in the West. In that memorandum I most certainly pointed to the fact that this Non-Aggression Pact existed. But all the rest were military considerations.

DR. NELTE: Were any military orders given at that time?

KEITEL: No. No orders were given at that time except, I think, for the improvement of lines of communications from the West to the East to permit speeding up troop transports, particularly to the Southeastern sector, in other words, north of the Carpathians and in the East Prussian sector. Apart from that no orders of any kind were given at that time.

DR. NELTE: Had the discussion with Foreign Minister Molotov already taken place at that time?

KEITEL: No. On the contrary, at that time, in October the idea of a discussion with the Russians was still pending. Hitler also told me that at the time, and he always emphasized in that connection that until such a discussion had taken place he would not give any orders, since it had been proved to him by General Jodl that in any case it was technically impossible to transfer strong troop units into the threatened sectors in the East which I have mentioned. Accordingly, nothing was done. The visit or rather discussion with the Russian delegation was prepared, in which connection I would like to say that I made the suggestion at that time that Hitler should talk personally with M. Stalin. That was the only thing I did in the matter.

DR. NELTE: During that conference were military matters discussed?

KEITEL: I did not take any part in the discussions with M. Molotov, although in this instance too I was present at the reception and at certain social meetings. I remember that on two occasions I sat next to Molotov at the table. I did not hear any political discussion, nor did I have any political discussions with my table companion.

DR. NELTE: What did Hitler say after these discussions had come to an end?

KEITEL: After the departure of Molotov he really said very little. He more or less said that he was disappointed in the discussion. I think he mentioned briefly that problems regarding the Baltic Sea and the Black Sea areas had been discussed in a general way and that he had not been able to take any positive or desired stand. He said he did not go into details. I asked him about military things which had a certain significance at the time – the strong forces, for instance, in the Bessarabian sector. I think Hitler evaded the answer and said that this was obviously connected with all these matters and that he had not gone into it too deeply, or something similar, I cannot remember exactly. At any rate, there was nothing new in it for us and nothing final.

DR. NELTE: After that conference were any military orders given?

KEITEL: I think not even then, but Hitler told us at the time that he wished to wait for the reaction to these discussions in the Eastern area after the delegation had returned to Russia. Certain orders had been given to the ambassador, too, in that respect, however not directly after the Molotov visit.

DR. NELTE: May I ask you to give the date when the first definite instructions were given?

KEITEL: I can only reconstruct it retrospectively, on the strength of the instruction Barbarossa which has been shown to me here and which came out in December. I believe it must have been during the first half of December that the orders were issued, the well-known order Barbarossa. To be precise, these orders were given at the beginning of December, namely, the orders to work out the strategic plan.

DR. NELTE: Did you know about the conference which took place at Zossen in December and which has been mentioned by the Prosecution here? Perhaps I may remind you that the Finnish General Heinrichs was present.

KEITEL: No, I knew nothing about the conference in Zossen, and I think General Buschenhagen was also there, according to the statements he has made here. I did not know anything about the Finnish General Heinrichs' presence in Zossen and have heard about it for the first time here. The only way I can explain this is that the General Staff of the Army wanted to get information or other things and that for that purpose they discussed that with the persons concerned. I did not meet

General Heinrichs until May 1941. At that time I had a conference with him and General Jodl at Salzburg. Before that I had never seen him and I had never talked to him.

DR. NELTE: Is there any significance in the fact that Directive Number 21 says that Hitler would order the actual deployment of the troops 8 weeks before the operational plan would become effective?

KEITEL: Yes, there was considerable significance attached to that. I have been interrogated about that by the Soviet Delegation here. The reason was that according to the calculations of the Army, it would take about eight weeks to get these troops, which were to be transported by rail, into position; that is to say, if troops from Reich territory were to be placed in position on an operative starting line. Hitler emphasized when the repeated revisions of the plan were made that he wanted to have complete control of such deployment. In other words, troop movements without his approval were not to be made. That was the purpose of this instruction.

DR. NELTE: When did it become clear to you that Hitler was determined to attack the Soviet Union?

KEITEL: As far as I can recollect, it was at the beginning of March. The idea was that the attack might be made approximately in the middle of May. Therefore the decision regarding the transport of troops by rail had to be made in the middle of March. For that reason, during the first half of March a meeting of generals was called, that is to say, a briefing of the generals at Hitler's headquarters and the explanations given by him at that time had clearly the purpose of telling the generals that he was determined to carry out the deployment although an order had not yet been given. He gave a whole series of ideas and issued certain instructions on things which are contained in these directives here for the special parts of *Fall* Barbarossa. This is Document 447-PS, and these are the directives which were eventually also signed by me. He then gave us the directive for these guiding principles and ideas, so that the generals were already informed about the contents, which in turn caused me to confirm it in writing in this form, for there was nothing new in it for any one who had taken part in the discussions.

DR. NELTE: It appears to me, however, that what Hitler told the generals in his address was something new; and it also seems to me that you who were concerned with these matters, that is to say, who had to work them out, understood or had to understand that now a completely abnormal method of warfare was about to begin, at least when seen from your traditional point of view as a soldier.

KEITEL: That is correct. Views were expressed there regarding the administration and economic exploitation of the territories to be conquered or occupied. There was the completely new idea of setting up Reich commissioners and civilian administrations. There was the definite decision to charge the Delegate for the Four Year Plan with the supreme direction in the economic field; and what was for me the most important point, and what affected me most was the fact that besides the right of the military commander to exercise the executive power of the occupation force, a policy was to be followed here in which it was clearly expressed that *Reichsführer-SS* Himmler was to be given extensive plenipotentiary powers concerning all police actions in these territories which later on became known. I firmly opposed that, since to me it seemed impossible that there should be two authorities placed side by side. In the directives here it says: "The authority of the Commander-in-Chief of the Army is not affected by this."

That was a complete illusion and self-deception. Quite the opposite happened. As long as it was compatible with my functions, I fought against this. I think I ought to say that I have no witness to that other than General Jodl, who shared these experiences with me. Eventually, however, Hitler worked out those directives himself, more or less, and gave them the meaning he wanted. That is how these directives came about.

That I had no power to order the things which are contained in these directives is clear from the fact that it says that the *Reichsmarschall* receives this task... the *Reichsführer-SS* receives that task, *et cetera*. I had no authority whatever to give orders to them.

DR. NELTE: Was it never actually discussed that if one wanted to launch an attack on the Soviet Union, one would previously have to take diplomatic steps or else send a declaration of war, or an ultimatum?

KEITEL: Oh, yes, I discussed that. As early as the winter of 1940-1941, whenever there were discussions regarding the strength of the Russian forces on the demarcation line, that is, in December-January, I asked Hitler to send a note to the Soviet Union so as to bring about a cleaning-up of the situation, if I may express it so. I can add now that the first time he said nothing at all, and the second time he refused, maintaining that it was useless, since he would only receive the answer that this was an internal affair and that it was none of our business, or something like that. At any rate, he refused. I tried again, at a later stage, that is to say I voiced the request that an ultimatum should be presented before we entered upon an action, so that in some form the basis would be created for a preventive war, as we called it, for an attack.

DR. NELTE: You say "preventive war". When the final decisions were made, what was the military situation?

KEITEL: I am best reminded of how we, or rather the Army judged the situation, by a study or memorandum. I believe it is Document 872-PS, dated the end of January or the beginning of February, a report made by the Chief of the General Staff of the Army to Hitler on the state of operative and strategic preparations. And in this document I found the information we then had on the strength of the Red Army and other existing information known to us, which is dealt with fully in this document.

Apart from that, I have to say too that the intelligence service of the OKW, Admiral Canaris, placed at my disposal or at the Army's disposal very little material because the Russian area was closely sealed against German intelligence. In other words, there were gaps up to a certain point. Only the things contained in Document 872-PS were known.

DR. NELTE: Would you like to say briefly what it contained, so as to justify your decision?

KEITEL: Yes, there were – Halder reported that there were 150 divisions of the Soviet Union deployed along the line of demarcation. Then there were aerial photographs of a large number of airdromes. In short, there was a degree of preparedness on the part of Soviet Russia, which could at any time lead to military action. Only the actual fighting later made it clear just how far the enemy had been prepared. I must say, that we fully realized all these things only during the actual attack.

DR. NELTE: You were present during Hitler's last speech to the commanders in the East, made on 14 June 1941, in the Reich Chancellery, were you not? I ask you, without going over old ground, to state briefly what Hitler said on that occasion, and what effect it had on the generals.

THE PRESIDENT: Isn't there a document in connection with this? It must all be in the document. Isn't that so?

DR. NELTE: I wanted to ask one question on that subject and then submit the document; or, if the Tribunal so desires, I will not read the document at all, but will merely quote the short summaries which are at the end of the document. Will the Tribunal agree to that?

THE PRESIDENT: But what you did was to ask the defendant what was in the document.

DR. NELTE: The document contains, if I may indicate it briefly, the following: The developments, and the ever increasing influence of organizations alien to the Wehrmacht on the course of the war. It is the proof that the Wehrmacht, during this war, which must be called a degenerate war, tried, as far as possible, to keep within the limits of international law and that when the...

THE PRESIDENT: I only want to know what your question is, that is all.

DR. NELTE: My question to Field Marshal Keitel was to tell me about the speech on 14 June 1941, and what Hitler ordered the generals to do and what the effect on them was. With that, I intended to conclude the preparations for the Russian campaign.

THE PRESIDENT: He can tell what the effect was upon himself, but I don't see how he can tell what the effect was upon the other generals.

DR. NELTE: He can only assume of course, but he can say whether the others reacted in one way or another. One can talk and one can take an opposing stand. I merely wanted to know whether this happened or not.

THE PRESIDENT: Perhaps you had better ask him what happened that day at the conference; if you want to know what happened at the conference, why don't you ask him?

DR. NELTE: Please, tell us about it.

KEITEL: After short reports regarding the operational orders to the individual commanders, there followed a recapitulation, which I must describe as a purely political speech. The main theme was that this was the decisive battle between two ideologies, and that this fact made it impossible – that the leadership in this war, the practices which we knew as soldiers, and which we considered to be the only correct ones under international law, had to be measured by completely different standards. The war could not be carried on by these means. This was an entirely new kind of war, based on completely different arguments and principles.

With these explanations, the various orders were then given to do away with the legal system in territories which were not pacified, to combat resistance with brutal means, to consider every local resistance movement as the expression of the deep rift between the two ideologies. These were decidedly quite new and very impressive ideas, but also thoughts which affected us deeply.

DR. NELTE: Did you, or did any other generals raise objections to or oppose these explanations, directives, and orders?

KEITEL: No, I personally made no remonstrances, apart from those which I had already advanced and the objections I had already expressed before. However, I have never known which generals, if any of the generals, addressed the *Führer*. At any rate, they did not do so after that discussion.

DR. NELTE: Mr. President, I think that now the time has come to decide whether you will accept the affidavits of the Defendant Keitel contained in my Document Book Number 2 under the Numbers 3 and 5, as exhibits. Perhaps the Prosecution can express an opinion on this.

Up to now we have merely discussed the history before the actual Russian war. Insofar as the Defendant Keitel and the OKW is concerned, I should like to shorten the examination by submitting these two affidavits. The affidavit Number 3 is an exposé of the conditions governing the authority for issuing orders in the East. The extent of the territory and the numerous organizations led to an extremely complicated procedure for giving orders. To enable you to ascertain whether the Defendant Keitel, or the OKW, or some other department might be responsible, the conditions governing the authority to issue orders in the East have been presented in detail. I believe it would save a great deal of time if you would accept this document as an exhibit.

SIR DAVID MAXWELL-FYFE: My Lord, Mr. Dodd and I have no objection to this procedure used by the Defence and we believe that it might probably help the Tribunal to have in front of them the printed accounts.

THE PRESIDENT: Does Dr. Nelte intend to read or only summarize these affidavits?

DR. NELTE: I intend merely to submit it to you after I have asked the defendant whether the contents of the affidavit have been written and signed by him.

THE PRESIDENT: And the Prosecution, of course, have had these affidavits for some time?

SIR DAVID MAXWELL-FYFE: Yes.

DR. NELTE: The same applies, if I understand Sir David correctly, to affidavit Number 5.

SIR DAVID MAXWELL-FYFE: Yes.

THE PRESIDENT: Dr. Nelte, it would be convenient, I think, if you gave these affidavits numbers in the sequence of your exhibit numbers and gave us also their dates so that we can identify them. Can you give us the dates of the affidavits?

DR. NELTE: May I be permitted to arrange the matter in the secretary's office during the recess?

THE PRESIDENT: Yes. The first is dated 8 March, isn't it? The other is the 18th, is it? Dr. Nelte, you can do it at the recess and give them numbers. You can give them numbers at the recess.

It is nearly 1 o'clock now, and we are just going to adjourn. You can give them numbers then. Does that conclude your examination?

DR. NELTE: We come now to the individual cases which I hope, however, to conclude in the course of the afternoon. Mr. President, I am sorry but I must discuss the prisoner-of-war affairs and several individual matters. I think I still need this afternoon for myself. I believe that if I bear in mind the interests of the Defendant Keitel, I am limiting myself a good deal.

THE PRESIDENT: Do you desire to put your questions to him now or not?

DR. NELTE: I think – I do not know how the President feels about it – it would be convenient if we had a recess now so that in the meantime I can put the affidavits in order. I have not yet finished the discussion of this subject.

THE PRESIDENT: We will adjourn now.

[The Tribunal recessed until 1400 hours.]

AFTERNOON SESSION

DR. NELTE: Mr. President, of the two documents mentioned this morning, the first document, Number 3 of Document Book Number 2, entitled "The Command Relationships in the East", will be given the number 10 of the Keitel Documents.

THE PRESIDENT: That is dated the 14 March 1946?

DR. NELTE: Yes, 14 March 1946.

THE PRESIDENT: The document that I have got is headed the 23 February 1946, and at the end, the 14 March 1946. Is that the one?

DR. NELTE: The document was first written down and later attested. There is, therefore, a difference in the two dates.

THE PRESIDENT: I only wanted to identify which it is, that is all.

DR. NELTE: It is the document of 14 March 1946.

THE PRESIDENT: Very well.

DR. NELTE: The affidavit is dated 14 March.

THE PRESIDENT: And you are giving it what number?

DR. NELTE: I give it Number Keitel-10. The second document, which is fifth in the document book, is dated at the head 18 March 1946 and has at the end the defendant's attestation as of 29 March 1946. This document has received the number Keitel-12. Permit me to read a summary of a few points on Pages 11 and 12 of the German copy. This, as it appears to me, is of very great importance for this Trial.

THE PRESIDENT: Of which document?

DR. NELTE: Document Number 12.

THE PRESIDENT: Yes.

DR. NELTE: The question in this document…

THE PRESIDENT: Just a minute. I do not think the interpreters have found the document yet, have they? It comes just after a certificate, by Catherine Bedford, and I think it is about halfway through the book, and, although the pages are not numbered consecutively, it appears to have the figure 51 on it.

DR. NELTE: I shall begin where it says, "In summing up… Those are the last three pages of this document:

"In summing up it must be established that:

"1. In addition to the Wehrmacht as the legal protector of the Reich internally and externally (as in every State)" – I interpolate, 'in the SS organizations' – "a particular, completely independent power factor arose and was legalized, which politically, biologically, in police and administration matters actually drew the powers of the State to itself.

"2. Even at the beginning of military complications and conflicts the SS came to be the actual forerunner and standard bearer of a policy of conquest and power.

"3. After the commencement of the military actions the *Reichsführer-SS* devised methods which always appeared appropriate, which were concealed at first, or were hardly apparent, at least from the outside, and which enabled him in reality to build up his power under the guise of protecting the annexed or occupied territories from political opponents.

"4. From the occupation of the Sudeten territory, beginning with the organization of political unrest, that is, of so-called liberation actions and 'incidents', the road leads straight through Poland and the Western areas in a steep curve into the Russian territory.

"5. With the directives for Barbarossa for the administration and utilization of the conquered Eastern territories, the Wehrmacht was, against its intention and without knowledge of the conditions, drawn further and further into the subsequent developments and activities.

"6. I (Keitel) and my colleagues had no deeper insight into the effects of Himmler's full powers, and had no idea of the possible effect of these powers.

"I assume without further discussion that the same holds true for the OKH, which according to the order of the *Führer* made the agreements with Himmler's officials and gave orders to the subordinate army commanders.

"7. In reality, it was not the Commander-in-Chief of the Army who had the executive power assigned to him and the power to decree and to maintain law in the occupied territories, but Himmler and Heydrich decided on their own authority the fate of the people and prisoners, including prisoners of war in whose camps they exercised the executive power.

"8. The traditional training and concept of duty of the German officers, which taught unquestioning obedience to superiors who bore responsibility, led to an attitude – regrettable in retrospect, – which caused them to shrink from rebelling against these orders and these methods even when they recognized their illegality and inwardly refuted them.

"9. The *Führer*, Hitler, abused his authority and his fundamental Order Number 1 in an irresponsible way with respect to us. This Order Number 1 read, more or less:

"'1. No one shall know about secret matters which do not belong to his own range of assignments.

"'2. No one shall learn more than he needs to fulfil the tasks assigned to him.

"'3. No one shall receive information earlier than is necessary for the performance of the duties assigned to him.

"4. No one shall transmit to subordinate offices, to any greater extent or any earlier than is unavoidable for the achievement of the purpose, orders which are to be kept secret.'

"10. If the entire consequences which arose from granting Himmler authority in the East had been foreseen, in this case the leading generals would have been the first to raise an unequivocal protest against it. That is my conviction.

"As these atrocities developed, one from the other, step by step, and without any foreknowledge of the consequences, destiny took its tragic course, with its fateful consequences."

Witness, Defendant Keitel, did you yourself write this statement, that is, dictate it as I have just read it? Are you perfectly familiar with its contents and did you swear to it?

KEITEL: Yes.

DR. NELTE: I shall submit the document in the original.

[Turning to the defendant]: We had stopped at Document C-50, which deals with the abolition of military jurisdiction in the Barbarossa area. I do not know whether you still want to express your opinion on it, or whether that is now superfluous after what has just been read.

KEITEL: I should like to say to this only that these documents, C-50 and 884-PS, beginning at Page 4, are the record of the directives that were given in that General Staff meeting on 14 June. In line with military regulations and customs they were given the form of written orders and then sent to the subordinate offices.

DR. NELTE: I have a few more short questions regarding the war against America. The Prosecution assert that Japan was influenced by Germany to wage war against America and have, in the course of their presentation, accused you of participation and cooperation in this plan.

Would you like to make some statement regarding this?

KEITEL: Document C-75 is a directive by the Supreme Command of the Wehrmacht which deals with cooperation with Japan. Of course, I participated in the drawing-up of this order and signed it by order. The other document, Number 1881-PS, regarding a conference between the *Führer* and Matsuoka, I do not know, and I did not know anything about it. I can say only the following for us soldiers:

In the course of all this time, until the Japanese entry into the war against America, there were two points of view that were the general directives or principles which Hitler emphasized to us. One was to prevent America from entering the war under any circumstances; consequently to renounce military operations in the seas, as far as the Navy was concerned. The other, the thought that guided us soldiers, was the hope that Japan would enter the war against Russia; and I recall that around November and the beginning of December 1941, when the advance of the German armies west of Moscow was halted and I visited the front with Hitler, I was asked several times by the generals, "When is Japan going to enter the war?" The reasons for their asking this were that again and again Russian Far East divisions were being thrown into the fight via Moscow, that is to say, fresh troops coming from the Far East. That was about 18 to 20 divisions, but I could not say for certain.

I was present in Berlin during Matsuoka's visit, and I saw him also at a social gathering, but I did not have any conversation with him. All the deductions that might be made from Directive 24, C-75, and which I have learned about from the preliminary examination during my interrogation, are without any foundation for us soldiers, and there is no justification for anyone's believing that we were guided by thoughts of bringing about a war between Japan and America, or of undertaking anything to that end.

In conclusion, I can say only that this order was necessary because the branches of the Wehrmacht offered resistance to giving Japan certain things, military secrets in armament production, unless she were in the war.

DR. NELTE: There was also a letter submitted by the Prosecution, a letter from Major Von Falkenstein to the Luftwaffe Operations Staff. *Reichsmarschall* Göring testified to this in his interrogation. I only wanted to ask you if you knew of this letter, or if you have anything to add to *Reichsmarschall* Göring's testimony?

KEITEL: I have nothing to add, for I never saw this letter by Von Falkenstein until I saw it here during my interrogation.

DR. NELTE: We come now to the individual facts with which you and the OKW are charged by the Prosecution. Because of the vast number of points brought up by the Prosecution I can naturally choose only individual groups and those with the most serious charges, in order to elucidate whether and to what extent you were involved and what your attitude was to the ensuing results. In most cases it is a question of orders from Hitler, but in your statement on the actual happenings you have admitted to a certain participation in these things and knowledge of them. Therefore, we must discuss these points. One of the most important is that of hostages. In this connection I want to show you Document C-128. These are orders for operations in the West. Let me ask you, however, first of all, what is the basis for the taking of hostages as it was usually carried out by the Wehrmacht?

KEITEL: These are the printed regulations "Secret G-2" (Army Service Regulation G-2) and headed, according to the order: "Service Instructions for Army Units."

DR. NELTE: I ask you, Mr. President, to turn to Document Book Number 1, Number 7 on Page 65 of my document book. I ask you to establish that this is a copy from the afore-mentioned Army Regulations, Section 9, which deals with the question of hostages. This is Document K-7, and it reads as follows:

> "Hostages may be taken only by order of a regimental commander, an independent battalion commander or a commander

of equal rank. With regard to accommodation and feeding, it is to be noted that, though they should be kept under strictest guard, they are not convicts. Furthermore, only senior officers holding at least the position of a division commander can decide on the fate of hostages."

That is, if you want to call it so, the Hostage Law of the German Wehrmacht.

KEITEL: I might say in this connection that in Document C-128, which is the preparatory operational order of the Army for the battle in the West, this is mentioned specially under the heading: "3a. Security measures against the population of occupied territory. A) Hostages."

THE PRESIDENT: Dr. Nelte, are you offering that as Keitel-7?

DR. NELTE: I ask to have these printed Army Instructions put in evidence as Exhibit Keitel-7 (Document Number Keitel-7).

THE PRESIDENT: Would you kindly say what you are putting it in as each time, because if you simply say "7" it will lead to confusion.

DR. NELTE: Keitel-7.
[Turning to the defendant]: Was Document C-128 the order of the High Command of the Army on the occasion of the march into France?

KEITEL: Yes.

DR. NELTE: Now I have here another document, Document Number 1585-PS, which contains an opinion expressed by the OKW. It is a letter to the Reich Minister for Air and Commander-in-Chief of the Luftwaffe; and in this letter, I assume, are contained the convictions held by the office of which you were head.

KEITEL: Yes.

DR. NELTE: What do you say today in connection with this letter?

KEITEL: I can say only that it is precisely the same standpoint that I represent today, because there is here, with reference to the above-mentioned order, the following paragraph, beginning with the words, "For the protection against any misuse…" and so on. Then the order is quoted.

DR. NELTE: This is in reference to Regulation G-2, and further, that the "decision regarding the fate of hostages…"

KEITEL: It says, "According to which the decision on the fate of hostages is reserved to senior officers holding at least the position of a division commander."

DR. NELTE: Is it correct when I say that this letter was drawn up by the Legal Department of the OKW after examination of the situation as regards international law and its implications?

KEITEL: Yes, it is to be seen from the document itself that this point of view was taken into consideration.

DR. NELTE: Did you issue any general orders on this question of hostages in your capacity as chief of OKW, apart from those we have had up to now?

KEITEL: No, the OKW participated only in helping to draw up this order. No other basic orders or directions were issued on this question.

DR. NELTE: Did you nevertheless in individual cases have anything to do with this question of hostages? You and the OKW are charged by the Prosecution with having expressed yourselves in some way or having taken some kind of attitude when inquiries were made by Stülpnagel and Falkenhausen.

I show you Document 1594-PS.

KEITEL: This document, 1594-PS, is a communication from Von Falkenhausen, the Military Commander of Belgium, and is directed to the OKH, General Staff, Quartermaster General, and, further, to the Commander-in-Chief and Military Commander in France and for the information of the Wehrmacht Commander in the Netherlands and Luftgau Belgium.

I do not know this document nor could I know it, for it is directed to the Army. The assumption expressed by the French Prosecutor that I received a letter from Falkenhausen is not true. I do not know this letter and it was not sent to me. Official communication between the military commanders in France and Belgium took place only between the OKH and these two military commanders subordinate to it. These commanders were not subordinate either to the OKW or to me.

DR. NELTE: The French Prosecution has submitted Document Number UK-25 and has asserted that this document was the basis for the hostage legislation in France, that there is, in other words, a basic connection between the order you signed on 16 September 1941 and the treatment of hostages in France. I will show you these documents, 1587-PS and 1588-PS, in addition to UK-25 and request you to comment on them.

KEITEL: I must first answer the question as to whether I had any discussion on individual matters with military commanders regarding the question of hostages. Did you not ask me that?

DR. NELTE: With regard to Stülpnagel and Falkenhausen?

KEITEL: Yes, with regard to Stülpnagel and Falkenhausen. It is possible, and I do recall one such case, Stülpnagel called me up from Paris on such a matter because he had received an order from the Army to shoot a certain number of hostages for an attack on members of the

German Wehrmacht. He wanted to have this order certified by me. That happened and I believe it is confirmed by a telegram, which has been shown to me here. It is also confirmed that at that time I had a meeting with Stülpnagel in Berlin. Otherwise, the relations between myself and these two military commanders were limited to quite exceptional matters, in which they believed that with my help they might obtain certain support with regard to things that were very unpleasant for them, for example, in such questions as labour allocation, that is, workers from Belgium or France destined for Germany, where also, in one case, conflicts arose between the military commanders and their police authorities. In these cases I was called up directly in order to mediate.

Permit me, please, to look at the documents first.

DR. NELTE: You must begin with UK-25, 16 September 1941.

KEITEL: Yes.

THE PRESIDENT: It is impossible for the Tribunal to carry all these documents in their heads by reference to their numbers, and we do not have the documents before us. We do not know what documents you are dealing with here. It is quite impossible for us.

DR. NELTE: Mr. President, for this reason, I took the liberty of submitting to the Tribunal before the beginning of the sessions a list of documents. I am sorry if that was not done. I could not submit the documents themselves. You will always find a number to the left of this list.

THE PRESIDENT: Yes, I see that, but all that I see here is 1587-PS, which is not the one that you are referring to, apparently, and it is described as a report to the Supreme Command of the Army. That does not give us much indication of what it is about.

The next one is 1594-PS, a letter to OKH. That again does not give us much indication of what it is about, except that they have something to do with the hostage question.

DR. NELTE: It is concerned with the question which the Defendant Keitel is about to answer. Do you not also have the order bearing Document Number C-128?

THE PRESIDENT: Yes, I have that. That is directions for the operation in the West.

DR. NELTE: And UK-25?

THE PRESIDENT: Yes.

DR. NELTE: And 1588-PS?

THE PRESIDENT: We have got them all. The only thing that I was pointing out to you was that the description of them is inadequate to explain to us what they mean and what they are. Perhaps by a word or two you can indicate to us when you come to the document what it is about.

DR. NELTE: Document UK-25, about which the Defendant Keitel is about to testify, is an order of 16 September 1941, signed by him, regarding "Communist Uprisings in the Occupied Territories". It contains, among other things, the sentence, "The *Führer* has now ordered that most severe measures should be taken everywhere in order to crush this movement as soon as possible". The French Prosecution asserted that, on the basis of this order, hostage legislation was promulgated in France, which is contained in Document 1588-PS. If you have Document 1588-PS, you will find on the third page a regular code regarding the taking and treatment of hostages.

The defendant is to state whether such a causal relation did exist, and to what extent the OKW and he himself were at all competent in these matters.

KEITEL: Document UK-25, the *Führer* Order of the 16 September 1941, as has just been stated, is concerned with communist uprisings in occupied territories, and the fact that this is a *Führer* order has already been mentioned. I must clarify the fact that this order, so far as its contents are concerned, referred solely to the Eastern regions, particularly to the Balkan countries. I believe that I can prove this by the fact that there is attached to this document a distribution list, that is, a list of addresses beginning, "Wehrmacht Commander Southeast for Serbia, Southern Greece, and Crete". This was, of course, transmitted also to other Wehrmacht commanders and also to the OKH with the possibility of its being passed on to subordinate officers. I believe that this document, which, for the sake of saving time, I need not read here, has several indications that the assumption on the part of the French Prosecution that this is the basis for the hostage law to be found in Document Number 1588-PS is false, and that there is no causal nexus between the two. It is true that the date of this hostage law is also September – the number is hard to read – but, as far as its contents are concerned, these two matters are, in my opinion, not connected. Moreover, the two military commanders in France and Belgium never received this order from the OKW, but they may have received it through the OKH, a matter which I cannot check because I do not know.

Regarding this order of 16 September 1941, I should like to say that its great severity can be traced back to the personal influence of the *Führer*. The fact that it is concerned with the Eastern region is already to be seen from the contents and from the introduction and does not need to be substantiated any further. It is correct that this order of 16 September 1941 is signed by me.

DR. NELTE: We come now to the second individual fact, *"Nacht und Nebel"*. The Prosecution charges you of having participated in the *Nacht und Nebel* decree of 12 December 1941, Document Number L-90…

KEITEL: May I say one more thing regarding the other question?

DR. NELTE: Please, if it appears to be necessary. In the communication of 2 February 1942 we find the words, "In the annex are transmitted: 1) A decree of the *Führer* of 7 December 1941..." You wanted to say something more; if it is important, please. Do you have Document Number L-90?

KEITEL: L-90, yes.

DR. NELTE: What was the cause for this order, so terrible in its consequences?

KEITEL: I must state that it is perfectly clear to me that the connection of my name with this so-called *"Nacht und Nebel"* order is a serious charge against me, even though it can be seen from the documents that it is a *Führer* order. Consequently I should like to state how this order came about. Since the beginning of the Eastern campaign and in the late autumn of 1941 until the spring of 1942, the resistance movements, sabotage and everything connected with it increased enormously in all the occupied territories. From the military angle it meant that the security troops were tied down, having to be kept on the spot by the unrest. That is how I saw it from the military point of view at that time. And day by day, through the daily reports we could picture the sequence of events in the individual occupation sectors. It was impossible to handle this summarily; rather, Hitler demanded that he be informed of each individual occurrence, and he was very displeased if such matters were concealed from him in the reports by military authorities. He got to know about them all the same.

In this connection, he said to me that it was very displeasing to him and very unfavourable to establishing peace that, owing to this, death sentences by court-martial against saboteurs and their accomplices were increasing; that he did not wish this to occur, since from his point of view it made appeasement and relations with the population only more difficult. He said at that time that a state of peace could be achieved only if this were reduced and if, instead of death sentences – to shorten it – in case a death sentence could not be expected and carried out in the shortest time possible, as stated here in the decree, the suspect or guilty persons concerned – if one may use the word "guilty" – should be deported to Germany without the knowledge of their families and be interned or imprisoned instead of lengthy court-martial proceedings with many witnesses.

I expressed the greatest misgivings in this matter and know very well that I said at that time that I feared results exactly opposite to those apparently hoped for. I then had serious discussions with the legal adviser of the Wehrmacht, who, had similar scruples, because there was an elimination of ordinary legal procedures. I tried again to prevent this order from being issued or to have it modified. My efforts were in vain. The threat was made to me that the Minister of Justice would be commissioned to issue a corresponding decree, should the Wehrmacht not be able to do so. Now may I refer to details only insofar as these ways were provided in this order, L-90, of preventing arbitrary application, and these were primarily as follows:

The general principles of the order provided expressly that such deportation or abduction into Reich territory should take place only after regular court-martial proceedings, and that in every case the officer in charge of jurisdiction, that is, the divisional commander must deal with the matter together with his legal adviser, in the legal way, on the basis of preliminary proceedings.

I must say that I believed then that every arbitrary and excessive application of these principles was avoided by this provision. You will perhaps agree with me that the words in the order, "It is the will of the *Führer* after long consideration…" put in for that purpose, were not said without reason and not without the hope that the addressed military commander would also recognize from this that this was a method of which we did not approve and did not consider to be right.

Finally we introduced a reviewing procedure into the order so that through the higher channels of appeal, that is, the Military Commander in France and the Supreme Command or Commander of the Army, it would be possible to try the case legally by appeal proceedings if the verdict seemed open to question, at least, within the meaning of the decree. I learned here for the first time of the full and monstrous tragedy, namely, that this order, which was intended only for the Wehrmacht and for the sole purpose of determining whether an offender who faced a sentence in jail could be made to disappear by means of this *Nacht und Nebel* procedure, was obviously applied universally by the police, as testified by witnesses whom I have heard here, and according to the Indictment which I also heard, and so the horrible fact of the existence of whole camps full of people deported through the *Nacht und Nebel* procedure has been proved.

In my opinion, the Wehrmacht, at least I and the military commanders of the occupied territories who were connected with this order, did not know of this. At any rate it was never reported to me. Therefore this order, which in itself was undoubtedly very dangerous and disregarded certain requirements of law such as we understood it, was able to develop into that formidable affair of which the Prosecution have spoken.

The intention was to take those who were to be deported from their home country to Germany, because Hitler was of the opinion that penal servitude in wartime would not be considered by the persons concerned as dishonourable in cases where it was a question of actions by so-called patriots. It would be regarded as a short detention which would end when the war was over.

These reflections have already been made in part in the note. If you have any further questions, please put them.

DR. NELTE: The order for the carrying out of this *Nacht und Nebel* decree states that the Gestapo was to effect the transportation to Germany. You stated that the people who came to Germany were to be turned over to the Minister of Justice, that is, to normal police custody. You will understand that, by the connection with the Gestapo, certain suspicions are raised that it was known from the start what happened to these people. Can you say anything in elucidation of that matter?

KEITEL: Yes. The order that was given at that time was that these people should be turned over to the German authorities of justice. This letter signed "by order" and then the signature, was issued 8 weeks later than the decree itself by the *Amt Ausland Abwehr* as I can see from my official correspondence. It indicates the conferences, that is, the agreements, which had to be reached at that time, regarding the method by which these people were to be taken from their native countries to Germany. They were apparently conducted by this *Amt Abwehr*, which evidently ordered police detachments as escorts. That can be seen from it.

I might mention in this connection – I must have seen it – that it did not seem objectionable at that time, because I could have, and I had, no reason to assume that these people were being turned over to the Gestapo, frankly speaking, to be liquidated, but that the Gestapo was simply being used as the medium in charge of the transportation to Germany. I should like to emphasize that particularly, so that there can be no doubt that it was not our idea to do away with the people as was later done in that *Nacht und Nebel* camp.

DR. NELTE: We come now to the question of parachutists, sabotage troops, and Commando operations. The French Prosecution treat in detail the origin and effect of the two *Führer* Orders of 18 October 1942 regarding the treatment of Commandos.

Does the Tribunal have a copy of this *Führer* Order? It is 498…

THE PRESIDENT: We haven't got a copy of the order. You mean 553-PS or 498?

DR. NELTE: The second is Document Number 553-PS.

THE PRESIDENT: We have not got that either, "Combating of Individual Parachutists, Decree of 4. 8. 42."

DR. NELTE: Could you please repeat your statement? What you just said did not come through.

THE PRESIDENT: 553-PS, "Combating of Individual Parachutists, Decree of 4. 8. 42." That is what we have, nothing else. You also have 498...

DR. NELTE: Document Number 553-PS is a memorandum signed by Keitel. The French Prosecution has assumed correctly that there is some connection between the Document 553-PS and the *Führer* Order of 18 October 1942. The defendant is to testify what were the reasons that lay behind this *Führer* Order and this notice.

KEITEL: First of all, Document 553-PS, the note: This memorandum was issued by me in August 1942. As I have already described in connection with the *Nacht und Nebel* Decree, sabotage acts, the dropping of agents by parachute, the parachuting of arms, ammunition, explosives, radio sets and small groups of saboteurs reached greater and greater proportions. They were dropped at night from aircraft in thinly populated regions. This activity covered the whole area governed by Germany at that time. It extended from the west over to Czechoslovakia and Poland, and from the East as far as the Berlin area. Of course, a large number of the people involved in these actions were captured and much of the material was taken. This memorandum was to rally all offices, outside the Wehrmacht, as well, police and civilian authorities, to the service against this new method of conducting the war, which was, to our way of thinking, illegal, a sort of "war in the dark behind the lines". Even today, after reading this document through again – it has already been given to me here – I consider this memorandum unobjectionable. It expressly provides that members of enemy forces, that is members of any enemy force, if captured by the police, should be taken to the nearest Wehrmacht office after being identified. I know that in the French sector the French police did their full share in arresting these troops and putting them in safe charge. They collaborated in preventing these acts of sabotage. It will perhaps make clear how extensive these activities were if I mention that on certain days there were as many as 100 railways blown up in this way. That is in the memorandum.

Now, as to the *Führer* orders of 18 October 1942, which have been mentioned very often here and which I may describe as the further development of the regulations mentioned in this memorandum: As to these methods, this way of conducting illegal warfare kept on increasing, and individual parachutists grew into small Commando units which landed from heavy aircraft or by parachute and were systematically employed, not to create disturbances or destruction in general, but to attack specific, vital, and important military objectives. In Norway, for instance, I recall that they had the task of blowing up the only aluminium works. It may sound strange, but during this period half to three-quarters of an hour of the daily discussion on the situation was devoted to the problem of how to handle these incidents. These incidents in all sectors caused the *Führer* to demand other methods, vigorous measures, to combat this activity, which he characterized as "terrorism" and said that the only method that could be used to combat it was severe countermeasures. I recall that in reply to our objections as soldiers the following words were spoken: "As long as the paratrooper or saboteur runs the danger only of being taken captive, he incurs no risk; in normal circumstances he risks nothing; we must take action against this." These were the reasons behind his thoughts. I was asked several times to express myself on this subject and to present a draft. General Jodl will also recall this. We did not know what we, as soldiers, were to do. We could make no suggestion.

If I may sum up briefly, we heard Hitler's bursts of temper on this subject almost every day, but we did nothing, not knowing what we could do. Hitler declared that this was against the Hague Convention and illegal, that it was a method of waging war not foreseen in the Hague Convention and which could not be foreseen. He said that this was a new war with which we had to contend, in which new methods were needed. Then, to make it short, as I have already testified in the preliminary investigation, these orders – this order itself and the well-known instructions that those who did not carry out the first order should be punished – were issued in a concise form and signed by Hitler. They were then distributed, I believe, by the Chief of the Operations Staff,

Jodl. I might add that many times the commanders who received these orders asked questions about how they were to be applied, particularly in connection with the threat that they would be punished if they did not carry them out. The only reply we could make was, "You know what is in the orders", for we were not in a position to change these signed orders.

DR. NELTE: The Prosecution have accused you personally of having issued the order to kill the English saboteurs captured in the Commando operations at Stavanger. In this connection I submit to you Documents 498-PS, 508-PS, and 527-PS. *[The documents were submitted to the defendant.]*

This, Mr. President, was a Commando mission in the vicinity of Stavanger. The troops who fell into German hands had to be killed, according to the *Führer* decree. There was a remote possibility of interrogating these persons, if that was demanded by military necessity. In this case the Commander-in-Chief in Norway, General Von Falkenhorst, dealt with the matter. He turned to the OKW, as he has already testified in the minutes of an interrogation.

[Turning to the defendant.] Would you make any statement in this connection?

KEITEL: I was interrogated on this subject, and in the course of the interrogation I was confronted with General Von Falkenhorst. As I recall, I did not remember his having asked me questions regarding the carrying out of this order. I did not know of it. Even the event itself was no longer in my memory, and I remembered it again only after I had seen the documents. During the interrogation, I told the interrogator that I had no authority to change that order, that I could refer any one concerned only to the order, as such. As regards my confrontation with General Von Falkenhorst, I should like to say only what is stated here in the minutes, "He obviously shelved the answers and altered his earlier statements, but did not deny them. Keitel did not deny having had this talk with me but denied that the subject of it was what I said."

DR. NELTE: Mr. President, I can only say that this is a summary of the interrogation of General Von Falkenhorst, a document which was submitted by the Prosecution without having a document number.

[Turning to the defendant.] Have you finished your statement?

KEITEL: Yes. I believe that suffices.

THE PRESIDENT: Dr. Nelte, the Prosecution did not put in this document, did they? They have not offered it in evidence?

DR. NELTE: I believe they did.

THE PRESIDENT: I think they must have put it to the Defendant Keitel in one of his interrogations, did they not? Isn't that right? That does not mean that it is put in evidence, because the interrogation itself, you see, need not be put in evidence. You must put it in now if you want it to go in.

DR. NELTE: Mr. President, there is some error here. This document was put in by the Prosecution here as proof of the assertion that the Defendant Keitel had given the order to kill these paratroopers. I received the document here.

THE PRESIDENT: The Prosecution will tell me if that is so, but I cannot think of any document having been put in here that has not had an exhibit number.

MR. DODD: We have no recollection of having put it in. Many of these interrogations did not have document numbers; but, of course, if they were put in, they would have USA or Great Britain exhibit numbers.

THE PRESIDENT: Well, perhaps the best way would be for Counsel for the Prosecution to verify whether it was read in evidence.

MR. DODD: That will take me a few minutes, Your Honour.

THE PRESIDENT: Yes, I mean at your leisure. Would that be a convenient time to break off for 10 minutes?

DR. NELTE: Yes.

[A recess was taken.]

THE PRESIDENT: The Tribunal will adjourn this afternoon at a quarter to 5. They will then sit again in this Court in closed session, and they desire that both Counsel for the Prosecution and Counsel for the Defence should be present then, as they wish to discuss with those counsels on both sides the best way of avoiding translating unnecessary documents.

There have, as you know, been a very great number of documents put in, and a great burden has fallen upon the Translation Division. That is the problem which the Tribunal wish to discuss in closed session with Counsel for the Prosecution and Counsel for the Defence. They will, therefore, as I say, sit here in closed session where there is room for all the Defence Counsel. That is at 5 o'clock.

DR. NELTE: Do you remember an inquiry of the Commander-in-Chief West, in June 1944, regarding the treatment of sabotage troops behind the invasion front? A new situation had been created by the invasion and, therefore, by the problem of the Commandos.

KEITEL: Yes, I remember, since these documents too have been submitted to me here, and there were several documents. It is true that the Commander-in-Chief West, after the landing of Anglo-American forces in Northern France, considered that a new situation had arisen with reference to this *Führer* Order of 18 October 1942 directed against the parachute Commandos.

The inquiry was, as usual, reported, and General Jodl and I

represented the view of the Commander-in-Chief West, namely, that this order was not applicable here. Hitler refused to accept that point of view and gave certain directives in reply, which, according to the document, had at least two editions; after one had been cancelled as useless, the Document 551-PS remained as the final version as approved by the *Führer* during that report.

I remember all this so accurately because, on the occasion of presenting that reply during the discussion of the situation, this handwritten appendix was added by General Jodl with reference to the application in the Italian theatre, too. With that appendix, this version, which was approved and demanded by Hitler, was then sent out to the Commander-in-Chief West.

DR. NELTE: In this connection, was the question discussed as to how the active support of such acts of sabotage by the population could be judged from the point of view of international law?

KEITEL: Yes, that question arose repeatedly in connection with the order of 18 October 1942, and the well-known memorandum previously discussed. I am of the opinion that giving any assistance to agents or other enemy organs in such sabotage acts is a violation of the Hague Rules for Land Warfare. If the population takes part in, aids, or supports such action, or covers the perpetrators – hides them or helps them in any way or in any form – that, in my opinion, is clearly expressed in the Hague Rules for Land Warfare, namely that the population must not commit such actions.

DR. NELTE: The French Prosecution have submitted a letter of 30 July 1944, which is Document 537-PS. This document is concerned with the treatment of members of foreign military missions caught together with partisans. Do you know this order?

KEITEL: Yes I do. Yes, I have already been interrogated on this Document 537-PS during the preliminary investigation, and I made the statement which I will repeat here: It had been reported that, attached to the staffs of these partisans, particularly those of the leaders of the Serbian and Yugoslav partisans, there were military missions which, we believed, were certainly individual agents or teams for maintaining liaison with the states with which we were at war. It had been reported to me, and I had been asked what should be done if such a mission, as it was called, were captured. When this was reported to the *Führer* he decided to reject the suggestions of the military authority concerned, namely, to treat them as prisoners of war, since, according to the directive of 18 October 1942, they were to be considered as saboteurs and treated as such. This document is, therefore, the transmission of this order which bears my signature.

DR. NELTE: The problem of terror-fliers and lynch law has been mentioned during the examination of *Reichsmarschall* Göring. I shall confine myself to a few questions which concern you personally in connection with that problem. Do you know what we are concerned with in the conception of terror-fliers and their treatment? What was your attitude toward this question?

KEITEL: The fact that, starting from a certain date in the summer of 1944, machine-gun attacks from aircraft against the population as has already been mentioned here, increased considerably, with 30 to 40 dead on certain days, caused Hitler to demand categorically an adequate ruling on this question. We soldiers were of the opinion that existing regulations were sufficient, and that new regulations were unnecessary. The question of lynch law was dragged into the problem and the question of what was meant by the term terror-flier. These two groups of questions resulted in the very large quantity of documents which you all know, and which contain the text of the discussion on these subjects.

DR. NELTE: I think it will not be necessary to repeat the details which have already been discussed. In connection with your responsibility, I am interested in the words which you have written across this document. Please, will you explain those?

KEITEL: I merely wanted to state, first of all, that I had suggested, following the lines of the warning issued when German prisoners of war taken at Dieppe were shackled, that a warning should be issued here, too, in the form of a similar official note, saying that we should make reprisals unless the enemy commanders stopped the practice of their own accord. That was turned down as not being a suitable course of action.

And now let us turn to the documents, which are important to me.

DR. NELTE: Document 735-PS.

KEITEL: There are some notes in handwriting made by Jodl and myself. That is the record of a report written by me in the margin which runs as follows: "Courts-martial will not work"; at least that was the content. That was written at the time because the question of sentence by courts-martial came up for discussion since this very document laid down in detail for the first time what a terror-flier was, and because it stated that terror attacks were always attacks carried out from low-flying aircraft with machine guns. I was led to think that crews attacking in low-level flights could not, generally speaking, in 99 out of 100 cases be captured alive, if they crashed; for there is no possibility of saving oneself with a parachute from a low-level attack. Therefore, I wrote that remark in the margin. Furthermore, I considered, apart from the fact that one could not conduct proceedings against such a flier, one would, secondly, not be able to conclude a satisfactory trial or a satisfactory investigation if an attack had been carried out from a considerable height, because no court, in my opinion, would be able to prove that such a man had had the intention of attacking those targets which possibly were hit.

Finally, there was one last thought, which was that, in accordance with the rules, court-martial sentences against prisoners of war had to be communicated to the enemy state through the protecting power, and 3 months' grace had to be given during which the home state could object to the sentence. It was, therefore, out of the question that, through those channels the deterrent results desired could be achieved within a brief period. That was really what I meant. I also wrote another note, and this refers to lynch law. It states: "If you allow lynching at all, then you can hardly lay down rules for it."

To that I cannot say very much, since my conviction is that there is no possibility of saying under what circumstances such a method could be regulated or considered justified by mob justice, and I am still of the opinion that rules cannot be laid down, if such proceedings are tolerated.

DR. NELTE: But what was your attitude regarding the question of lynch law?

KEITEL: It was my point of view that it was a method completely impossible for us soldiers. One case had been reported by the *Reichsmarschall* in which proceedings against a soldier who had stopped such action were suppressed. I know of no case where soldiers, with reference to their duty as soldiers, behaved towards a prisoner of war in any way other than that laid down in the general regulations. That is unknown to me.

I should also like to state, and this has not been mentioned yet, that I had a discussion with *Reichsmarschall* Göring at the Berghof about the whole question, and he, at that time, quite clearly agreed with me: We soldiers must reject lynch law under any circumstances. I requested him in this awkward position in which we found ourselves to approach Hitler once more personally, to persuade him not to compel us to give an order in these matters or to draft an order. That was the situation.

DR. NELTE: We are now turning to questions relating to prisoners of war.

KEITEL: May I just say finally that an order from the OKW was never submitted and never issued.

DR. NELTE: There is hardly any problem in the law of warfare in which all nations and all people are so passionately interested as the prisoner-of-war question. That is why, here too, the Prosecution have stressed particularly those cases which were considered to be violations of laws for prisoners of war, according to the Geneva Convention, or to international law in general.

Since the OKW, and you as its Chief, were responsible for prisoner-of-war questions in Germany, I should like to put the following questions to you: What had been done in Germany to make all departments and offices of the Wehrmacht acquainted with international agreements which referred to prisoners of war?

KEITEL: There was a special military manual on that subject, which I think is available, and which contained all the clauses in the existing international agreements and the provisions for carrying them out. That is, I think, Directive Number 38, which applied to the Army and the Navy, and also to the Luftwaffe as a military manual. That was the basis, the basic order.

DR. NELTE: How was that put into practice? Were people who were concerned with such questions in practice instructed, or was it sufficient to draw their attention to the Army directives?

KEITEL: Every department right down to the smallest unit had these directives, and every soldier up to a certain point was instructed on them. Apart from that, no further explanations and regulations were issued at the beginning of the war.

DR. NELTE: I am thinking of the courses of instruction instituted in Vienna for that particular purpose. Do you know that they took place in Vienna?

KEITEL: It is known to me that such matters were the subject of courses of instructions suitable for those people who were actually in

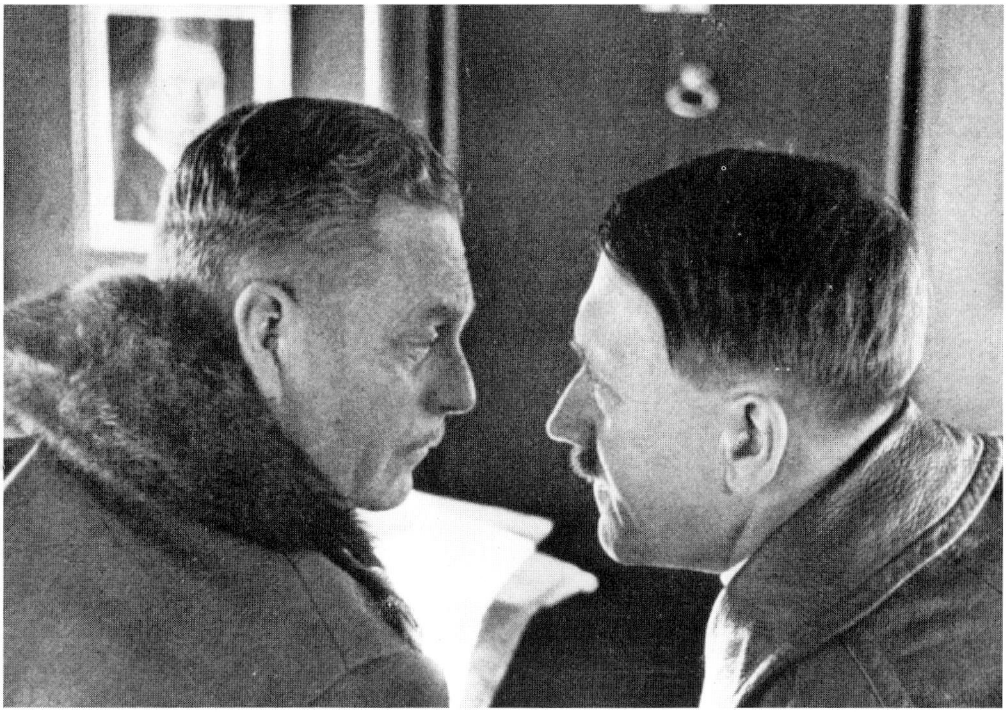

1938 – Wilhelm Keitel and Adolf Hitler deep in conversation. During the Second World War, Keitel was one of the primary planners of the Wehrmacht campaigns on the Western and the Eastern fronts.

The majority of his colleagues viewed Keitel with disdain for succumbing to Hitler's influence. He acquired the nickname 'Lakeitel', a pun on his name (in German, the word 'Lakai' means 'lackey').

September 1939 – Hitler receives a briefing on the tactical situation in Poland from General List (left). Behind Hitler are Keitel and General Alfred Jodl both of the Supreme Armed Forces HQ.

May-June 1940 – Keitel surveys an array of maps and documents as Adolf Hitler takes a phone call at Wolfsschlucht I – his headquarters at Bruly-de-Pesche, Belgium.

June 1940 – Senior General Georg von Küchler of Army Group B makes a situation report to Hitler, as Keitel (centre) listens on, paying close attention.

June 1940 – Keitel stands beside Hitler in silent contemplation before the Menin Gate.

June 1940 – Keitel and Hitler at Mount Kemmel. Both men had served in the First World War.

10 June 1940 – Hitler visits the First World War memorial to the Canadian soldiers killed at Vimy Ridge, France. He is flanked by Keitel (left) and Wehrmacht Field Marshal Gunther von Kluge (right).

July 1940 – Hitler in discussion with senior figures including Keitel, at a Berghof planning conference.

April 1941 – Keitel, Walther von Brauchitsch and Hitler during a meeting in Hitler's personal train.

20 April 1941 – (Left to right) Hermann Göring, Wilhelm Keitel, and Heinrich Himmler join Adolf Hitler for lavish celebrations on his birthday.

Keitel is shown here at the shoulder of Hitler as he plots news reports on a map during a meeting at his Eastern Front Headquarters that would become known as 'The Wolf's Lair'.

25 July 1941 – Adolf Hitler walks in the grounds of 'The Wolf's Lair' in the company of Wilhelm Keitel (left) and Hermann Göring (right).

Generalfeldmarschall Karl Rudolf Gerd von Rundstedt delivers a report to Hitler and Keitel.

6 April 1942 – Hitler studying a map with Göring, Keitel and an unidentified officer.

Nikola Mikhov, Hitler and Keitel meet in Berlin during 1943.

19 March 1943 – Adolf Hitler, accompanied by Heinz Guderian (left) and Keitel, touring the Rügenwalde testing grounds in Pomerania to see the giant railway gun "Dora".

18 May 1944 – Keitel is seen smiling (centre) as he stands next to Admiral Karl Dönitz and Himmler, who converses as he shakes hands with Adolf Hitler.

20 July 1944 – Keitel, Göring, Hitler and Martin Bormann photographed together shortly after the failed plot to assassinate Hitler known as Operation Valkyrie.

8 May 1945 – Field Marshal Keitel signing the unconditional surrender of the German Wehrmacht at the Soviet headquarters in Karlshorst, Berlin.

(Front row, from left to right) – Hermann Göring, Rudolf Hess, Joachim von Ribbentrop, Wilhelm Keitel. (Second row, from left to right) – Karl Dönitz, Erich Raeder, Baldur von Schirach, Fritz Sauckel.

Keitel photographed during the proceedings at Nuremberg.

(Left to right) Hess, von Ribbentrop, Göring and Keitel at Nuremberg.

Keitel looks out from the dock, seemingly uninterested in the proceedings.

Keitel as the trial nears its end at Nuremburg.

The body of Wilhelm Keitel after being hanged.

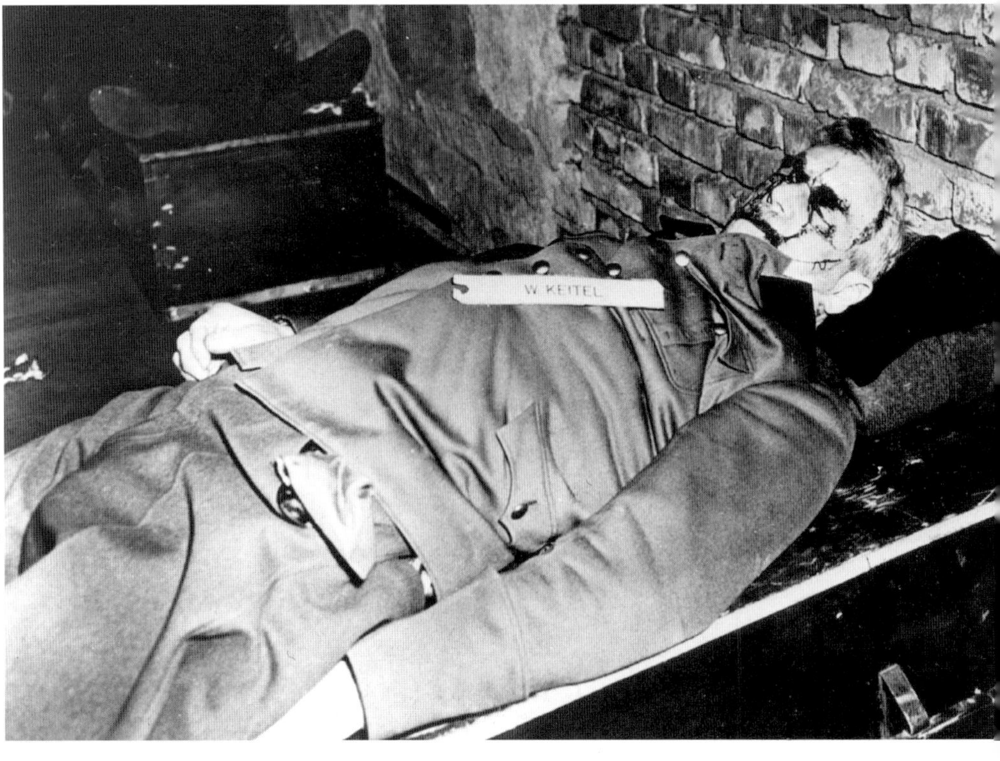

contact with prisoner-of-war matters. They took the form of training courses.

DR. NELTE: Is it, furthermore, correct that every soldier had a leaflet in his pay book?

KEITEL: Yes. That has already been confirmed by General Milch the other day, who had it with him.

DR. NELTE: When were the first instructions regarding prisoners of war given in our case?

KEITEL: As far as I know, the first instructions appeared after the beginning of the Polish campaign in the East, since every – I should like to say – preparatory measure for reception of prisoners of war had been rejected by Hitler. He had prohibited it. Afterwards things had to be improvised at very short notice.

DR. NELTE: What was ordered?

KEITEL: It was ordered that the three branches of the Wehrmacht, the Navy, Army and Luftwaffe – the latter had to do with it only to a limited extent – but particularly the Army should make appropriate preparations for camps, guards, and whatever was necessary for the establishment and the organization of such things.

DR. NELTE: Please tell us what the functions of the OKW were regarding the treatment and care of prisoners of war?

KEITEL: The principal instruction was treatment according to Directive KGV-38 (Prisoner of War Regulation 38) based on international agreements; in my opinion it contained absolutely everything which the people concerned should know. Apart from that, no additional instructions were issued at that time, but the above directive was applied.

DR. NELTE: I should like to know first of all how far the OKW had jurisdiction regarding the treatment of prisoners of war.

KEITEL: The OKW was, shall I say, the ministerial directing department which had to issue and prepare all basic regulations and directives concerning these questions. It was entitled to make sure, by means of inspections and surprise visits, that the instructions were carried out. In other words, it was the head office which issued directives and was entitled to make inspections, but was not in command of the camps themselves.

DR. NELTE: Should one not add the contact with the Foreign Office?

KEITEL: Of course, I forgot that. One of the main tasks of the entire Wehrmacht, and therefore of the Navy and Luftwaffe too, was to communicate with the protecting powers, through the Foreign Office and also to communicate with the International Red Cross and all agencies interested in the welfare of prisoners of war. I had forgotten that.

DR. NELTE: Therefore the OKW was, generally speaking, the legislator and the control organ.

KEITEL: That is correct.

DR. NELTE: What did the branches of the Wehrmacht have to do?

KEITEL: The Navy and the Luftwaffe had camps under their command, which were restricted to prisoners of war belonging to their own arms; and so did the Army. But owing to the large numbers belonging to the Army, the deputy commanding generals of the home front, that is, the commanders of the *Wehrkreise* were the commanding authorities who in their area were in charge of the camps.

DR. NELTE: Now, let us take the prisoner-of-war camps. Who was at the head of such a camp?

KEITEL: In the *Wehrkreis* command, there was a commander or a general responsible for questions relating to prisoners of war in the *Wehrkreis* concerned, and the camp itself was under the charge of a camp commandant who had a small staff of officers, among them an intelligence officer and similar personnel who were necessary for such matters.

DR. NELTE: Who was the superior officer of the general for prisoner-of-war affairs in the *Wehrkreis*?

KEITEL: The commander of the *Wehrkreis* was the superior officer of the commander for prisoner-of-war affairs in the *Wehrkreis*.

DR. NELTE: Who was the superior of the *Wehrkreis* commander?

KEITEL: The *Wehrkreis* commanders were under the Commander-in-Chief of the Home Army and the Reserve, and he in turn under the Commander-in-Chief of the Army.

THE PRESIDENT: The Tribunal will adjourn.

[The Tribunal adjourned until 5 April 1946 at 1000 hours.]

NUREMBERG TRIAL PROCEEDINGS
ONE HUNDREDTH DAY
FRIDAY, 5 APRIL 1946

MORNING SESSION

DR. NELTE: The last question I asked you yesterday concerned the channel through which orders were transmitted in matters concerning prisoners of war. You said that orders went from the camp commander to the army district commander and then by the commander of the reserve army to the OKH, the High Command of the Army. I should now like to have you tell me who was responsible if something happened in a PW camp which violated the Geneva Convention or was a breach of generally recognized international law. Was that your business? Was the OKW responsible?

KEITEL: The OKW was responsible in the case of incidents which violated general orders, that is, basic instructions issued by the OKW, or in the case of failure to exercise the right to inspect. In such circumstances I would say that the OKW was responsible.

DR. NELTE: How did the OKW exercise its right to inspect camps?

KEITEL: At first, in the early days of the war, through an inspector of the Prisoners of War Organization (the KGW), who was at the same time the office or departmental chief of the department KGW in the General Office of the Armed Forces. In a certain sense, he exercised a double function. Later on, after 1942 I believe, it was done by appointing an inspector general who had nothing to do with the correspondence or official work on the ministerial side.

DR. NELTE: What was the control by the protecting powers and the International Red Cross?

KEITEL: If a protecting power wished to send a delegation to inspect camps, that was arranged by the department or the inspector for the prisoner-of-war matters, and he accompanied the delegation. Perhaps I ought to say that, as far as the French were concerned, Ambassador Scapini carried out that function personally and that a protecting power did not exist in this form.

DR. NELTE: Could the representatives of the protecting powers and the Red Cross talk freely to the prisoners of war or only in the presence of officers of the German Armed Forces?

KEITEL: I do not know whether the procedure adopted in camps was always in accordance with the basic instructions, which were to render possible a direct exchange of views between prisoners of war and visitors from their own countries. As a general rule, it was allowed and made possible.

DR. NELTE: Did you as the chief of the OKW concern yourself personally with the general instructions on prisoner-of-war matters?

KEITEL: Yes. I did concern myself with the general instructions. Apart from that, my being tied to the *Führer* and to headquarters naturally made it impossible for me to be in continuous contact with my offices. There were, however, the KGW branch office and the inspector, as well as the Chief of the General Armed Forces Office who was, in any case, responsible to me and dealt with these matters. These three departments had to deal with the routine work; and I, myself, was called on when decisions had to be made and when the *Führer* interfered in person, as he frequently did, and gave orders of his own.

DR. NELTE: According to the documents presented here in Court,

Soviet prisoners of war seem to have received different treatment from the other prisoners. What can you say on that subject?

KEITEL: It is true that in this connection there was a difference in treatment due to the view, frequently stated by the *Führer*, that the Soviet Union on their part had not observed or ratified the Geneva Convention. It was also due to the part played by "ideological conceptions regarding the conduct of the war". The *Führer* emphasized that we had a free hand in this field.

DR. NELTE: I am now going to show you Document EC-388, Exhibit USSR-356. It is dated 15 September 1941.

Part 1 is the minutes of a report by the Foreign Intelligence Department of the OKW. Part 2 is a directive from the OKW, dated 8 September 1941, regarding the treatment of Soviet Russian prisoners of war. Part 3 is a memorandum on the guarding of Soviet prisoners of war, and the last document is a copy of the decree by the Council of People's Commissars regarding the prisoners of war matters dated 1 July 1941.

[The document was submitted to the defendant.]

KEITEL: Perhaps I can say by way of introduction that these directives were not issued until September, which can be attributed to the fact that at first an order by Hitler existed, saying that Russian prisoners of war were not to be brought back to Reich territory. This order was later on rescinded.

Now, regarding the directive of 8 September 1941, the full text of which I have before me, I should like to say that all these instructions have their origin in the idea that this was a battle of nationalities, for the initial phrase reads, "Bolshevism is the deadly enemy of National Socialist Germany." That, in my opinion, immediately shows the basis on which these instructions were made and the motives and ideas from which they sprang. It is a fact that Hitler, as I explained yesterday, did not consider this a battle between two states to be waged in accordance with the rules of international law but as a conflict between two ideologies. There are also several statements in the document regarding selection from two points of view: Selection of people who seem, if I may express it in this way, not dangerous to us; and the selection of those who, on account of their political activities and their fanaticism, had to be isolated as representing a particularly dangerous threat to National Socialism.

Turning to the introductory letter, I may say that it has already been presented here by the Prosecutor of the Soviet Union. It is a letter from the Chief of the Intelligence Service of the OKW, Admiral Canaris, reminding one of the general order which I have just mentioned and adding a series of remarks in which he formulates and emphasizes his doubts about the decree and his objections to it. About the memorandum which is attached I need not say any more. It is an extract, and also the orders which the Soviet Union issued in their turn I think on 1 July, for the treatment of prisoners of war, that is, the directives for the treatment of German prisoners of war. I received this on 15 September, whereas the other order had been issued about a week earlier; and after studying this report from Canaris, I must admit I shared his objections. Therefore I took all the papers to Hitler and asked him to cancel the provisions and to make a further statement on the subject. The *Führer* said that we could not expect that German prisoners of war would be treated according to the Geneva Convention or international law on the other side. We had no way of investigating it and he saw no reason to alter the directives he had issued on that account. He refused point-blank, so I returned the file with my marginal notes to Admiral Canaris. The order remained in force.

DR. NELTE: What was the actual treatment accorded to Soviet prisoners of war? Was it in compliance with the instructions issued or was it handled differently in practice?

KEITEL: According to my own personal observations and the reports which have been put before me, the practice was, if I may say so, very much better and more favourable than the very severe instructions first issued when it had been agreed that the prisoners of war were to be transported to Germany. At any rate, I have seen numerous reports stating that labour conditions, particularly in agriculture, but also in war economy and in particular in the general institution of war economy such as railways, the building of roads, and so on, were considerably better than might have been expected, considering the severe terms of the instructions.

DR. NELTE: Mr. President, may I refer on this occasion to Document Number 6 in the document book?

THE PRESIDENT: Which document book?

DR. NELTE: Document Number 6, in Document Book Number 1 – in my document book, Number 6 – "Conditions of employment for workers from the East, as well as Soviet Russian prisoners of war." In this document book I have included from the book I am submitting only those passages which concern the conditions of employment for Soviet Russian prisoners of war. I am submitting this book in evidence as Exhibit K-6, and beg the Tribunal to admit it in evidence without my having to read from it. These instructions refer expressly to the points which indicate that at a later period Soviet Russian prisoners of war were to be treated in accordance with the Geneva Convention as laid down by the OKW, author of the decree.

May I continue?

THE PRESIDENT: Yes, very well. You do not wish to read from it?

DR. NELTE: No, I do not want to.
[Turning to the defendant.] Please, will you explain to me just what relations existed between the police, or rather Himmler, on the one hand and the Prisoners of War Organization, the KGW, on the other?

KEITEL: May I say, first of all, that there was constant friction between Himmler and the corresponding police services and the departments of the Wehrmacht which worked in this sphere and that this friction never stopped. It was apparent right from the first that Himmler at least desired to have the lead in his own hands, and he never ceased trying to obtain influence of one kind or another over prisoner-of-war affairs. The natural circumstances of escapes, recapture by police, searches and inquiries, the complaints about insufficient guarding of prisoners, the insufficient security measures in the camps, the lack of guards and their inefficiency – all these things suited him; and he exploited them in talks with Hitler, when he continually accused the Wehrmacht behind its back, if I may use the expression, of every possible shortcoming and failure to carry out their duty. As a result of this Hitler was continually intervening, and in most cases I did not know the reason. He took up the charges and intervened constantly in affairs so that the Wehrmacht departments were kept in what I might term a state of perpetual unrest. In this connection, since I could not investigate matters myself, I was forced to give instructions to my departments in the OKW.

DR. NELTE: What was the underlying cause and the real purpose which Himmler attempted to achieve?

KEITEL: He wanted not only to gain influence but also, as far as possible, to have prisoner-of-war affairs under himself as Chief of Police in Germany so that he would reign supreme in these matters, if I may say so.

DR. NELTE: Did not the question of procuring labour enter into it?

KEITEL: Later on that did become apparent, yes. I think I shall have to refer to that later but I can say now that one observation at least was made which could not be misinterpreted: The searches and inquiries, made at certain intervals in Germany for escaped persons, made it clear that the majority of these prisoners of war did not go back to the camps from which they had escaped so that obviously they had been retained by police departments and probably used for labour under the jurisdiction of Himmler. Naturally, the number of escapes increased every year and became more and more extensive. For that, of course, there are quite plausible reasons.

DR. NELTE: The prisoner-of-war system, of course, is pretty closely connected with the labour problem. Which departments were responsible for the employment of prisoners of war?

KEITEL: The departments which dealt with this were the State Labour Offices in the so-called Reich Labour Allocation Service, which had originally been in the hands of the Labour Minister and was later on transferred to the Plenipotentiary for the Allocation of Labour. In practice it worked like this. The State Labour Offices applied for workers to the Army district commands which had jurisdiction over the camps. These workers were supplied as far as was possible under the existing general directives.

DR. NELTE: What did the OKW have to do with the allocation of labour?

KEITEL: In general, of course, they had to supervise it, so that allocation was regulated according to the general basic orders. It was not possible, of course, and the inspector was not in a position to check on how each individual was employed; after all, the army district commanders and their generals for the KGW were responsible for that and were the appropriate persons. The actual fight, as I might call it, for prisoner-of-war labour did not really start until 1942. Until then, such workers had been employed mainly in agriculture and the German railway system and a number of general institutions, but not in industry. This applies especially to Soviet prisoners of war who were, in the main, agricultural workers.

DR. NELTE: What was the actual cause for these labour requirements?

KEITEL: During the winter of 1941-42 the problem of replacing soldiers who had dropped out arose, particularly in the eastern theatre of war. Considerable numbers of soldiers fit for active service were needed for the front and the armed services. I remember the figures. The army alone needed replacements numbering from 2 to 2.5 million men every year. Assuming that about 1 million of these would come from normal recruiting and about half a million from rehabilitated men, that is, from sick and wounded men who had recovered, that still left 1.5 million to be replaced every year. These could be withdrawn from the war economy and placed at the disposal of the services, the Armed Forces. From this fact resulted the close correlation between the drawing off of these men from the war economy and their replacement by new workers. This manpower had to be taken from the prisoners of war on the one hand and Plenipotentiary Sauckel, whose functions may be summarized as the task of procuring labour, on the other hand. This connection kept bringing me into these matters, too, since I was responsible for the replacements for all the Wehrmacht – Army, Navy, and Air Force – in other words, for the recruiting system. That is why I was present at discussions between Sauckel and the *Führer* regarding replacements and how these replacements were to be found.

DR. NELTE: What can you tell me about the allocation of prisoners of war in industry and in the armament industry?

KEITEL: Up to 1942 or thereabouts we had not used prisoners of war in any industry even indirectly connected with armaments. This was due to an express prohibition issued by Hitler, which was made by him because he feared attempts at sabotaging machines, production equipment, *et cetera*. He regarded things of that kind as probable and dangerous. Not until necessity compelled us to use every worker in some capacity in the home factories did we abandon this principle. It was no longer discussed; and naturally prisoners of war came to be used after that in the general war production, while my view which I, that is the OKW, expressed in my general orders, was that their use in armament factories was forbidden; I thought that it was not permissible to employ prisoners of war in factories which were exclusively making armaments, by which I mean war equipment, weapons, and munitions.

For the sake of completeness, perhaps I should add that an order issued by the *Führer* at a later date decreed further relaxation of the limitations of the existing orders. I think the Prosecution stated that Minister Speer is supposed to have spoken of so many thousands of prisoners of war employed in the war economy. I may say, however, that many jobs had to be done in the armament industry which had nothing to do with the actual production of arms and ammunition.

DR. NELTE: The Prosecution have frequently stated that prisoners of war were detained by the police and even placed in concentration camps. Can you give an explanation about that?

KEITEL: I think the explanation of that is that the selection process already mentioned took place in the camps. Furthermore there are documents to show that prisoners of war in whose case the disciplinary powers of the commander were not sufficient were singled out and handed over to the Secret State Police. Finally, I have already mentioned the subject of prisoners who escaped and were recaptured, a considerable number of whom, if not the majority, did not return to their camps. Instructions on the part of the OKW or the Chief of Prisoners of War Organization ordering the surrender of these prisoners to concentration camps are not known to me and have never been issued. But the fact that, when they were handed over to the police, they frequently did end up in the concentration camps has been made known here in various ways, by documents and witnesses. That is my explanation.

DR. NELTE: The French Prosecution have presented a document which bears the Number 1650-PS. This is an order, or, rather, an alleged order, from the OKW ordering that escaped prisoners of war who are not employed are to be surrendered to the Security Service. After what you have just told us, you will have to give an explanation of that. I am showing you, in addition, Document 1514-PS, an order from the *Wehrkreiskommando VI* (Area Command), from which you will be able to see the procedure adopted by the OKW in connection with the surrender of prisoners of war to the Secret State Police.

KEITEL: First of all, I want to discuss Document 1650-PS. To begin with, I have to state that I did not know of that order, that it was never in my hands, and that so far I have not been able to find out how it came to be issued.

DR. NELTE: Wouldn't you like to say, first of all, that the document as such is not a document of the OKW?

KEITEL: I am coming to that.

DR. NELTE: I am afraid you must start with that in order to clear up the matter.

KEITEL: The document starts like a document which has been confiscated in a police department. It starts with the words, "The OKW has ordered as follows:"; after that come the Numbers 1, 2, 3 and then it goes on to say, "In this connection I order…", and that is the Supreme Police Chief of the Reich Security Head Office; it is signed by Müller, not Kaltenbrunner but Müller. I have certainly not signed this order OKW 1 to 3, and I have not seen it; there is no doubt about that. The fact that technical expressions, "Stage 3b" *et cetera*, are used proves that in itself. These are terms used by the police and they are unknown to me. I must say, therefore, that I am not sure how this document was drafted. I cannot explain it. There are assumptions and possibilities, and I should like to mention them briefly because I have given a great deal of thought to the matter. First, I do not believe that any department of the OKW, that is, the Chief of Prisoners of War Organization or the Chief of the

General Wehrmacht Office, could have issued this order independently without instructions to do so. I consider that quite impossible, as it was completely contrary to the general tendency. I have no recollection that I have ever received any instructions of this kind from Hitler or that I have passed any such instruction on to anybody else. I conclude that even if this may look like an excuse, there were, of course, other channels which the *Führer* used without regard to competency. And, if I must supply an explanation, such orders could have been given through an adjutant without my knowledge. I emphasize that this is a supposition and that it cannot absolve me from blame.

There is only one thing that I would like to say, and that is with reference to the Document 1514-PS. This is a captured order from the *Wehrkreiskommando VI*, at Münster, dated 27 July 1944, in other words, the summer of 1944. It deals with escaped prisoners of war and how they are to be dealt with. It says "Reference", and then it quotes seven different orders from the year 1942 up to the beginning of July 1944. This order deals with the question of escaped prisoners of war and ought to have been incorporated in this document, if the military office of *Wehrkreis VI* had had such an OKW order. That fact is remarkable, and it led me to the conclusion that there never was a written order and that the military authorities in question never received such an order at all. I cannot say more about it since I cannot prove it.

DR. NELTE: You know that the Prosecution have submitted an order, according to which Soviet Russian prisoners of war were to be marked by means of tattooing, so that they could be identified. Would you please make a statement on that?

KEITEL: The facts are as follows: During the summer of 1942, the *Führer* called the Quartermaster General of the Army to headquarters for a report lasting several hours, at which the *Führer* asked him to report on conditions in the Eastern rear army territory. I was suddenly called in and told that the Quartermaster General was saying that thousands of Russian prisoners of war were escaping every month, that they disappeared among the population, immediately discarded their uniforms, and procured civilian clothes, and could no longer be identified. I was ordered to make investigations and to devise some means of identification which would enable them to be identified even after they had put on civilian clothing. Thereupon I sent instructions to Berlin, saying that such an order should be prepared but that investigations should first be made by the international law department of the Foreign Office to find out whether such an order could be given at all; and, secondly, whether it could be carried out technically.

I should like to say that we were thinking of tattoo marks of the kind found on many seamen and bricklayers in Germany. But I heard no more about it. One day I met the Foreign Minister at headquarters and talked to him about the question. Foreign Minister Von Ribbentrop knew about the inquiry submitted to the Foreign Office and considered the measure extremely questionable. That was the first news I had about the subject. I gave immediate instructions, whether personally or through the adjutant I cannot remember, that the order was not to go out. I had neither seen a draft nor had I signed anything. At any rate I gave an unmistakable order: "The order is in no circumstances to be issued." I received no further detailed information at the time. I heard nothing more about it and I was convinced that the order had not been issued.

When I was interrogated, I made a statement on those lines. I have now been told by my Defence Counsel that the woman secretary of the Chief of the Prisoners of War Organization has volunteered to testify that the order was rescinded and was not to be issued and, further, that she had received those instructions personally. She said in her statement, however, that this did not happen until several days after the order had actually gone out and that that was the only possible explanation of how that order came to be found in the police office as still valid.

DR. NELTE: Mr. President, I shall submit the affidavit of the witness which has been received at the appropriate time.

[Turning to the defendant.] We now turn to the case of Sagan. The Prosecution originally accused you of giving the order for the killing of 50 Royal Air Force officers who escaped from Stalag Luft III at Sagan.

I am no longer clear as to whether the Prosecution still maintain this grave accusation since *Reichsmarschall* Göring and the witness Westhoff have been interrogated, the latter outside these proceedings. I have the report of Westhoff's interrogation before me and I have also submitted it to you. I should like to ask you now to amplify the statement which the witness Westhoff made during the preliminary proceedings and which he will make shortly in this court, and to say what you yourself know about this extremely grave incident.

KEITEL: The facts are that one morning it was reported to me that the escape had taken place. At the same time I received the information that about 15 of the escaped officers had been apprehended in the vicinity of the camp. I did not intend to report the case at the noon conference on the military situation held at Berchtesgaden, or rather, at the Berghof, as it was highly unpleasant, being the third mass escape in a very short period. As it had happened only 10 or 12 hours before, I hoped that in the course of the day the majority of them would be caught and that in this way the matter might be settled satisfactorily.

While I was making my report Himmler appeared. I think that it was towards the end of my report that he announced the incident in my presence, as he had already started the usual general search for the escaped prisoners. There was an extremely heated discussion, a serious clash between Hitler and myself, since he immediately made the most outrageous accusations against me on account of this incident.

Things are sometimes incorrectly represented in Westhoff's account, and that is why I am making a detailed statement. During this clash the *Führer* stated in great excitement, "These prisoners are not to be sent back to the Armed Forces; they are to stay with the Police." I immediately objected sharply. I said that this procedure was impossible. The general excitement led Hitler to declare again and with considerable emphasis, "I am ordering you to retain them, Himmler; you are not to give them up."

I put up a fight for the men who had already come back and who should, according to the original order, be brought out again and handed over to the police. I succeeded in doing it; but I could not do anything more.

After that very grave clash...

DR. NELTE: Will you tell me, please who was present during that scene?

KEITEL: As far as I remember, Colonel General Jodl was certainly present, at least for part of the time, and heard some of it, though perhaps not every word, since he was in the adjoining room at first. At any rate, Jodl and I returned to our quarters together. We discussed the case and talked about the extremely unpleasant consequences which the whole matter would have. On returning to my quarters I immediately ordered General Von Graevenitz to report to me the following morning.

In this connection I must explain that *Reichsmarschall* Göring was not present. If I was a little uncertain about that during my interrogation it was because I was told that witnesses had already stated that Göring was present. But right from the beginning I thought it improbable and doubtful. It is also incorrect, therefore, that Göring raised any accusations against me at the time. There had not been a conference in Berlin either. These are mistakes which I think I can explain by saying that Graevenitz, who came with Westhoff and saw me for the first time, was present during the report and witnessed a scene of a kind unusual in military life, because of the violence of my remarks in connection with the incident.

Do you want me to say anything more about the discussion with Graevenitz?

DR. NELTE: The only thing which interests me in this connection is, whether you repeated to Graevenitz the order previously given by Hitler in such a way that both Graevenitz and Westhoff who was also present, might get the impression that you yourself had issued the order for the shooting of the escaped officers.

KEITEL: According to the record of Westhoff's interrogation, which I have seen, I can explain it, I think, as follows: First of all, I made serious accusations. I myself was extraordinarily excited, for I must say that even the order that the prisoners were to be retained by the police caused me extreme anxiety regarding their fate. I frankly admit that the possibility of their being shot while trying to escape remained in my subconscious mind. I certainly spoke in extreme agitation at the time and did not weigh my words carefully. And I certainly repeated Hitler's words, which were, "We must make an example," since I was afraid of some further serious encroachments upon the Prisoners of War Organization in other ways, apart from this single case of the prisoners not being returned to the Wehrmacht. On reading the interrogation report I saw the statement by Graevenitz, or rather, Westhoff, to the effect that I had said, "They will be shot, and most of them must be dead already." I probably said something like, "You will see what a disaster this is; perhaps many of them have been shot already."

I did not know, however, that they had already been shot; and I must confess that in my presence Hitler never said a word about anybody being shot. He only said, "Himmler, you will keep them; you will not hand them over." I did not find out until several days later that they had been shot. I saw among other papers also an official report from the British Government stating that not until the 31st – the escape took place on the 25th – that not until the 31st were they actually shot.

Therefore Westhoff is also wrong in thinking that orders had already been issued saying that an announcement was to be made in the camp stating that certain people had been shot or would not return and that lists of names were to be posted. That order did not come until later, and I remember it; I remember it because of the following incident:

A few days afterwards, I think on or about the 31st, before the situation report, one of the adjutants told me that a report had been received that some had been shot. I requested a discussion alone with

Hitler and told him that I had heard that people had been shot by the police. All he said was that he had received it too – naturally, since it was his report. In extreme disgust I told him my opinion of it. At that time he told me that it was to be published in the camp as a warning to the others. Only upon this the announcement in the camp was ordered. In any case, Westhoff's recollection of some of the facts, which he has sworn to, is not quite accurate, even if such expressions as those used by him and explained by me here may have occurred. We shall hear his own account of that.

DR. NELTE: Did Hitler ever tell you that he had ordered those men to be shot?

KEITEL: No, he never told me that. I never heard it from him. I heard it very much later, as far as I can remember, from *Reichsmarschall* Göring, with whom the whole incident was, of course, the subject of discussions and conversations, especially as an Air Force camp was involved.

DR. NELTE: I should like to say in conclusion: Are you stating under oath, here, that you yourself neither ordered these Royal Air Force officers to be shot, nor did you receive and pass on such an order, nor did you yourself learn who gave the order?

KEITEL: That is correct. I neither received that order nor did I know or hear of it; nor did I pass on such an order. I can repeat this herewith under oath.

DR. NELTE: We now turn to deportations. What the Prosecution refer to as deportation of workers is the removal of bodily fit citizens of the occupied territories to Germany or other occupied territories for the purpose of using them for "slave labour" on defence work or other tasks connected with warfare. That is the accusation which I have read to you.

The Prosecution have repeatedly coupled your name with these accusations and have said that you, that is, the OKW, had cooperated in supplying workers for the German war economy. You know that in fact the Defendant Sauckel was the Plenipotentiary in that field. I should like to ask you whether workers had been taken from the occupied territories and brought to Germany before Plenipotentiary Sauckel was appointed.

KEITEL: As far as I know, workers came from occupied territories, especially those in the West: Belgium, Holland – I do not know about Holland, but certainly France – to Germany. According to what I heard, I understood at the time that it was done by recruiting volunteers. I think I remember that General Von Stülpnagel, the military commander of Paris, told me in Berlin once during a meeting that more than 200,000 had volunteered, but I cannot remember exactly when that was.

DR. NELTE: Was the OKW the competent authority on these matters?

KEITEL: No, the OKW had nothing to do with it. These questions were handled through the usual channels, the OKH, the Military Commanders in France and in Belgium and Northern France with the competent central authorities of the Reich at home, the OKW never had anything to do with it.

DR. NELTE: What about civilian administration in occupied territories?

KEITEL: In occupied territories with civilian administration, the Wehrmacht was excluded from any executive powers in the administration, so that in these territories the Wehrmacht and its services had certainly nothing to do with it. Only in those territories which were still operational areas for the Army were executive powers given to military troops, high commanders, army commanders, *et cetera*. The OKW did not come into the official procedure here either.

DR. NELTE: According to an interrogation report submitted here the Defendant Sauckel said that you, that is, the OKW, were responsible for giving instructions to the military commanders in the occupied territories and that he, Sauckel, was to have their support in his recruiting campaigns for getting the quotas. What can you say about that?

KEITEL: The view held by Plenipotentiary Sauckel can obviously be explained by the fact that he knew neither the official service channels nor the functions of the Wehrmacht, that he saw me at one or two discussions on the furnishing of manpower, and, thirdly, that he sometimes came to see me when he had made his report and received his orders alone. He had probably been given orders to do so, in Hitler's usual way: Go and see the Chief of the OKW; he will do the rest. The OKW had no occasion to do anything. The OKW had no right to give orders, but in Sauckel's case I did take over the job of informing the OKH or the technical departments in the General Quartermaster's office. I have never issued orders or instructions of my own to the military commanders or other services in occupied territories. It was not one of the functions of the OKW.

DR. NELTE: A document has been submitted here according to which Generals Stapf and Nagel had agreed to ask you to exercise pressure or coercion during the recruiting campaigns in the East. That, at any rate, is the assertion by the Prosecution. Do you know of this happening?

KEITEL: I remembered it when the document was presented. It was obviously an attempt on the part of Stapf, who had worked with me in the Army for many years, to get the *Führer*'s support or assistance through my mediation. Stapf, who was the director of the Economic Staff East at the time, and General Nagel, who was also mentioned in this connection and who was in charge of the Economic Inspectorate Department in the East, had obviously tried to involve me in the matter. According to the document, some pressure had to be applied from higher quarters; but I took no steps at all as I had nothing to do with these things.

DR. NELTE: I am now going to deal with the question of the pillage of art treasures.

THE PRESIDENT: Perhaps we might adjourn now.

[A recess was taken.]

DR. NELTE: The French Prosecution have accused you, among other things, of issuing directives regarding the safeguarding and confiscation of objects of art, libraries, *et cetera*. Were any military orders, directives, or instructions laid down before the campaign in the West or in the East, with regard to objects of art, libraries, and their treatment in occupied territories?

KEITEL: No, as far as I know, there was nothing at all about these matters, although thorough provision had been made for everything else which might happen in the course of a war. I am not aware of any orders which were given with that in mind.

DR. NELTE: I am going to show you three documents submitted by the French Prosecution, which mention you in connection with Rosenberg's special staff, which has already been mentioned here on various occasions. These are Documents 137-PS, 138-PS, and 140-PS. These are documents from the Chief of the OKW to the Commander-in-Chief of the Army in France and in the Netherlands.

KEITEL: The first two documents, 137-PS and 138-PS, came from headquarters. They were dictated in part by myself and sent to offices of the Army. One says "To the Commander-in-Chief of the Army", the other one "To the Commander-in-Chief of the Army in Occupied France" and to the "Commander of the Wehrmacht in the Netherlands". They originated partly in answers to queries from various military offices which considered themselves responsible for the safekeeping or guarding of whatever was in the occupied territories, and also from offices which obviously were going to collect, inspect, to register, or otherwise investigate these art treasures, libraries, *et cetera*, and to confiscate them. In one case I was called up on the phone by the Commander-in-Chief of the Army, I think, who protested against this, at other times by *Reichsleiter* Rosenberg. The *Führer* directed me to instruct military services to acquiesce in this and to state their agreements, as they were directives which he had issued and approved himself. The way in which the documents are drawn up shows, in itself, that they did not emanate from an OKW office. My adjutant signed them; but I myself dictated them on the *Führer's* orders and sent them out. These queries may have been made just because no provision had been made and no orders given. I did not know what was to be done with these art treasures, *et cetera*; but I naturally took the view that the object was to safeguard them. No mention was made of transport, or confiscation, or expropriation; and the question did not occur to me; I merely gave these instructions in quite a brief form and did not bother any further about the matter. I took them to be precautionary measures and they did not seem to me to be unjustified.

DR. NELTE: Then you mean the OKW had no jurisdiction over these affairs?

KEITEL: No.

DR. NELTE: It was a question of merely transmitting letters to the military authorities to make known Hitler's wishes to assist Rosenberg in his task?

KEITEL: That is correct.

DR. NELTE: I should like to put a personal question to you in this connection. Have you ever appropriated to yourself any of the art treasures from public or private ownership in the occupied countries, or did any office whatever assign any work of art to you?

KEITEL: No, I never had anything to do with these things.

DR. NELTE: We now come to the so-called economic exploitation of occupied territories. You are accused of participating, in your official position as Chief of the OKW, in the economic exploitation of the occupied Eastern countries and the Western occupied countries. This question has already been discussed in *Reichsmarschall* Göring's examination, so I can treat it relatively briefly. It is, however, necessary for you to clarify the extent to which the OKW, and yourself in particular, were connected with these matters, for both the OKW and yourself are mentioned in this connection, as well as the *Wirtschaftsrustungsamt* (Economic Armament Office), which was a branch of the OKW. General Thomas of that office prepared a compilation which was produced by the Prosecution. What can you say about this question, if I have Document 1157-PS and USSR-80 shown to you?

KEITEL: 1157-PS deals with "Plan Barbarossa Oldenburg". I would like to say this:

The *Wehrwirtschaftsamt* (War Economy Office), which even then was no longer known as the *Wirtschaftsrustungsamt* carried out under its chief, General Thomas, certain organizational preparations, first for the campaign in the West and later for campaign Barbarossa in the East. They were made by the military economic organization at home, in the Reich, which had teams attached to all *Wehrkreiskommandos*. As a result, advisers and some personnel with experience in problems of war economy supplies and a few small detachments called *Feldwirtschaftskommandos* (Field Economic Detachments) were assigned to the Army Commands (the A.O.K.s).

The personnel attached to the Quartermaster Staffs at the A.O.K. were responsible for securing, or causing to be secured, supplies, fuel, and food stuffs found in occupied or conquered territories, as well as other articles suitable for the immediate requirements of the troops. They should then cooperate with the Senior Quartermaster, who looks after my army supplies, and the intendant in charge of the transport of supplies, in making them available for the fighting troops. Information obtained regarding war economy in the important areas of France and Belgium, as far as such information could be obtained, was kept for later use. The East, as I believe *Reichsmarschall* Göring has already explained at length, was organized on quite a different basis with a view not only to supplying the troops, but also to exploiting the conquered territories. An organization serving this aim was built up, called *Wirtschaftsorganisation Ost*-Oldenburg (Economic Organization East-Oldenburg). Its connection with the OKW lay in the fact that the necessary preparations for organizing and developing panels of experts and technical branch offices had to be discussed with the Ministry of Economics, the Four Year Plan, and the Ministry of Food and Agriculture. That was *Wirtschaftsorganisation* Oldenburg. The OKW and its Chief, that is myself, had no power to give orders or instructions affecting its activities. The organization was created and placed at the disposal of those responsible for putting it in action, giving it instructions and working with it. If General Thomas wrote in his book, which was produced here as a document...

DR. NELTE: 2353-PS (Exhibit Number USA-35), Page 386. Perhaps, you will just read that, so that you can give us a summary.

KEITEL: Yes. This is an excerpt from the book of General Thomas, where he describes in detail his own functions and those of the organization which he directed in the OKW, from its origin until far into the war. He says here:

"The functions exercised by the Economic Armament Office (*Wirtschaftsrustungsamt*) while the Eastern campaign was going on consisted mainly in the organizational management of the economic machinery set in motion and in advising the Operational Staff for War Economy East."

DR. NELTE: You need read only Paragraph 4 for your summary.

KEITEL: The Operational Staff for Military Economy East, attached to the Four Year Plan as Barbarossa-Oldenburg, was responsible for the entire economic direction of the whole of the Eastern area. It was responsible for the technical instructions of the State Secretaries in the Operational Staff for Military Economy, for the organization of Thomas' Economic Armament Office, and for applying all measures to be taken by the Operational Staff for Military Economy East under the direction and command of the *Reichsmarschall*.

DR. NELTE: How were conditions in the West?

KEITEL: I described very briefly the small group of experts attached to the High Command quartermaster departments in the West. Later on, as I have already stated, at the beginning of June, the entire economic direction was transferred to the Four Year Plan and the plenipotentiaries for the Four Year Plan, as far as anything passed beyond current supplies intended to cover daily requirements, fuel, *et cetera*. This was done by a special decree, which has already been mentioned by the *Reichsmarschall* and which had been issued by the *Führer*.

DR. NELTE: That was laid down by General Thomas on Page 304 in Document 2353-PS, which we have already mentioned. There is no need for me to read this; and I request the Tribunal to allow me to present the defendant's affidavit in Document Book Number 2 for, the Military Economic Armament Office of the OKW, as Document Keitel-11 in evidence, so that no further questions on the subject may be necessary. I assume that the Prosecution will agree to this procedure.

THE PRESIDENT: What number is it in Book 2?

DR. NELTE: Number 4 in this Document Book Number 2. It is

Page 27 and following, in Document Book 2, submitted to the Court. The document is dated 29 March 1946.

THE PRESIDENT: What date did you say it is?

DR. NELTE: 29 March 1946. I do not think there is any date in the document book. I will present the original which I have here.

THE PRESIDENT: How is it described in the document itself? We have a document dated 4 March 1946, "The Economic Armament Office of the Supreme Command of the Wehrmacht." Is that right?

DR. NELTE: The document was written on 4 March 1946, but the affidavit was added on 29 March 1946.

THE PRESIDENT: But that appears to have been 8 March? Is it that document?

DR. NELTE: The *Wirtschaftsrustungsamt* in the OKW. It is possible.

THE PRESIDENT: That's here.

DR. NELTE: In any case, there is no doubt about the identity of the document.

[Turning to the defendant.] Now I come to a topic which is presented again and again before the high Tribunal and which is very difficult because the reason for these questions is not properly understood.

The charge has been made against you that in your capacity as a member of the government, as the Prosecution contend, you knew, or must have known of the happenings in the concentration camps. I am therefore compelled to ask you what you know about the existence of the concentration camps, how much you knew and what you had to do with them. Did you know of their existence? Did you know that concentration camps existed?

KEITEL: Yes, I knew already before the war that concentration camps existed; but at that time I knew only two of them by name; and I supposed and assumed that there were other concentration camps besides the two I knew. I had no further particulars about the existence of concentration camps. As far as internees in such camps were concerned, I knew that they included habitual criminals and political opponents. As *Reichsmarschall* Göring has said, that was the basis of the institution.

DR. NELTE: Did you hear anything about the treatment of internees?

KEITEL: No, I heard nothing precise about it. I assumed that it was a severe form of detention, or one which brought severe measures in its train, under certain specific circumstances. I knew nothing about the conditions found there, especially in-treatment of internees, tortures, *et cetera*.

I tried in two cases to free individuals who were in concentration camps. One was Pastor Niemoller, by intervention of *Großadmiral* Raeder. With the help of Canaris and at the request of *Großadmiral* Raeder, I tried to get Pastor Niemoller out of the concentration camps. The attempt was unsuccessful. I made a second attempt at the request of a family in my home village, in a case where a peasant was in a concentration camp for political reasons; and in this case I succeeded. The individual involved was set free. That was in the autumn of 1940. I had a talk with this man; and when I asked him what things were like there, he gave me a non-committal reply to the effect that he had been all right. He gave me no details. I know of no other cases...

DR. NELTE: When you talked to this man did you have the impression that anything had happened to him?

KEITEL: Undoubtedly he did not give that impression. I did not see him directly after his release. I saw him later when I was at home. The reason that I talked to him was because he came to thank me. He said nothing about being badly treated or anything like that at all.

DR. NELTE: It has been stated here that now and again these concentration camps were visited by members of the Wehrmacht, by officers – and high ranking officers, too. How do you explain that?

KEITEL: I am convinced that these visits took place on Himmler's invitation. I myself once received a personal invitation from him to pay a visit to the Dachau Camp from Munich. He said he would like to show it to me. I know also that large and small groups of officers and commissions were shown through the camps. I think I need scarcely say how these visits were handled as regards the things that were shown to them. To supplement my statement I would like to say it was not uncommon to hear such remarks as "You'll end up in a concentration camp!" or "All sorts of things go on there." I do know, however, that whenever anyone came to me with these rumours and stories and I asked what exactly they knew and where the information came from, the reply was always: "I really do not know; I just heard it." So that whatever one might think, one never got at the facts and never could get at them.

DR. NELTE: You heard that medical experiments were made on these internees, and that this was done by agreement with higher quarters. I ask you whether you had knowledge of that, either personally or from the Supreme Command of the Wehrmacht.

KEITEL: No, I never heard anything about the medical experiments on internees, which have been described here in detail, either officially or otherwise. Nothing.

DR. NELTE: I turn now to a group of questions relating to the Prosecution's assertion that you intended to have General Weygand and General Giraud assassinated or, at least, were participating in plans to that end. You know that witness Lahousen, on 30 November 1945 stated that Admiral Canaris had been pressed by you for some time, November-December 1940, to do away with the Chief of the French General Staff, General Weygand.

Lahousen added that Canaris told his departmental heads that after a talk with you. Did you discuss the case of General Weygand with Canaris?

KEITEL: That is probably correct, for there were reports at the time that General Weygand was travelling in North Africa, visiting the troops, and inspecting the colonial troops. I consider it quite natural that I told Canaris, who was the Chief of Counterintelligence, that it should be possible to determine the object of General Weygand's journey, the places at which he stopped in North Africa, and whether any military significance could be attached to this visit, as regards putting colonial troops into action or the introduction of other measures concerning them in North Africa. He is sure to have received instructions to try to get information through his Intelligence Department as to what was taking place.

DR. NELTE: I assume, also to keep an eye on him?

KEITEL: Yes.

DR. NELTE: Could the Counterintelligence department send members of its staff to North Africa?

KEITEL: I believe that certain channels of information existed via Spanish Morocco; and I know that Canaris maintained intelligence links with Morocco by way of Spain.

DR. NELTE: My question was meant to find out whether it was officially possible to visit North Africa in agreement with France.

KEITEL: Of course it was possible. After the Armistice, there were

Disarmament Commissions in North Africa, as well as in France. We had several Army departments there in connection with checking up the armaments of the North African troops.

DR. NELTE: What was the point, or was there any point, in wishing General Weygand ill? Was he a declared opponent of the policy Germany wished to carry through? What was the reason?

KEITEL: We had no reason to think that General Weygand might be, shall we say, inconvenient. In view of the connection with Marshal Petain, which was started about the end of September and the beginning of October of that year, and the well-known collaboration policy which reached its height in the winter of 1940-41, it was absurd even to think of doing away with the Marshal's Chief of Staff. An action of this kind would not have fitted into the general policy followed in dealing with the situation in North Africa. We released a large number of officers in the regular French Colonial Army from French prisoner-of-war camps in the winter of 1940-1941 for service with the colonial forces. There were generals among them; I remember General Juin in particular who, as we knew at the time, had been Chief of the General Staff in North Africa for many years. At my suggestion he was put at the disposal of the Marshal by Hitler, obviously with the aim of utilizing him in the colonial service. There had not been the slightest motive for wishing General Weygand ill or to think of anything of the sort.

DR. NELTE: Is it correct that conferences even took place with the French General Staff and Laval about cooperating in operations in Africa and the strengthening of West Africa?

KEITEL: Yes. Among the documents of the French Armistice Delegation there ought to be a large number of documents asking for all sorts of concessions in connection with North Africa and more especially Central and West Africa, owing to the fact that during the winter of 1940-41 riots had taken place in French Central Africa against which the French Government wanted to take measures. I believe that in the spring of 1941 a conference lasting several days took place in Paris with the French General Staff, in order to prepare measures in which the German Wehrmacht, which already had troops stationed in Tripoli in the Italian area, would participate.

DR. NELTE: So there is no apparent motive?

KEITEL: No.

DR. NELTE: Something must have been said, however, in this conversation with Canaris, which led to this misunderstanding. Can you suggest anything which might have caused this misunderstanding?

KEITEL: It can only be that, according to the very comprehensive details given by Lahousen in his testimony, I said at a later meeting, "What about Weygand?" That was the phrase Lahousen used; and he might have drawn the conclusion that, perhaps, in that sense of the word, as he represented it, he kept on saying "in that sense of the word," and when asked what that meant, he said "To kill him." It is due only to that, it can be due only to that. I must say that Canaris was frequently alone with me. Often he brought the chiefs of his departments along. When we discussed matters by ourselves, I thought he was always perfectly frank with me. If he had misunderstood me, there would certainly have been discussions about it, but he never said anything like that.

DR. NELTE: Is it clear to you that if there had been any idea of putting Weygand out of the way, it would have constituted an act of high political significance?

KEITEL: Yes, of course. In the collaboration of the *Führer* Adolf Hitler and Marshal Petain an act of that kind would have had the greatest imaginable political significance.

DR. NELTE: Then you still believe that if it had happened, it would have meant the breaking-off of the policy initiated by Hitler?

KEITEL: Certainly one would have had to expect that.

DR. NELTE: Only with regard to the great importance of General Weygand's personality?

KEITEL: Yes.

DR. NELTE: Can you give any other explanation, or any proof that the designs attributed to you, but thanks be to God were never put into practice, had no foundation in fact?

KEITEL: Although it was at a much later date that General Weygand was taken to Germany, on the occupation of the hitherto unoccupied zone of Southern France, I was told by the *Führer* himself that he had given orders only for the general to be interned in his own home, without being inconvenienced by guards – an honourable arrest and not the treatment accorded to an ordinary prisoner of war. Of course, that was in 1942.

DR. NELTE: Therefore, you finally and repeatedly deny under oath that you gave any order or expressed yourself in any way which might lead your hearers to conclude that you intended or wished General Weygand to be put out of the way?

KEITEL: Yes. I can expressly reaffirm that.

DR. NELTE: The witness Lahousen also spoke of Giraud and described the case much in the same way as that of Weygand. In neither case was he in a position to say from his own first-hand knowledge that you had given such an order, but he reported what Canaris had told him and illustrated his testimony by means of later inquiries. I ask you to tell us what you know about the case of Giraud, which created a sensation at the time and also here, and to say what part you took in discussions regarding Giraud.

KEITEL: Giraud's successful escape from the Fortress of Konigstein near Dresden on 19 April 1942 created a sensation; and I was severely reprimanded about the guard of this general's camp, a military fortress. The escape was successful despite all attempts to recapture the general, by police or military action, on his way back to France. Canaris had instructions from me to keep a particularly sharp watch on all the places at which he might cross the frontier into France or Alsace-Lorraine, so that we could recapture him. The police were also put on to this job; 8 or 10 days after his escape it was made known that the general had arrived safely back in France. If I issued any orders during this search I probably used the words I gave in the preliminary interrogations, namely, "We must get the general back, dead or alive." I possibly did say something like that. He had escaped and was in France.

Second phase: Efforts, made through the Embassy by Abetz and Foreign Minister Ribbentrop to induce the general to return to captivity of his own accord, appeared not to be unsuccessful or impossible, as the general had declared himself willing to go to the occupied zone to discuss the matter. I was of the opinion that the general might possibly do it on account of the concessions hitherto made to Marshal Petain regarding personal wishes in connection with the release of French generals from captivity. The meeting with General Giraud took place in occupied territory, at the staff quarters of a German Army Corps, where the question of his return was discussed. The Military Commander informed me by telephone of the general's presence in occupied territory, in the hotel where the German officers were billeted.

The commanding general suggested that if the general would not return voluntarily it would be a very simple matter to apprehend him if he were authorized to do so. I at once refused this categorically for I considered it a breach of faith. The general had come trusting to receive proper treatment and be returned unmolested.

Third phase: The attempt or desire to get the general back somehow into military custody arose from the fact that Canaris told me that the general's family was residing in territory occupied by German troops; and it was almost certain that the general would try to see his family, even if only after a certain period of time and when the incident had been allowed to drop. He suggested to me to make preparations for the recapture of the general if he made a visit of this kind in occupied territory. Canaris said that he himself would initiate these preparations through his Counterintelligence office in Paris and through his other offices. Nothing happened for some time; and it was surely quite natural for me to ask on several occasions, no matter who was with Canaris or if Lahousen was with him, "What has become of the Giraud affair?" or, in the same way, "How is the Giraud case getting on?" The words used by Mr. Lahousen were, "It is very difficult; but we shall do everything we can." That was his answer. Canaris made no reply. That strikes me as significant only now; but at the time it did not occur to me.

Third phase: At a later stage – Shall I continue?

DR. NELTE: Fourth phase.

KEITEL: Fourth phase. This began with Hitler's saying to me: "This is all nonsense. We are not getting results. Counterintelligence is not capable of this and cannot handle this matter. I will turn it over to Himmler and Counterintelligence had better keep out of this, for they will never get hold of the general again." Admiral Canaris said at the time that he was counting on having the necessary security measures taken by the French secret state police in case General Giraud went to the occupied zone; and a fight might result, as the general was notoriously a spirited soldier, a man of 60 who lowers himself 45 metres over a cliff by means of a rope – that is how he escaped from Konigstein.

Fifth phase: According to Lahousen's explanation in Berlin, Canaris' desire to transfer the matter to the Secret State Police, which Lahousen said was done as a result of representations from the departmental heads, was because I asked again how matters stood with Giraud and he wanted to get rid of this awkward mission. Canaris came to me and asked if he could pass it on to the Reich Security Main Office or to the police. I said yes, because the *Führer* had already told me repeatedly that he wanted to hand it over to Himmler.

Next phase: I wanted to warn Canaris some time later, when Himmler came to see me and confirmed that he had received orders from Hitler to have Giraud and his family watched unobtrusively and that I was to stop Canaris from taking any action in the case. He had been told that Canaris was working along parallel lines. I immediately agreed.

Now we come to the phase which Lahousen has described at length. I had asked about "Gustav" and similar questions. I wanted to direct Canaris immediately to stop all his activities in the matter, as Hitler had confirmed the order. What happened in Paris according to Lahousen's detailed reports, that excuses were sought, *et cetera*, that the matter was thought to be very mysterious, that is, Gustav as an abbreviation for the G in Giraud, all this is fancy rather than fact. I had Canaris summoned to me at once, for he was in Paris and not in Berlin. He had done nothing at all, right from the start. He was thus in a highly uncomfortable position with regard to me for he had lied to me. When he came I said only, "You will have nothing more to do in this matter; keep clear of it."

Then came the next phase: The general's escape without difficulty to North Africa by plane, which was suddenly reported – if I remember correctly – before the invasion of North Africa by the Anglo-American troops. That ended the business. No action was ever taken by the Counterintelligence whom I had charged to watch him, or by the police; and I never even used the words to do away with the general. Never!

The final phase of this entire affair may sound like a fairy tale, but it is true nevertheless. The general sent a plane from North Africa to Southern France near Lyons in February or March 1944, with a liaison officer who reported to the Counterintelligence and asked if the general could return to France and what would happen to him on landing in France. The question was turned over to me. *Generaloberst* Jodl is my witness that these things actually happened. The chief of the Counterintelligence Office involved in this matter was with me. The answer was: "Exactly the same treatment as General Weygand who is already in Germany. There is no doubt that the *Führer* will agree."

Nothing actually did happen, and I heard no more about it. But these things actually happened.

DR. NELTE: To complete our information, I must ask you a few questions for the French Prosecution have mentioned that later, in a later phase, the family of General Giraud suffered inconveniences or losses of a rather serious nature. When you were searching for Giraud did you cause any trouble to his family, who were living in occupied France? Did you give any directives which would confine or inconvenience the family in any way?

KEITEL: No. I had only an unobtrusive watch kept on the family's residence in order to receive information of any visit which he might have planned. But no steps of any kind were ever taken against the family. It would have been foolish in this case.

DR. NELTE: Foolish of you?

KEITEL: Yes.

DR. NELTE: To make matters quite clear: You had no knowledge of anything having happened later on?

KEITEL: No, none at all.

DR. NELTE: Well, General Giraud is still alive and I will only ask you, in conclusion, under your oath: Can you confirm that you did not, at any time, give an order or a directive which might be interpreted to mean that General Giraud was to be killed?

KEITEL: No. I never gave such an order, unless the phrase "We must have him back, dead or alive" may be considered of weight in this respect. I never gave orders that the general was to be killed or done away with, or anything of the kind. Never.

DR. NELTE: I have concluded my direct examination of the Defendant Keitel. May I ask you to permit me to submit in evidence the affidavit, that last one, Number 6 in Document Book Number 2. I would like to submit that affidavit in evidence. It is on Page 51 and following and is Document K...

THE PRESIDENT: Didn't you put that in as K-12 yesterday?

DR. NELTE: Today I submit Keitel-13...

THE PRESIDENT: This affidavit that you want to submit now, where is it and what is the date of it?

DR. NELTE: It is Page 51 and following, and it is dated 9 March 1946.

THE PRESIDENT: Yes, I see.

DR. NELTE: This affidavit has also been attested to by *Generaloberst* Jodl. I ask permission to question him about the affidavit or to show it to him for confirmation when he is called to the witness stand.

THE PRESIDENT: Very well.

MR. DODD: If the Court please, we have looked into the matter of the so-called interrogation of General Von Falkenhorst referred to yesterday by Dr. Nelte. Insofar as we can determine, this paper was never offered in evidence by any members of the Prosecution. It was referred to by M. Dubost – I mean, it was not referred to by him, but it was included in his brief. I did not refer to it, and I did not offer it in evidence. That is how it came into the hands of Dr. Nelte, but not in evidence.

THE PRESIDENT: Does Dr. Nelte want to offer it in evidence now?

DR. NELTE: I ask to submit it as Document Number Keitel-14.

THE PRESIDENT: Has it got a PS number or another number?

DR. NELTE: No, Mr. President, it has no other number.

THE PRESIDENT: Thank you.
Now, do any of the other Defence Counsel want to ask questions?

DR. STAHMER: Mr. Defendant, as you have corrected your former statement by answering the question put by your counsel with a statement that *Reichsmarschall* Göring was not present at the conference in which Hitler gave orders for the airmen who had escaped from the Sagan Camp should be held by the police and since you further said that a conference with *Reichsmarschall* Göring in Berlin did not take place, I have only the following questions on this subject: Some weeks after that escape, did you receive a letter from the Quartermaster General of the General Staff of the Luftwaffe informing you that the Luftwaffe wanted to hand over their prison camps to the OKW?

KEITEL: Yes, I received this letter and following an interview with Hitler I declined the offer.

DR. STAHMER: I have no more questions.

DR. SEIDL: At the beginning of the war, the Defendant Dr. Frank was a lieutenant of the 9th Infantry Regiment; is that correct?

KEITEL: Yes.

DR. SEIDL: Do you remember receiving a letter from Dr. Frank, who was then Governor General, in 1942, saying that he wanted to rejoin the Wehrmacht?

The purpose of that letter was, of course, that he be relieved of his office as Governor General in this way. Is that correct?

KEITEL: Yes, I received such a letter and handed it to the *Führer* who merely made a movement with his hands and said "Out of the question". I informed Frank of that decision through the liaison officer who was temporarily with him at the time.

DR. SEIDL: That is all.

DR. DIX: Your Lordship, it is 3 minutes to one and it will not take me very long, but it might take me beyond 1 o'clock, so it might be better to adjourn now. I would then put my question to the witness after the recess.

THE PRESIDENT: Very well, we will adjourn until 2:00 o'clock.

[The Tribunal recessed until 1400 hours.]

AFTERNOON SESSION

DR. DIX: May it please the Tribunal, this witness is competent and an expert who can give the Tribunal definite figures about the armament expenditures of the Reich. However, the witness is certainly not in a position to remember these figures just at the moment. Professor Kraus, my colleague, therefore, during my absence, was kind enough to mark these figures down and to check them in cooperation with the witness. The written deposition was signed by the witness at that time, in order to avoid any misunderstanding. In order to help him recollect these figures, I now ask your permission to have submitted to the witness this deposition which he has signed. I have had translations made of this deposition into the three languages in question and I now submit to the Tribunal eight copies. I also have four copies for the four delegations of the Prosecution, and German copies for the counsels of the Defendants Keitel, Jodl, Raeder, Doenitz, and the OKW.

May I ask for just one moment so that the witness can read it?

[Turning to the defendant.] Witness, would you please look at the first column only, which bears the heading "Total Expenditures". The second and the third columns show which of those sums were raised through the Reichsbank, on the one hand, and which were raised from other sources, on the other hand. These figures I should like to have certified during the interrogation of Schacht himself, because they were the results of Schacht's calculations and the witness here can therefore give no information about them. May I ask you concerning these armament expenditures of the Reich, beginning with the fiscal year of 1935, the fiscal year running from 1 April to 31 March: The figures stated herein are: 5,000 millions for 1935, 7,000 millions for 1936, 9,000 millions for 1937, 11,000 millions for 1938, and 20,500 millions for 1939. Are these figures correct?

KEITEL: According to my conviction these figures are correct. May I add that at the beginning of my captivity I also had an opportunity to speak to the Reich Finance Minister about these figures and to coordinate our opinions.

DR. DIX: Now, a question about the armament strength of the Reich on 1 April 1938. Is it correct to say that at that time there existed: 24 infantry divisions, 1 armoured division, no motorized division, 1 mountain division, 1 cavalry division, and that in addition 10 infantry divisions and 1 armoured division were being formed? I wish to add, that of the 3 reserve divisions none had been completed on 1 April 1938; and only 7 to 8 were in the process of being formed and expected to be complete by 1 October 1938.

KEITEL: I consider these figures correct and I have therefore confirmed them in this affidavit.

DR. DIX: That is as far as the deposition goes. I would like to put two more questions to the witness which have not been discussed with him so that I do not know whether he remembers the figures in question.
I consider it possible that the Tribunal would be interested in the proportion of strength between the Reich, on the one hand, and Czechoslovakia, on the other hand, at the time of Hitler's march into Czechoslovakia; that is the relation of strength (a) concerning the armed might and (b) concerning the civilian population.

KEITEL: I do not remember the accurate figures about that. In the preliminary interrogation I have been questioned about it and I believe the figures will be correct if I say that in the fall of 1938, going by military units, that is, divisions…

DR. DIX: I mean now the time when Hitler marched into Czechoslovakia, in the spring of 1939.

KEITEL: That was in the same year of mobilization, that is to say at that time, as far, as figures are concerned, there were fewer divisions than Czechoslovakia had at her disposal. In the fall of 1938 the number of formations, that is, divisions, was probably equal. In the spring of 1939, when we marched in, the strength which was used then was less than that which stood ready in the fall of 1938. Accurate figures, if they are important to this Tribunal, you could get rather from General Jodl.

DR. DIX: As to the number of divisions which Czechoslovakia had at her disposal in March 1939, could you not tell us anything about that?

KEITEL: No, I do not know that exactly.

DR. DIX: Then I shall possibly ask General Jodl about that later.

THE PRESIDENT: Perhaps you will actually offer this document in evidence when the Defendant Schacht gives evidence. Is that what you intend to do?

DR. DIX: I am going to submit it in evidence and it will be included in my document book. It is not necessary to keep it now because I have to take it up again when Schacht will be examined and you will find it then in the document book. However, I would like to suggest that the copy which I have given to the witness should become a part of the record, because my questions have referred to this document. For this reason it might be useful to make this copy a part of the record.

THE PRESIDENT: If you want to make it a part of the record it had better be given a number now. It had better be S-1 had it not?

DR. DIX: Yes. Your Lordship, may I suggest Schacht-1?

THE PRESIDENT: Yes.

DR. STAHMER (Representing Dr. Robert Servatius, Counsel for Defendant Sauckel, and the Leadership Corps of the Nazi Party): Witness, on 4 January 1944, a conference allegedly took place between the *Führer* and Sauckel about the procuring of manpower. Were you present at this conference?

KEITEL: Yes.

DR. STAHMER: Did Sauckel on this occasion state that he could not fill, to the extent demanded, the manpower demands of those who asked for it?

KEITEL: Yes, he discussed it thoroughly and also gave his reasons for it.

DR. STAHMER: What reasons did he give?

KEITEL: He pointed out the great difficulties encountered in the areas from which he was supposed to draft or recruit manpower; the strong activity of guerillas and partisans in these areas, the great obstacles in obtaining sufficient police forces for protecting the action, and similar reasons. I do not remember any details.

FLOTTENRICHTER KRANZBÜHLER: Field Marshal, were you the leader of the German delegation which signed the capitulation with which the war in Europe was terminated?

KEITEL: Yes.

FLOTTENRICHTER KRANZBÜHLER: When and where did that take place?

KEITEL: In Berlin on 8 May, that is to say during the night from 8 to 9 May 1945.

FLOTTENRICHTER KRANZBÜHLER: Were you asked for full powers which would authorize you to negotiate about the capitulation?

KEITEL: Yes. I took the full powers with me to Berlin. They had been signed by *Großadmiral* Doenitz in his capacity as Chief of State and Commander-in-Chief of the Wehrmacht and stated in a few words that he had authorized and ordered me to conduct the negotiations and to sign the capitulation.

FLOTTENRICHTER KRANZBÜHLER: Were these full powers examined and acknowledged by the Allies?

KEITEL: In the course of the afternoon of 8 May I was asked to present the full powers. Obviously they were examined and several hours later they were returned to me by a high ranking officer of the Red Army who said that I had to show them again when signing.

FLOTTENRICHTER KRANZBÜHLER: Did you show them again?

KEITEL: I did have my credentials at hand during the act of capitulation and handed them over to become part of the record.

PROFESSOR DR. HERMANN JAHRREISS (Counsel for Defendant Jodl): Witness, during your testimony you have explained the organization of the Supreme Command of the Wehrmacht. This organization was based on a decree of the *Führer* and Reich Chancellor of 4 February 1938. In that decree the OKW was designated as the military staff of the Supreme Commander of the Armed Forces. So, in that aspect you were the Chief of Staff. Now, the Prosecution have repeatedly named Jodl as your Chief of Staff. Is that correct?

KEITEL: No, General Jodl never was my Chief of Staff, he was the Chief of the Armed Forces' Operations Staff and one of the departmental chiefs of the Armed Forces High Command as I have already stated, although the first among equals.

DR. JAHRREISS: That is to say, the Chief of several collateral coordinated offices?

KEITEL: Yes; I never had a Chief of Staff.

DR. JAHRREISS: Mention was made here about the discussion between Hitler and Schuschnigg at Obersalzberg on 12 February 1938. Do you remember that? A diary entry by Jodl referring to this conversation has been submitted to the Tribunal. Was Jodl present at this conference?

KEITEL: No, he was not present and his knowledge is derived from the conference which I described before and which I held with him and Canaris about the news to be disseminated as to certain military preparations during the days following the Schuschnigg conference; it is therefore an impression gained by General Jodl as a result of the description made to him.

DR. JAHRREISS: In the course of the preparations to make the German-Czechoslovakian question acute, that is, the Sudeten question, the plan to stage an incident played a great role. Did you ever give an order to the department Abwehr II (Counterintelligence) under Canaris, to stage such an incident in Czechoslovakia or on the border?

KEITEL: No, such orders were never given to the Abwehr, anyway, not by myself.

DR. JAHRREISS: After Munich, that is in October 1938, Field Marshal, the then Chief of National Defence, Defendant Jodl, left this position and was transferred to Vienna. Who was his successor?

KEITEL: Jodl was transferred to active service. He became chief of an artillery division in Vienna and his successor was Warlimont, at that time Colonel Warlimont.

DR. JAHRREISS: That is to say his successor…

KEITEL: Yes.

DR. JAHRREISS: If I understood you correctly, that is to say Jodl was not only sent on leave but he definitely left his office?

KEITEL: Jodl had definitely left the High Command of the Armed Forces and was personnel officer of a division; Warlimont was not his representative but successor in Jodl's position.

DR. JAHRREISS: Now, the Prosecution has said that at the occasion of that famous conference of 23 May 1938 – no, 1939 – Warlimont was present as deputy designate for Jodl. What had Jodl to do with that conference?

KEITEL: Nothing at all, he was at that time a front-line officer and commander in Vienna.

DR. JAHRREISS: Why did you choose Jodl to be chief of the Armed Forces Operations Staff?

KEITEL: That was in consequence of our cooperation from 1935 to 1938. My opinion was that I could not find a better man for that position.

DR. JAHRREISS: How did Jodl picture his military career, once his command as artillery commander in Vienna or Brunn had ended?

KEITEL: I knew about his passion and his desire to become commander of a mountain division. He has frequently told me about it.

DR. JAHRREISS: Well, would there have been any chance to get such a command?

KEITEL: Yes, I tried to use my influence with the Commander-in-Chief of the Army and I remember that during the summer of 1939, I wrote him that his wish to become the commander of a mountain division in Reichenhall – I do not remember the number – would come true. I was glad to be able to give him that information.

DR. JAHRREISS: Was it up to you to make the decision or was it up to the OKH?

KEITEL: I had made a request to the Commander-in-Chief of the Army and he had made the decision.

DR. JAHRREISS: And if I understand correctly, you yourself notified Jodl?

KEITEL: I wrote him a letter because I knew that I would make him very happy.

DR. JAHRREISS: May I ask, Field Marshal, did you correspond regularly with Jodl?

KEITEL: No; I believe that was the only letter which I wrote to him during that year.

DR. JAHRREISS: I ask that for a definite reason: Jodl leaves the OKW. He knows that if the necessity arises he will become chief of the future so-called Armed Forces Operations Staff, that is to say, a rather important position. He goes on active service, as you say. One should think that then he would not only receive a private letter once from you but would be kept informed by you regularly.

KEITEL: That was certainly not done by me and, according to my personal opinion, every general staff officer who goes on active service is very happy if he is not bothered with such things any longer.

DR. JAHRREISS: Yes, but fate does not grant us everything which would make us happy. It could be that somebody received the official order for instance, to keep this gentleman informed.

KEITEL: I certainly did not do it. I do not believe that it happened, but I do not know for sure whether or not somebody tried to do it.

DR. JAHRREISS: During the period when Jodl was in Vienna and Brunn, that is, away from Berlin, was he repeatedly in Berlin in order to get information?

KEITEL: I did not see him and he did not come to see me. I believe it is very unlikely because if such were the case he would have visited me.

DR. JAHRREISS: Then I have to understand from what you say, that when he came to Berlin shortly before the beginning of the war, in response to a telegram, he first had to be informed as to what was going on?

KEITEL: Yes, and that was the first thing done between him and myself.

DR. JAHRREISS: You informed him?

KEITEL: Yes.

DR. JAHRREISS: Another thing, Field Marshal. You remember, perhaps, the somewhat stormy morning in the Reich Chancellery after the Simovic Putsch; that was 27 March 1941, was it not?

KEITEL: Yes, Yugoslavia.

DR. JAHRREISS: If one reflects on the politics and the history of the wars of the last 200 years in Europe, one asks: Was there nobody at that conference in the Reich Chancellery who might have suggested that instead of attacking immediately, it would be better to march to the borders of a state whose attitude was completely uncertain and then clarify the situation by an ultimatum?

KEITEL: Yes, during all these pros and cons under turbulent conditions in that morning session, Jodl, himself, to my knowledge, brought that point up in the debate. Proposal: To march and to send an ultimatum; that is about the way it was.

DR. JAHRREISS: If I am correctly informed, you were in the East in October 1941 for the purpose of an inspection or a visit to Army Group North; is that correct?

KEITEL: Yes, in the autumn of 1941 I frequently went by plane to Army Group North in order to get information for the *Führer*.

DR. JAHRREISS: Was Field Marshal Von Leeb the commander of Army Group North?

KEITEL: Yes, he was.

DR. JAHRREISS: Did Von Leeb tell you about particular worries which he had at that time?

KEITEL: I think it was my last or the next to the last visit to Von Leeb where the questions of capitulation, that is to say, the question of the population of Leningrad, played an important role, which worried him very much at that time because there were certain indications that the population was streaming out of the city and infiltrating into his area. I remember that at that time he asked me to make the suggestion to the *Führer* that, as he could not take over and feed 1 million civilians within the area of his army group, a sluice, so to speak, should be made towards the east, that is, the Russian zone, so that the population could flow out in that direction. I reported that to the *Führer* at that time.

DR. JAHRREISS: Well, did the population turn in any other direction?

KEITEL: Yes, especially to the south into the Southern forests. According to Von Leeb a certain pressure exerted by the population to get through the German lines made itself felt at the time.

DR. JAHRREISS: And that would have impeded your operations?

KEITEL: Yes.

DR. JAHRREISS: Field Marshal, you are aware, I suppose, since it has been mentioned this morning, of the order issued by the *Führer* and Supreme Commander about the Commandos, dated 18 October 1942, that is Document Number 498-PS which has been submitted here. It had been announced publicly beforehand that an order of that kind would be issued. Do you know that?

KEITEL: Yes; the item in question was included in one of the daily communiqués of the Wehrmacht.

DR. JAHRREISS: We are dealing with the Wehrmacht communiqué of 7 October 1942, which, below the usual report, states with reference to what has happened, "The High Command of the Armed Forces therefore considers itself obliged to issue the following orders." The first item is of no interest here, and then, at the second item appears the following sentence:
"In the future all terror and sabotage Commandos of the British

and their accomplices who do not behave like soldiers, but rather like bandits, will be treated as such by the German troops and will be killed in combat without mercy wherever they appear."
Field Marshal, who drafted this wording?

KEITEL: The *Führer* personally. I was present when he dictated and corrected it.

DR. LATERNSER: Witness, I should like to continue at the point which was last mentioned by Professor Jahrreiss. The order about Commandos, Document Number 498-PS, was discussed. In this order on Commandos, under Number VI, Hitler threatened that all commanders would be court-martialed if they did not carry out this order. Do you know what considerations prompted Hitler to include this particular passage in the order?

KEITEL: Yes, they are actually quite clear; I should think that the purpose was to put emphasis on the demand that this order should actually be carried out, since it was definitely considered by the generals and those who were to carry it out, as a very grave order; and for that reason compliance was to be enforced by the threat of punishment.

DR. LATERNSER: Now, I should like to ask you several questions concerning the nature of the so-called Groups of the General Staff and the OKW. What do you understand to be the German General Staff?

KEITEL: By the General Staff I understand those officers who are especially trained to be assistants to the higher leadership.

THE PRESIDENT: The defendant has already spent a very long time in explaining the difference between the OKW and the staff of the various commands, and the Prosecution have defined specifically and quite clearly what the group is, which they are asking the Court to declare as criminal; and therefore, I do not see what relevance any further evidence on the subject can have. What are you trying to show by asking him now about what he understands by the General Staff?

DR. LATERNSER: This question was purely preparatory. I intended to connect this question with another one; and, by the answer to the second question, I wanted to prove that under the alleged group, a group has been accused under a wrong name.

THE PRESIDENT: I do not see how it matters if it is a wrong name if the group is specified. But, anyhow, the defendant has already told us what he understands by the General Staff. Will you put your second question.

DR. LATERNSER: Witness, if the higher military leaders are considered collectively to form one group which is designated as General Staff and OKW, do you consider this designation to be correct or misleading?

KEITEL: According to our German military concepts this designation is misleading, because to us the General Staff always means a body of assistants, whereas the commanders of armies and army groups and the commanding generals represent the leadership corps.

DR. LATERNSER: The military hierarchy has been discussed sufficiently in this Trial. I want to know only the following from you: Was the relation of these echelons to each other that of military superiors and subordinates or did there exist an additional organization involving these ranks which went beyond purely professional military duties?

KEITEL: No, the General Staff, that is to say, the General Staff officers as assistants to the leaders, could be recognized by their uniforms as such. The leaders or so-called commanders themselves had no relation to each other through any interoffice channels or through any other organizations of any kind.

DR. LATERNSER: Yesterday the affidavit made by *Generaloberst* Halder was put to you. I would like to discuss now the last sentence of that affidavit; I shall read it to you, "That was the actual General Staff and the highest leadership of the Armed Forces." Is the statement in that sentence correct or incorrect?

KEITEL: I understand it this way, that Halder wanted to say that those few officers who had General Staff positions were the ones who did the real work in the General Staff of the Army, while the rest of the far more than 100 General Staff officers in the OKH had nothing to do with these matters. That is what I think he wanted to say, a small group which was concerned with these problems.

DR. LATERNSER: Do you know of a single incident where Hitler ever consulted a military leader on a political matter?

KEITEL: No, that did not happen.

DR. LATERNSER: I assume that you were present at most of the conferences with Hitler when the situation was discussed. Could you tell me anything about protests made, with or without success, by any commanders who had come from the front and who happened to be present?

KEITEL: As a rule front commanders who were present were silent listeners at the general discussion of the situation; and afterwards, according to circumstances, such commanders used to make a special report to Hitler about their respective areas. Then there was also an opportunity, as I believe was already mentioned by Kesselring, to discuss these things personally and to advance opinions. But otherwise nobody had anything to say in these matters.

DR. LATERNSER: Witness, were you ever present when particularly emphatic objections were raised, by any commander, to Hitler?

KEITEL: During the discussion of the situation?

DR. LATERNSER: No, I mean, whatever the occasion may have been.

KEITEL: I was not, of course, present at every conference which Hitler had with high ranking commanders in his quarters, but I do not know of any such incidents. I have related in detail those cases which played a role in this war, namely the opposition of the generals in the West, before the beginning of the war, and I understood your question to mean whether I knew of any cases beyond that.

DR. LATERNSER: Yes.

KEITEL: I have related all that and must emphasize once more that the Commander-in-Chief of the Army at that time went to the limit of anything which could be justified from the military viewpoint.

DR. LATERNSER: What was the attitude of Hitler toward the General Staff of the Army?

KEITEL: It was not a good one. One may say that he held a prejudice against the General Staff and thought the General Staff was arrogant. I believe that is sufficient.

THE PRESIDENT: We have heard all this once, if not more than once.

DR. LATERNSER: Mr. President, I do not believe that this witness has been asked about that. As far as I remember, this particular witness has not been asked about these points.

THE PRESIDENT: The Tribunal thinks he has been asked about it.

DR. LATERNSER: I would have paid special attention to this point and would have crossed off this question already if one of my colleagues had put it before.

[To the defendant.] Would Hitler in case an application for resignation was tendered by one or more front commanders have been willing to take back an order which he had once given...

THE PRESIDENT: Dr. Laternser, nearly every officer who has come and given evidence to this Court has spoken about that subject, certainly many of them.

DR. LATERNSER: Mr. President, does your objection refer to the question I have put now?

THE PRESIDENT: Nearly all the officers who have been examined in this Court have told us it was impossible to resign. That is what you are asking about, isn't it?

DR. LATERNSER: Yes. I will be glad to forego that question, if I can assume that the Tribunal accepts those facts which I wanted to prove, as true.

THE PRESIDENT: The Tribunal thinks it is cumulative; whether they accept its truth or not, is a different question.

DR. LATERNSER: Mr. President, I should like to say something also to this question. I do not believe that it can be considered cumulative, since as has already been pointed out by my colleague, Dr. Dix, the same question when put to two different witnesses is in each case a different question, because the subjective answer of the individual witness to this particular point is desired. But I will forego that question.

THE PRESIDENT: Is there any other question you want to ask?

DR. LATERNSER: Yes, I have a few more questions.

[Turning to the defendant.] Witness, to what extent was the headquarters of the *Führer* protected against attacks during the war?

KEITEL: There was a special guard detachment of the Army and also I believe one company of the Waffen-SS. Very thorough security measures had been taken with every kind of safety device such as fences, obstacles, and similar things. It was very well secured against any surprise attack.

DR. LATERNSER: Were there several zones?

KEITEL: Yes, there was an inner zone and an outer zone and several areas which were fenced in separately.

DR. LATERNSER: Yes. You have already stated that the commanders of the army groups and armies in the East did not have any authority outside their area of operation. Was there a tendency to keep that operational area as small as possible, or as large as possible?

KEITEL: Originally the tendency definitely was to have large areas of operation in order to assure the greatest possible freedom of movement in the rear of the armies and army groups. The *Führer* was the first who, by drastic means, caused the limitation of these zones to make them as small as possible.

DR. LATERNSER: For what reasons?

KEITEL: As he said, in order to free military officers from administrative measures and get them out of the extended space they had sought for their equipment and to concentrate them into narrowly limited areas.

DR. LATERNSER: You mentioned during your interrogation, units of the Waffen-SS which were assigned to the Army for operational, that is, for combat purposes. I am particularly interested in getting that point clear because, as far as I see, there still prevails some confusion. Did the forces of the SD have anything to do with the units of the Waffen-SS which were subordinated to army units for the purpose of operational assignments?

KEITEL: No, the formations of the Waffen-SS within divisions were incorporated as such into the armies and had nothing to do with anything else. They were in that case purely Army Forces.

DR. LATERNSER: Was it possible for a commander to punish an SS man for any offence?

KEITEL: If the man was caught in the act I believe no commander would have hesitated; but apart from that, the last resort for disciplinary measures and jurisdiction was the *Reichsführer* Himmler, and not the commander of the army.

DR. LATERNSER: Did the executives of the *Einsatzgruppen* of the SD have to report to the commanders of the armies upon what they did on Himmler's orders?

KEITEL: This question has been dealt with here in great detail by the witness Ohlendorf, and I am not informed about the connections which existed between the commanders and the *Einsatzgruppen* and commands. I was not involved and took no part in it.

DR. LATERNSER: I wanted to know from you whether the *Einsatzgruppen* of the SD, according to your knowledge of the regulations, were obliged to report to the military commanders in whose rear areas they operated.

KEITEL: I do not believe so; I do not know the orders which were in force in this respect; I have not seen them.

DR. LATERNSER: Do you know whether the higher military commanders at any time were informed of the intention of Hitler or Himmler to kill the Jews?

KEITEL: According to my opinion, that was not the case, since I personally was not informed either.

DR. LATERNSER: Now, I have only one more question, on the subject of the prisoners of war. It had already become known during the war that the conditions relating to the food supply of Soviet Russian prisoners of war during the first period of the eastern campaign were miserable. What was the reason for these conditions which prevailed during that first period?

KEITEL: I can base my statement only on what the Commander-in-Chief of the Army said during the situation report conferences. As I recall, he repeatedly reported that it was clearly a problem of large masses which required extraordinary efforts of organization to provide food supply, housing, and security.

DR. LATERNSER: Now, these conditions were without doubt actually chaotic during a certain period of time. I am thinking of a particular reason which existed, and in order to refresh your memory, Witness, I would like to mention the following:

The Army had already prepared camps in the homeland for the future prisoners of war, because it was planned in the beginning that these prisoners should be transferred to the homeland. In spite of these preparations, however, as has been stated here, this was stopped by a sudden order from Hitler which prohibited the transfer of these Russian prisoners into the homeland.

KEITEL: I explained that this morning; and I said that during a certain period until September, the transfer of Soviet Russian prisoners of war into the Reich was prohibited and only after that the transfer into the home camps was made possible in order to utilize the manpower.

DR. LATERNSER: And the deficiencies which appeared during this first period could not be remedied by the means at the disposal of the troops?

KEITEL: That I do not know. I am not informed about that. Only the OKH, which had the exclusive responsibility, would know that.

DR. LATERNSER: I have only a few more questions about the position of the Deputy Chief of the Armed Forces Operations Staff. When was that position set up?

KEITEL: I believe in 1942.

DR. LATERNSER: 1942. What was the rank connected with that position?

KEITEL: It could be a colonel or a general.

DR. LATERNSER: What I mean is whether it was about the same as the position of a commander of a division?

KEITEL: Well, I would say it was equal to the position of the commander of a brigade or a division, a section chief.

DR. LATERNSER: How many section chiefs were there in the OKW?

KEITEL: I could not say that at present from memory. By way of estimate I had eight department chiefs, each of which had one, two, three or four sections. Therefore there would have been about 30 or 35 section chiefs.

DR. LATERNSER: The Deputy Chief of the Armed Forces Operations Staff was one of the eight or of the 30 section chiefs?

KEITEL: No, I would not like to say that definitely. We had among the department chiefs so-called department group chiefs, who combined several small sections. That was about his position.

DR. LATERNSER: What were the official duties connected with that position?

KEITEL: Naturally the supervision and direction of all the work of that part of the Armed Forces Operations Staff which was attached to the *Führer*'s headquarters. It was his task to direct that work in accordance with the directives given by Jodl, the Chief of the Armed Forces Operations Staff.

DR. LATERNSER: Was the Deputy Chief of the Armed Forces Operations Staff responsible for the strategic planning to a particularly high degree, as is maintained by the Prosecution?

KEITEL: He was, of course, not responsible for that in this capacity, but as a matter of fact he belonged to the small group of high ranking and outstanding general staff officers who were concerned with these things, as Halder has pointed out.

DR. LATERNSER: Now, I have one last question. Was, therefore, the position of the Deputy Chief of the Armed Forces Operations Staff, not equal in importance to the other positions which are included in this group or alleged group of the General Staff and the OKW?

KEITEL: I said chief of a group of departments in the Armed Forces Operations Staff and co-worker in the small group of those who had to deal with operational and strategical questions, but subordinate to General Jodl and director of the work supervisor in the *Arbeitsstab*.

DR. LATERNSER: Field Marshal, I believe that the question which I have put to you was not completely answered. I have asked you whether the importance of that position was equal to or even approached equality with that of the other offices which are included in the group of the general staff and the OKW.

KEITEL: No, certainly not, because in the group of the General Staff and the OKW there were the commanders-in-chief, the supreme commanders, and the chiefs of the general staff. He certainly did not belong to those.

DR. LATERNSER: Thank you.

HERR LUDWIG BABEL (Counsel for SS): Witness, you have said in your Affidavit Keitel-12 that the SS, at the beginning of the war, became the champions and standard bearers of a policy of conquest and force. In order to exclude any misunderstandings, I should like to clarify the following: What did you mean by SS in this case?

KEITEL: I can say to that, that what has been read here by my counsel was a short summary of a much longer affidavit. If you read the latter you would find for yourself the answer to your question. To state it in a more precise way: It concerned the Reich SS Leadership under Himmler and under those functionaries within his sphere of command, police and SS, who appeared and were active in the occupied territories. The concept of the so-called general SS in the homeland had nothing to do with that. I hope that makes it clear.

HERR BABEL: Yes, thank you.

DR. FRIEDRICH BERGOLD (Counsel for Defendant Bormann): Witness, the Prosecution in their trial brief have charged the Defendant Bormann also with his activity in the so-called *Volkssturm*. In that connection, I would like to put a few questions to you.

Was an offensive or defensive activity planned for the *Volkssturm* as it was formed by decree of the *Führer* of 18 October 1944?

KEITEL: To that I can only say that *Reichsleiter* Bormann refused to give the military authorities any advice, any cooperation, and any information on the *Volkssturm*.

DR. BERGOLD: You mean to say that you were not at all informed of the purpose of the *Volkssturm*?

KEITEL: Only that I saw it as the last levy of men to defend their own homesteads.

DR. BERGOLD: That means that, within the framework of the Wehrmacht, the *Volkssturm* was not designed for any offensive purpose?

KEITEL: No, but all services of the Wehrmacht which encountered the *Volkssturm* units in their areas, either incorporated them or sent them home.

DR. BERGOLD: Did I understand you correctly that you wanted to say that that institution, the *Volkssturm*, was a product of Bormann's brain or did it originate with Hitler?

KEITEL: I do not know that, perhaps from both.

DR. BERGOLD: Hitler did not tell you about it, either?

KEITEL: No, he spoke only about the *Volkssturm* and similar things, but military authorities had nothing to do with it.

DR. BERGOLD: Did Bormann report any other military matters to the *Führer* besides the odd things about the *Volkssturm*?

KEITEL: He has often accused the Wehrmacht of all sorts of things; I can conclude that only from what I was told, and assume that it originated with Bormann. I do not know it.

DR. BERGOLD: Thank you.

DR. HORN: Is it correct that the Defendant Von Ribbentrop, after his return from Moscow in August 1939, on account of the changed foreign political situation – the guarantee pact between England and Poland had been ratified – advised Hitler to stop the military measures which had been set in motion?

KEITEL: I had the impression at that time that the orders given to me by Hitler were based upon a conversation between him and his foreign minister. I was not present at that conversation.

DR. HORN: Is it correct that Von Ribbentrop, just like the other ministers with portfolio, was as a rule not informed about the strategic plans?

KEITEL: I can say only for myself and for the Chief of the Armed Forces Operations Staff, that we were not authorized to do it and that we never did it. If the Reich Foreign Minister was informed about such questions, that information could have come only from Hitler himself. I doubt that he made an exception here.

DR. HORN: The Prosecution have submitted a letter of 3 April 1940, concerning the impending occupation of Denmark and Norway which you sent to the then Reich Foreign Minister. In that letter you informed the Reich Foreign Minister of the impending occupation and requested him to take the necessary political steps. Had you already instructed Von Ribbentrop before that date about the intended occupation of Norway and Denmark?

KEITEL: No, I would not have been allowed to do that, according to the way in which the *Führer* worked with us. That letter was an unusual method of giving information about this, by the *Führer's* order, to the Reich Foreign Minister, who knew nothing about these things. I was ordered to write it to him.

DR. HORN: In connection with the testimony by General Lahousen, I want to ask you one question. At the time of the Polish campaign, was there a directive or an order by Hitler to exterminate the Jews in the Polish Ukraine?

KEITEL: I cannot recall any such things. I know only that during the occupation of Poland – that is after the occupation – the problem of the Polish Jews played a part. In that connection I also put a question once to Hitler to which, I believe, he answered that that area was well suited for settling the Jews there. I do not know or remember anything else.

DR. HORN: At the time of the Polish campaign, was there any plan to instigate a revolt in the Polish Ukraine in the rear of the Poles?

KEITEL: I cannot answer that question, although I have heard such things said here by Lahousen. I do not know or remember anything about it.

DR. HORN: Thank you.

HERR GEORG BOHM (Counsel for the SA): Field Marshal, you were Chief of the OKW and thereby also the Chief of the KGF, that is, Prisoners of War Organization. Did you ever issue orders or have orders issued on the basis of which members of the SA or units of the SA were detailed to guard prisoners of war or prisoner-of-war camps, or were to be used for that purpose?

KEITEL: I cannot remember that any such directive had been issued by the OKW. I believe that certainly was not the case.

HERR BOHM: In that respect, was a report ever made to you that any such guard duty was performed?

KEITEL: I cannot remember but I do not mean to deny that some units of the army in some particular place may have used SA men temporarily to assist in guard duty, which I would not know.

HERR BOHM: Thank you.

THE PRESIDENT: Perhaps we had better adjourn now for 10 minutes.

[A recess was taken.]

THE PRESIDENT: The Tribunal will sit in open session tomorrow morning at 10 o'clock. At 1230 it will take the supplementary applications for witnesses and documents, and after that at a quarter to 1 it will adjourn into a closed session.

GEN. RUDENKO: Defendant Keitel, I would like you to tell me exactly when you received your first commission as an officer?

KEITEL: On 18 August 1902.

GEN. RUDENKO: What military training did you receive?

KEITEL: I came into the army as an officer candidate. Starting as a simple private I advanced through the various ranks of private first class, corporal and ensign to lieutenant.

GEN. RUDENKO: I asked you about your military training.

KEITEL: I was an army officer until 1909, and then for almost 6 years regimental adjutant; then during the World War I, battery commander, and then after the spring of 1915 I served on the general staff.

GEN. RUDENKO: You were evidently not given a correct translation. Did you pass the Staff College or any other college, that is to say, did you receive preliminary training?

KEITEL: I never attended the War Academy. Twice I participated in so-called Great General Staff trips as regimental adjutant and in the summer of 1914 I was detailed to the Great General Staff and returned to my regiment later when the war broke out in 1914.

GEN. RUDENKO: What military training and military rank did Hitler possess?

KEITEL: Only a few years ago I found out from Hitler himself that after the end of World War I, he had been a lieutenant in a Bavarian infantry regiment. During the war he was a private, then private first class and maybe corporal during the last period.

GEN. RUDENKO: Should we not, therefore, conclude that you, with your thorough military training and great experience, could have had an opportunity of influencing Hitler, very considerably, in solving questions of a strategic and military nature, as well as other matters pertaining to the Armed Forces?

KEITEL: No. I have to declare in that respect that, to a degree which is almost incomprehensible to the layman and the professional officer, Hitler had studied general staff publications, military literature, essays on tactics, operations, and strategy and that he had a knowledge in the military fields which can only be called amazing. May I give an example of that which can be confirmed by the other officers of the Wehrmacht. Hitler was so well informed concerning organization, armament, leadership, and equipment of all armies, and what is more remarkable, of all navies of the globe, that it was impossible to prove any error on his part; and I have to add that also during the war, while I was at his headquarters and in his close proximity, Hitler studied at night all the big general staff books by Moltke, Schlieffen, and Clausewitz and from them acquired his vast knowledge by himself. Therefore we had the impression: Only a genius can do that.

GEN. RUDENKO: You will not deny that by reason of your military training and experience you were Hitler's adviser in a number of highly important matters?

KEITEL: I belonged to his closest military entourage and I heard a lot from him; but I pointed out yesterday to the question of my counsel that even in the simple, everyday questions concerning organization and equipment of the Wehrmacht, I must admit openly that I was the pupil and not the master.

GEN. RUDENKO: From what date do you consider that your cooperation with Hitler began?

KEITEL: Exactly from the day when I was called into that position, 4 February 1938.

GEN. RUDENKO: That means that you were working with Hitler during the entire period of preparation for and realization of aggressive warfare?

KEITEL: Yes. I have already given all the necessary explanations as to how, after I entered my new position in the beginning of February, events followed in quick succession, often in a very surprising manner.

GEN. RUDENKO: Who, besides you, among the military leaders of the OKW and the OKH had the rank of Reich Minister?

KEITEL: The rank of Reich Minister was given to the three commanders-in-chief of the sections of the Armed Forces, and among these the Commander-in-Chief of the Air Force, *Reichsmarschall* Göring, was also Reich Minister of Aviation; likewise I received, as I said yesterday, the rank but not the authority and title of a minister.

GEN. RUDENKO: Who, besides you, among the military collaborators of the OKH and the OKW, signed decrees together with Hitler and the other Reich Ministers?

KEITEL: In the ministerial sector of the Reich Government, there was the method of the signatures of the *Führer* and Reich Chancellor and the Ministers immediately involved, and, finally of the Chief of the Reich Chancellery. This did not hold good for the military sector, for according to the traditions of the German Army and the Wehrmacht the signatures were given by the principal experts who had worked on the matter, by the Chief of Staff, or by whoever had given or at least drafted the order, and an initial was added on the margin.

GEN. RUDENKO: Yesterday you said that you signed such decrees together with other Ministers of the Reich.

KEITEL: Yes, yesterday I mentioned individual decrees and also gave the reasons why I signed them, and that in so doing I was not Reich Minister and did not receive the function of a minister in office.

GEN. RUDENKO: What organization exercised the function of the War Ministry from February 1938 on?

KEITEL: Until the last days of January, or the first days of February, it was the former Reich Minister for War, Von Blomberg. Beginning with 4 February there was neither a Minister for War nor a War Ministry.

GEN. RUDENKO: That is precisely why I asked you what

government organization had replaced the War Ministry and exercised its function, since I knew that this Ministry did not exist.

KEITEL: I, myself, with the *Wehrmachtsamt*, the former Staff of the War Ministry, whose chief I was, carried on the work and distributed it, as I described in detail yesterday, that is, I transferred all command functions to the commanders-in-chief of the branches of the Wehrmacht. But this was not an order of mine but an order of Hitler's.

GEN. RUDENKO: From the diagram you have submitted to the Tribunal it would appear that the OKW was the central, coordinating, and supreme military authority of the Reich and that it was directly under Hitler's control. Would this conclusion be correct?

KEITEL: Yes, that was the military staff of Hitler.

GEN. RUDENKO: Who, in the OKW, directly supervised the drafting of military and strategic plans? I am referring specifically to the plans for the attack on Austria, Czechoslovakia, Poland, Belgium, Holland, France, Norway, Yugoslavia, and the Soviet Union.

KEITEL: I believe that yesterday I stated that very precisely, saying that the operational and strategic planning, after an order had been given by Hitler, was prepared and then submitted to Hitler by the commanders-in-chief of the branches of the Wehrmacht; that is to say, for the Army, by the High Command of the Army and the General Staff of the Army, and then further decisions were made with respect to it.

GEN. RUDENKO: With regard to Yugoslavia I should like to ask you the following question: Do you admit that a directive issued under your signature, for the preliminary partition of Yugoslavia, is per se a document of great political and international importance, providing for the actual abolition of Yugoslavia as a sovereign state?

KEITEL: I did nothing more or less than to write down a decree by the *Führer* and forward it to those offices which were interested and concerned. I did not have any personal or political influence whatsoever in these questions.

GEN. RUDENKO: Under your own signature?

KEITEL: As to the signatures which I have given, I made a complete explanation yesterday, as to how they came about and what their significance is.

GEN. RUDENKO: Yes, we did talk about it, we did hear about it, and I shall ask some more questions on the subject later on. I should now like to determine with greater precision your own position in the question of Yugoslavia. Do you agree that you, with the direct participation of the OKW, organized acts of provocation in order to find a reason for aggression against Yugoslavia and a justification for this aggression in the eyes of the world?

KEITEL: This morning, in response to questions of the counsel of other defendants, I answered clearly that I did not participate in any preparation of an incident and that Hitler did not wish either that any military offices should ever participate in the discussion, preparation, deliberation, or the execution of incidents. I use "incident" here in the sense of provocation.

GEN. RUDENKO: Undoubtedly. What part did the OKW take to ensure the arming of the Free Corps in the Sudetenland?

KEITEL: Which Free Corps, General? I do not know to which Free Corps you refer.

GEN. RUDENKO: The Free Corps of the Sudetenland.

KEITEL: I am not informed as to whether any military office did any gun-running, if I may say so, or secretly sent arms there. I have no knowledge concerning that. An order to that effect was not given, or at any rate did not pass through my hands. I cannot remember that.

GEN. RUDENKO: By whom and for what reason was the order issued to occupy Ostrau in Moravia and Witkovitz by German troops, on 14 March 1939, in the afternoon, while President Hacha was still on the way to Berlin for negotiations with Hitler?

KEITEL: The order was eventually released and decided by the *Führer*. There had been preparations to occupy by a *coup de main* that area where the well-known big and modern steel works were located near Mahrisch Ostrau – I cannot remember the name now – before the date of the march into Czechoslovakia as originally set. As a justification for that decision, Hitler had told me that it was done in order to prevent the Poles from making a surprise attack from the north, and thereby perhaps taking possession of the most modern rolling mill in the world. This he gave as a reason, and the operation, that is, the occupation, actually took place in the late hours of 14 March.

GEN. RUDENKO: Yes, but during the same time, President Hacha was on the way to Berlin to negotiate which Hitler?

KEITEL: Yes, that is correct.

GEN. RUDENKO: This is treachery!

KEITEL: I do not believe that I need to add my judgement to the facts. It is true that the occupation was carried out on that evening. I have given the reasons, and President Hacha learned about it only after he arrived in Berlin.
Now I remember the name. The rolling mill was Witkovitz.

GEN. RUDENKO: I have a few more questions to ask you in connection with the aggression against the Soviet Union. You testified to the Tribunal yesterday on the subject. You explained your position with regard to the attack on the Soviet Union. But you informed the Tribunal that the orders for preparing Plan Barbarossa were given at the beginning of December 1940. Is that right?

KEITEL: Yes.

GEN. RUDENKO: Do you definitely remember and confirm this?

KEITEL: I do not know of, or do not remember, any specific order by the High Command of the Wehrmacht which called for the drawing up of this plan called Barbarossa any earlier than that. I explained yesterday, however, that some order had been issued, probably in September, concerning transport and railway facilities and similar matters. I cannot recall whether I signed that order, but yesterday I mentioned such a preparatory order to improve transport conditions from the West to the East.

GEN. RUDENKO: In September?

KEITEL: It may have been in September or October, but I cannot commit myself as to the exact time.

GEN. RUDENKO: I wish to know the exact time.

KEITEL: More accurate information may probably be obtained at a later stage from General Jodl, who ought to know it better.

GEN. RUDENKO: Of course we shall ask him about it during the course of his interrogation. I should like you to recollect the following briefly: Did you first learn of Hitler's schemes to attack the Soviet Union in the summer of 1940?

KEITEL: No. In the summer of 1940 this conversation which is mentioned in Jodl's diary – I believe that is what you are referring to, you mean the conversation from Jodl's diary – I was not present at this obviously very casual and brief conversation and did not hear it. My recollections concerning that period also justify my belief that I was not present, because I was on the move almost every day by airplane and was not present at the discussions of the situation at that time.

GEN. RUDENKO: And when did your conversation with Ribbentrop take place?

KEITEL: That may have been during the last days of August; I believe, it was in the beginning of September, but I cannot give the exact date any more. I reconstruct the date by the fact that I did not return to Berchtesgaden until 10 August, and that I wrote the memorandum which I mentioned yesterday at a later date.

GEN. RUDENKO: And so you assure the Tribunal that you first heard about Hitler's schemes to attack the Soviet Union from the conversation with Ribbentrop?

KEITEL: No, no. After having been absent from Berchtesgaden for about two weeks, partly on leave and partly on duty in Berlin, I returned to headquarters at Berchtesgaden; and then on one of the subsequent days, probably during the middle of August, I heard for the first time ideas of that kind from Hitler. That was the basis for my deliberation and my memorandum.

GEN. RUDENKO: In that case, have I put my question correctly in asking whether you learned of Hitler's schemes in the summer of 1940?

KEITEL: Yes. The middle of August, after all, is still summer.

GEN. RUDENKO: August is still summer, we will not quibble about that. Further, I should like to remind you of the evidence of the witness Paulus, which he gave here before the Tribunal, on 11 February of this year. Paulus, as you will remember, informed the Tribunal that when he entered the OKH on 3 September 1940, he found among other plans an unfinished preliminary operational draft of a plan for attacking the Soviet Union, known under the name of Barbarossa. Do you remember that part of Paulus' testimony?

KEITEL: I remember it only insofar as he stated that it was a study or a draft for a manoeuvre, and that he found a document on the occasion of his transfer to the OKH, to the General Staff of the Army. This is not known to me, and it could not be known to me because the documents, files, and other reports of the General Staff of the Army were never at my disposal; and I never had an opportunity to look at them.

GEN. RUDENKO: I wish to establish one fact. Do you deny that the OKH, in September 1940, was elaborating plans in connection with Plan Barbarossa?

KEITEL: If we go by the testimony of Meld Marshal Paulus, then I could not say that it is not true, since I cannot know whether it actually was true. I can neither deny nor affirm it.

GEN. RUDENKO: All right. You informed the Tribunal that you were opposed to the war with the Soviet Union.

KEITEL: Yes.

GEN. RUDENKO: You also stated that you went to Hitler with the suggestion that he should change his plans with regard to the Soviet Union. Is that correct?

KEITEL: Yes, not only to change them, but to drop this plan and not to wage war against the Soviet Union. That was the content of my memorandum.

GEN. RUDENKO: That is precisely what I asked you. I would like to ask you now about a conference, evidently known to you, which was held 3 weeks after Germany had attacked the Soviet Union, the conference of 16 July 1941. Do you remember that conference, which dealt with the tasks for the conduct of the war against the Soviet Union?

KEITEL: No, at the moment I do not know what you mean. I do not know.

GEN. RUDENKO: I do not intend to submit that document to you at this particular minute. You may remember that I submitted it to the Defendant Göring, when the question of the dismemberment and of the annexation of the Soviet Union arose. Do you remember?

KEITEL: That is a document which I know. I believe it is marked on top "BO-FU", and during my interrogation here I have identified it as a memorandum from *Reichsleiter* Bormann.

GEN. RUDENKO: That is correct.

KEITEL: I made that statement. At that time I also testified that I was called in only during the second part of the conference and that I had not been present during the first part of it. I also testified that it was not the minutes but a free summary made by *Reichsleiter* Bormann, dictated by him.

GEN. RUDENKO: But you do remember that even then, on 16 July, the question was already being advanced about the annexation by Germany of the Crimea, the Baltic States, the regions of the Volga, the Ukraine, Belorussia and other territories?

KEITEL: No, I believe that was discussed at the first part of the conference. I can remember the conference, from that stage on where questions of personnel were discussed, that is, certain personalities who were to be appointed. That I remembered. I have seen the document here for the first time and did not know of it before; and did not attend the first half of the conference.

GEN. RUDENKO: In that case may I put the question differently: What were the final aims pursued by Hitler and his entourage at that time, against the Soviet Union?

KEITEL: According to the explanations which Hitler had given me, I saw the more profound reasons for this war in the fact that he was convinced that a war would break out some way or other within the next years between the Greater Slav Empire of Communism and the German Reich of National Socialism. The reasons which were given to me were something like this: If I believe or rather if I am convinced that such a conflict between these two nations will take place, then it would be better now than later. That is how I can put it. But I do not remember, at least not at the moment, the questions which are in this document about the dismemberment of several areas. Perhaps they were constructions of fantasy.

GEN. RUDENKO: And you tell the Tribunal under oath that you did not know of the Hitlerite plans to seize and colonize the territories of the Soviet Union?

KEITEL: That has not been expressed in that form. It is true that I believed that the Baltic provinces should be made dependents of the Reich, and that the Ukraine should come into a closer connection from the point of view of food supply or economy, but concrete plans for conquest are not known to me and if they were ever touched upon I never considered them to be serious problems. That is the way I looked at it at that time. I must not explain how I see it today, but only how I saw it at that time.

GEN. RUDENKO: Did you know that at this conference of 16 July Hitler announced the necessity of razing the city of Leningrad to the ground?

KEITEL: I do not believe that during that conference – I have read that document here again. That it is contained in the document I cannot remember now. But I have had this document here in my hands; I have read it in the presence of the American Prosecutor; and if it is stated therein, then the question of whether or not I have heard it depends entirely on the moment at which I was called to that conference.

GEN. RUDENKO: I do not intend to hand you the document now, because it has already been submitted several times. But in the minutes previously quoted to the Defendant Göring, who read them himself, it is said, "The Leningrad region is claimed by the Finns. The *Führer* wants to raze Leningrad to the ground and then cede it to the Finns."

KEITEL: I can only say that it is necessary to establish from what moment on I attended that conference. Whatever was said before that moment I did not hear, and I can indicate that only if I am given the document or if one reads the record of my preliminary interrogation. That is what I told the interrogating officer at that time.

GEN. RUDENKO: Very well. We shall give you the minutes of the conference of 16 July immediately. While the passages required are being found, I shall ask you a few more questions, and by that time the passages will have been found.

With regard to the destruction of Leningrad, did you not know about it from other documents?

KEITEL: I have been asked about that by the Russian Delegation and the general who is present here in this courtroom. He has called my attention to a document.

GEN. RUDENKO: That was during the preliminary investigation, that is quite right.

KEITEL: I know the document which came from the Navy, from an admiral, as well as a second document which contained a short directive, I believe on the order of Jodl, concerning Leningrad. I have been interrogated regarding both documents. As to that I can state only that neither through artillery operations during the siege, nor by operations of the Air Force, could the extent of destruction be compared with that of other places we know about. It did not materialize, we did not carry it out. It never came to a systematic shelling of Leningrad, as far as I know. Consequently, only that can be stated which I said at that time under oath to the gentlemen of the Soviet Delegation.

GEN. RUDENKO: According to your knowledge was Leningrad never shelled?

KEITEL: Certainly artillery was also used in the Leningrad area, but it never went so far as to constitute shelling for the purposes of destruction. That would have occurred, General, if it had come to an attack on Leningrad.

GEN. RUDENKO: Look at this document, and I shall then ask you a few supplementary questions.

[The document was submitted to the defendant.]

KEITEL: It is very simple. My entry is exactly after the moment after this remark had been made. I told the American interrogator at the time that I just heard the discussion about the appointment of *Gauleiter* Lohse when I entered the room. The preceding remarks I did not hear.

GEN. RUDENKO: Have you acquainted yourself with those minutes of the report on the conference of 16 July that deal with Leningrad?

KEITEL: Yes, that is where I entered.

GEN. RUDENKO: You saw that there was such an entry in the minutes of the meeting. You arrived at the conference just as they had finished talking about Leningrad?

KEITEL: Yes. I entered the room when they were talking about the qualifications of *Gauleiter* Lohse, whether or not he was suitable for an administrative office. These were the first words which I heard. A debate was going on about that subject just when I entered.

GEN. RUDENKO: It states there quite clearly: "Raze the city of Leningrad to the ground."

KEITEL: Yes, I have read that here.

GEN. RUDENKO: The same is stated in the decree, is it not?

KEITEL: Yes; but there is no direct connection with me. Do you mean the order of the Navy, the order which was found with the Navy?

GEN. RUDENKO: Do you know that there were two decrees, one issued by the naval command and the other by the OKW, signed by Jodl? You do know that, do you not?

KEITEL: Yes, I have seen both these decrees here. They were submitted by the Russian Delegation.

GEN. RUDENKO: And you know that the decree signed by the Defendant Jodl also refers to the destruction of the city of Moscow.

KEITEL: That I do not remember exactly, any more since only Leningrad was referred to at that time, when I glanced at it. But if it is stated there, I will not doubt it at all.

GEN. RUDENKO: I am asking you: Did the OKW issue decrees for the purpose of having them obeyed?

KEITEL: The order or communication of the Navy is first of all no OKW order and how it originated is not known to me. The short order of the OKW, signed "By order of Jodl", was not drafted in my presence, as I already stated yesterday. I would have signed it but I was absent and therefore do not know either to which reasons or discussions this order was due.

GEN. RUDENKO: You have not replied to my question. I am asking you: The directives issued by the OKW were given out to be obeyed? Can you reply to me briefly?

KEITEL: This is a directive but not an order, because an order can be given only by the office of the local command of the army. It was therefore a directive, an aim, an intention.

GEN. RUDENKO: And are directives from the OKW not meant to be carried out?

KEITEL: Certainly they are meant to be carried out.

GEN. RUDENKO: As to your statement that no one shelled Leningrad, it does not even call for further denial, since it is a well-known fact.

KEITEL: May I at least say that I did not issue that order. That is why I do not know anything about it.

GEN. RUDENKO: Do you know that before the beginning of the war against the Soviet Union the Defendant Göring issued a so-called Green Folder containing directives on the economic matters in the territories of the U.S.S.R. intended for occupation?

KEITEL: Yes, that is known to me.

GEN. RUDENKO: Do you affirm that in your directive of 16 June 1941 you instructed all the German troops to obey these directives implicitly?

KEITEL: Yes, there is a directive which makes known to all units of the Army the organizations which are assigned for important tasks and what their responsibilities are, and that all the military commands of the Army must act in compliance therewith. That I passed on; it was not my order, I passed it on.

GEN. RUDENKO: Was it your own order or were you merely obeying the *Führer*'s instructions?

KEITEL: I merely passed on the orders received from the *Führer*, and I could not give any orders at all to *Reichsmarschall* Göring in that respect.

GEN. RUDENKO: You did not issue an order to Field Marshal Göring, but addressed your order to the troops?

KEITEL: I could not give him any orders either; I could only communicate the will of the *Führer* to the Commander-in-Chief of the Army, and he had to pass it on to his army groups.

GEN. RUDENKO: You did not disagree with this will of the *Führer*'s?

KEITEL: I did not raise any objection, since this did not concern a duty of the OKW. I followed the order and passed it on.

GEN. RUDENKO: Do you admit that this order gave you instructions for the immediate and complete economic exploitation of the occupied regions of the Soviet Union in the interest of German war economy?

KEITEL: I did not give such an order containing the aims and tasks which were to be carried out by the organization Economic Staff Oldenburg, since I had nothing to do with that. I only passed on the contents of the Green Folder – it is known what this name stands for – to the High Command of the Army for appropriate action.

GEN. RUDENKO: Do you admit that the directives contained in Göring's Green Folder were aimed at the plunder of the material wealth of the Soviet Union and all her citizens?

KEITEL: No. In my opinion nothing was said about destruction in the Green Folder. Instead of destruction one ought to say, to make good use of surplus, especially in the field of the food supply and the utilization of raw materials for the entire war economy of Germany, but not the destruction of them.

GEN. RUDENKO: Please repeat what you have said.

KEITEL: I said that in the Green Folder there were principles for the utilization of present and future reserves which were considered surplus, but never for their destruction. To let the Soviet population starve at the same time, on account of this, that was not the case. I have seen these things on the spot and therefore I am qualified to speak about them.

GEN. RUDENKO: You do not consider that plunder?

KEITEL: The quibble about words, whether booty, or exploitation of reserves found during the war, or looting, or the like, is a matter of concepts which I believe need not be defined here. Everyone uses his own expressions in this respect.

GEN. RUDENKO: Very well, do not let us argue about it. I have one last question to ask you with regard to the attack on the Soviet Union: Do you agree that the methods of warfare adopted by the German Army in the East stood in striking contrast with the simplest concept of military honour of an army and the exigencies of war?

KEITEL: No, I cannot admit that in this form. I would rather say, the fact that the brutalizing – I have used this term before – that the brutalizing of the war against the Soviet Union and what occurred in the East, is not to be attributed to instigation by the German Army but to circumstances which I have stated in an affidavit submitted by my counsel to the Tribunal. I would furthermore like to ask the Russian Prosecutor to read it so that he can see my opinion about it.

GEN. RUDENKO: Very well. To conclude the question of aggression and to pass to the question of atrocities, I have to ask you the following question, and I trust you will impart to the Tribunal the information you possess in your capacity as Hitler's closest adviser on the conduct of the war.
My question is the following: What tasks did the High Command of the Armed Forces entrust to the German Army in case Germany fought to the finish a victorious war against the Soviet Union?

KEITEL: I do not know what you mean by that. Which demands were put to the military leadership in case the war would be a success? May I ask you to put this question differently. I did not understand it.

GEN. RUDENKO: I have in mind tasks for the further conduct of the war after a successful conclusion of the Eastern campaign.

KEITEL: Then could have occurred what actually did occur later, that is, the landing of the British and American forces in France, in Denmark, or in Germany, *et cetera*. There were various possibilities of warfare which might occur and which could not be anticipated at all.

GEN. RUDENKO: I am not asking this question in general. You are evidently acquainted with a document entitled, Manual of Naval Warfare, which had already been drafted on 8 August 1941 and contained plans for the subsequent conduct of the war after the conclusion of the Eastern campaign. I refer here to the drafting of plans for an attack on Iraq, Syria, and Egypt. Do you know this document?

KEITEL: It has not been submitted to me so far. It is a surprise at the moment, and I cannot recall it.

GEN. RUDENKO: You do not know this document.
This document, Your Honours, is Number S-57; it was submitted to the Tribunal as Exhibit Number USSR-336. I shall show it to you in a minute. Please hand this document to the defendant.

[The document was submitted to the defendant.]

KEITEL: I see this document for the first time, at any rate here during the proceedings. It begins with the sentence, "A draft of directives concerning further plans after the end of the Eastern campaign was submitted to the Naval Operations Staff." This order or directive of the Navy I have never seen nor could I have seen it. It is a draft of directives which could come only from the High Command of the Wehrmacht. In the Armed Forces Operations Staff there were officers from the Army, the Navy, and the Air Force, and it is quite possible that ideas which took the shape of drafts of directives were made known at the time to the officers of the Wehrmacht Operations Staff. I cannot remember any such draft of directives of the Wehrmacht Operations Staff, but perhaps *Generaloberst* Jodl may possibly be in a position to give information about that. I cannot remember it.

GEN. RUDENKO: You do not remember it? I shall not examine you about it closely but you see that the document plans the seizure of Gibraltar with the active participation of Spain. In addition it provides for an attack on Syria, Palestine, Egypt, and so forth. And you say that you know nothing of this document?

KEITEL: I shall be glad to give information about that. An attack to seize Gibraltar, the entrance to the Mediterranean straits, had already been planned for the preceding winter but had not been carried out, that is, during the winter of 1939-40. It was nothing new and the other topics which have been mentioned were those which developed ideas based on the situation existing north of the Caucasus as a result of the operations. I do not at all mean to say that these ideas were not given any thought, but I do not remember it and I did not read every document or paper of the Wehrmacht Operations Staff when it was in the drafting stage.

GEN. RUDENKO: If you consider as mere scraps of paper documents concerning the seizure of foreign countries, then what documents do you consider as important?

KEITEL: I can state only the following, which is true and sincere. In wartime one makes many plans and considers various possibilities which are not and cannot be carried out in the face of the hard facts of reality; and therefore it is not permissible to regard such papers afterwards from an historical point of view, as representing throughout the will and intention of the operational and strategic war leadership.

GEN. RUDENKO: I agree with you that from a historical point of view this document is at present of no importance whatsoever. But taken in conjunction with the plan of the German General Staff at a time when this Staff thought it was going to defeat the Soviet Union, the document does acquire a very different meaning. However, I shall not examine you any further about this document, for the time being.

I now pass on to the subject of atrocities and of your attitude towards these crimes. Your counsel, Dr. Nelte, has already handed you the principal documents of the Prosecution on the subject of atrocities. I do not therefore intend either to submit them again or to enter into any detailed argument on the subject. I shall merely examine you on the basic principles of these documents which were submitted by your counsel when he interrogated you.

I shall first of all refer to a document entitled, "Directive on the Introduction of Military Jurisdiction in Region Barbarossa and on the Adoption of Special Military Measures." Do you remember that document? It was drawn up on 13 May 1941 more than a month before the outbreak of war against the Soviet Union. Do you remember that in that document, drawn up before the war, instructions were given that suspect elements should immediately be brought before an officer and that he would decide whether they were to be shot? Do you remember that directive? Did you sign the document?

KEITEL: Yes, I have never denied that. But I have given the necessary explanations as to how the document came into being and who was its originator.

THE PRESIDENT: What is the number of the document?

GEN. RUDENKO: Document C-50, dated 13 May 1941.

THE PRESIDENT: Very well.

GEN. RUDENKO: *[To the defendant]*: Although you declare that you have already elucidated the matter to your counsel, I am nevertheless obliged to put this question to you in a slightly different form: Did you consider that an officer had a right to shoot people without trial or investigation?

KEITEL: In the German Army there have always been courts-martial for our own soldiers as well as for our enemies, which could always be set up, consisting of one officer and one or two soldiers all three of whom would act as judges. That is what we call a court-martial

(*Standgericht*); the only requisite is always that an officer must preside at this court. But as a matter of principle I have to repeat the statement which I have made yesterday…

GEN. RUDENKO: One moment! Please reply to this question. Did not this document do away with judicial proceedings in the case of so-called suspects, at the same time leaving to an officer of the German Army the right to shoot them? Is that correct?

KEITEL: In the case of German soldiers it was correct and was permitted. There is a military tribunal with judicial officers and there is a court-martial which consists of soldiers. These have the right to pass and to execute an appropriate sentence against any soldier of the German Army in court-martial proceedings.

THE PRESIDENT: You are not answering the question. The question is, what right does this document give, not what the orders in the German Army are.

GEN. RUDENKO: Can you reply to the following question? Did this document do away with judicial proceedings and did it give the German officer the right to shoot suspects, as stated herein?

KEITEL: That was an order which was given to me by Hitler. He had given me that order and I put my name under it. What that means, I explained in detail yesterday.

GEN. RUDENKO: You, a Field Marshal, signed that decree. You considered that the decree was irregular; you understood what the consequences of that decree were likely to be. Then why did you sign it?

KEITEL: I cannot say any more than that I put my name to it and I thereby, personally, assumed in my position a degree of responsibility.

GEN. RUDENKO: And one more question. This decree was dated 13 May 1941, almost a month before the outbreak of war. So you had planned the murder of human beings beforehand?

KEITEL: That I do not understand. It is correct that this order was issued about 4 weeks before the beginning of the campaign Barbarossa, and another 4 weeks earlier it had been communicated to the generals in a statement by Hitler. They knew that weeks before.

GEN. RUDENKO: Do you know how this decree was actually applied?

KEITEL: I have also told my opinion to the interrogating General of the Soviet Army in the preliminary interrogations; whether generals discussed this order with me has not been mentioned, but I wish to point out that it says specifically here that the higher commanders have the right to suspend this order concerning court jurisdiction as soon as their area is pacified. I have given the same answer to every general who has asked me about the reasons for this order and its effect. I said that it provides that they were allowed to suspend this order as soon as they considered their area to be pacified. That is an individual subjective question for the discretion of the commanders and it is provided therein.

GEN. RUDENKO: And now for the final question in connection with this order or directive. This order actually assured German soldiers and officers impunity for arbitrary actions and actions of lawlessness?

KEITEL: Within certain limits, within certain limits! The limit was strictly defined in the oral order to the generals, namely, application of severest disciplinary measures among their own troops.

GEN. RUDENKO: I think, Defendant Keitel, that you have seen these "certain limits" in the documents submitted to the Tribunal and in the documentary films.

I shall now ask you the following question: On 12 May 1941 the question of the treatment of captured Russian political commissars and military prisoners was under consideration. Do you remember that document?

KEITEL: At the moment I cannot recall which one you mean. It is not clear to me what you are referring to at the moment.

GEN. RUDENKO: I refer to the document dated 12 May 1941, which established that the political leaders of the Red Army should not be recognized as prisoners of war but should be destroyed.

KEITEL: I have seen only notes on it. I do not recall the document at present but I know the facts. I cannot recall the document at the moment. May I see it please?

GEN. RUDENKO: If you please.

[The document was handed to the defendant.]

THE PRESIDENT: What number is it?

GEN. RUDENKO: Number 884-PS. It is a document dated 12 May 1941 and entitled: "Treatment of Political and Military Russian Functionaries."

KEITEL: It is not an order but a memorandum on a report by the Department of National Defence, with the remark that decisions by the *Führer* are still required. The memorandum probably refers to a suggested order, I remember this now; I saw it at the time and the result of the report is not mentioned but merely a suggestion which was put down for the ruling. As far as I know, the ruling was taken on those lines then communicated to the High Command of the Army as having been approved by the *Führer* or having been attended to, or discussed, or agreed upon, directly between the *Führer* and the Commander-in-Chief of the Army.

GEN. RUDENKO: What do you mean when you speak of "regulation"? We have learned so many expressions from German Army terminology, such as "regulation", "special treatment", "execution", but they all, translated into vulgar parlance, mean one thing, and one thing only – murder. What are you thinking of when you say "regulation"?

KEITEL: I did not say "regulation". I do not know which word was understood to mean regulation. I said that, in the sense of that memorandum, according to my recollection, directives had been issued by Hitler to the Army at that time, that is, an approval to the suggestion which has been made in the memorandum.

GEN. RUDENKO: In that case you do not deny that as far back as May, more than a month before the outbreak of war, the document had already been drafted which provided for the annihilation of Russian political commissars and military personnel? You do not deny this?

KEITEL: No, that I do not deny. That was the result of the directives which had been communicated and which had been worked out here in writing by the generals.

THE PRESIDENT: The Tribunal will adjourn now.

[The Tribunal adjourned until 6 April 1946 at 1000 hours.]

NUREMBERG TRIAL PROCEEDINGS
ONE HUNDRED AND FIRST DAY
SATURDAY, 6 APRIL 1946

MORNING SESSION

GEN. RUDENKO: Defendant Keitel, I am asking you about the directive concerning the so-called communist insurrectionary movement in the occupied territories. Yesterday your counsel showed you this directive. It is an order of 16 September 1941, Number R-98. I shall remind you of one passage from this order. It states:

> "In order to nip in the bud any conspiracy, the strongest measures should be taken at the first sign of trouble in order to maintain the authority of the occupying power and to prevent the conspiracy from spreading…";

and furthermore:

> "…one must bear in mind that in the countries affected human life has absolutely no value and that a deterrent effect can be achieved only through the application of extraordinarily harsh measures."

You remember this basic idea of the order, that human life absolutely does not amount to anything. Do you remember this statement, the basic statement of the order, that "human life has absolutely no value"? Do you remember this sentence?

KEITEL: Yes.

GEN. RUDENKO: You signed the order containing this statement?

KEITEL: Yes.

GEN. RUDENKO: Do you consider that necessity demanded this extremely evil order?

KEITEL: I explained some of the reasons for this order yesterday and I pointed out that these instructions were addressed in the first place to the Commander-in-Chief of the Wehrmacht offices in the Southeast; that is, the Balkan regions, where extensive partisan warfare and a war between the leaders had assumed enormous proportions, and secondly, because the same phenomena had been observed and established on the same or similar scale in certain defined areas of the occupied Soviet territory.

GEN. RUDENKO: Does this mean that you consider this order to have been entirely correct?

KEITEL: I have already explained in detail, in replying to questions, my fundamental standpoint with regard to all orders concerning the treatment of the population. I signed the order and by doing so I assumed responsibility within the scope of my official jurisdiction.

THE PRESIDENT: The Tribunal considers that you are not answering the question. The question was perfectly capable of an answer "yes" or "no" and an explanation afterwards. It is not an answer to the question to say that you have already explained to your counsel.

GEN. RUDENKO: I ask you once more, do you consider this order, this particular order – and I emphasize, in which it is stated that "human life has absolutely no value" – do you consider this order correct?

KEITEL: It does not contain these words; but I knew from years of experience that in the Southeastern territories and in certain parts of the Soviet territory, human life was not respected to the same degree.

GEN. RUDENKO: You say that these words do not exist in the order?

KEITEL: To my knowledge those exact words do not appear; but it says that human life has very little value in these territories. I remember something like that.

GEN. RUDENKO: According to your recollection now, you remember that you were interrogated by General Alexandrov on 9 November 1945. To a question in regard to the meaning of this sentence you replied: "I must admit that this sentence is authentic, although the *Führer* himself inserted this sentence in the order."

Do you remember your explanation?

KEITEL: That is correct. That is true.

GEN. RUDENKO: I can produce this order for you. I did not produce it because you were familiarizing yourself with it yesterday.

KEITEL: I did not read through all the points yesterday. I merely admitted its actual existence.

THE PRESIDENT: It would help the Tribunal if you got a translation of the document. When you are cross-examining upon a document and as to the actual words of it, it is very inconvenient for us not to have the document before us.

GEN. RUDENKO: Mr. President, I shall at once present this order to the defendant.

[Handing the document to the defendant.]

THE PRESIDENT: Is it Document 389-PS?

GEN. RUDENKO: Yes, this is Document 389-PS.

THE PRESIDENT: When you are citing a document it would be a good thing if you would cite the number rather slowly because very often the translation does not come through accurately to us.

GEN. RUDENKO: All right, I shall observe this in the future, Mr.

President. I numbered this document R-98, but it has a double number, R-98 and 389-PS. I cited Subparagraph 3b) of this order.

Defendant Keitel, have you familiarized yourself with the document?

KEITEL: Yes. The text in the German language says that "in the countries affected human life frequently has no value…"

GEN. RUDENKO: And further?

KEITEL: Yes, "… and a deterrent effect can be obtained only by extreme harshness. To atone for the life of a German soldier…"

GEN. RUDENKO: Quite clear. And in this same order, in this same Subparagraph "b", it is stated that:

"To atone for the life of one German soldier, 50 to 100 Communists must, as a rule, be sentenced to death. The method of execution should strengthen the measure of determent."

Is that correct?

KEITEL: The German text is slightly different. It says: "In such cases in general, the death penalty for 50 to 100 Communists may be considered adequate."

That is the German wording.

GEN. RUDENKO: For one German soldier?

KEITEL: Yes. I know that and I see it here.

GEN. RUDENKO: That is what I was asking you about. So now I ask you once more…

KEITEL: Do you want an explanation of that or am I not to say any more?

GEN. RUDENKO: I shall now interrogate you on this matter. I ask you whether, when signing this order you thereby expressed your personal opinion on these cruel measures? In other words, were you in agreement with Hitler?

KEITEL: I signed the order but the figures contained in it are alterations made personally by Hitler himself.

GEN. RUDENKO: And what figures did you present to Hitler?

KEITEL: The figures in the original were 5 to 10.

GEN. RUDENKO: In other words, the divergence between you and Hitler consisted merely in the figures and not in the spirit of the document?

KEITEL: The idea was that the only way of deterring them was to demand several sacrifices for the life of one soldier, as is stated here.

GEN. RUDENKO: You…

THE PRESIDENT: That was not an answer to the question. The question was whether the only difference between you and Hitler on this document was a question of figures. That admits of the answer "yes" or "no". Was the only difference between you and Hitler a question of figures?

KEITEL: Then I must say that with reference to the underlying principle there was a difference of opinion, the final results of which I no longer feel myself in a position to justify, since I added my signature on behalf of my department. There was a fundamental difference of opinion on the entire question.

GEN. RUDENKO: All right. Let us continue.
I would like to remind you of one more order. It is the order dated 16

December 1942, referring to the so-called "Fight against the Partisans". This document was submitted to the Tribunal as Exhibit Number USSR-16; I shall not examine you in detail with regard to this order. It was presented to you yesterday by your defence counsel.

KEITEL: I do not remember that at the moment.

GEN. RUDENKO: You do not remember?

KEITEL: Not the one that was presented yesterday.

GEN. RUDENKO: All right. If you do not remember I can hand you this document in order to refresh your memory.

THE PRESIDENT: What was the PS number of this document?

GEN. RUDENKO: This is the document submitted by the Soviet Prosecution as Exhibit Number USSR-16 (Document Number USSR-16).

THE PRESIDENT: I just took down that it was USA-516, but I suppose I was wrong in hearing. It is USSR-16, is it?

GEN. RUDENKO: Yes, USSR-16.

THE PRESIDENT: Very well.

GEN. RUDENKO: *[Handing the document to the defendant.]* I shall interrogate you, Defendant Keitel, only on one question in connection with this order. In Subparagraph 1 of this order, Paragraph 3, it is stated, and I would draw your attention to the following sentence:
"The troops are therefore authorized and ordered in this struggle to take any measures without restriction even against women and children, if that is necessary to achieve success."

Have you found this passage?

KEITEL: Yes.

GEN. RUDENKO: Have you found the order calling for the application of any kind of measures you like without restriction, also against women and children?

KEITEL: "To employ without restriction any means, even against women and children, if it is necessary." I have found that.

GEN. RUDENKO: That is exactly what I am asking you about. I ask you, Defendant Keitel, Field Marshal of the former German Army, do you consider that this order is a just one, that measures may be employed at will against women and children?

KEITEL: Measures, insofar as it means that women and children were also to be removed from territories where there was partisan warfare, never atrocities or the murder of women or children. Never!

GEN. RUDENKO: To remove – a German term – means to kill?

KEITEL: No. I do not think it would ever have been necessary to tell German soldiers that they could not and must not kill women and children.

GEN. RUDENKO: You did not answer my question.
Do you consider this order a just one in regard to measures against women and children or do you consider it unjust? Answer "yes" or "no". Is it just or unjust? Explain the matter later.

KEITEL: I considered these measures to be right and as such I admit them; but not measures to kill. That was a crime.

GEN. RUDENKO: "Any kind of measures" includes murder.

KEITEL: Yes, but not of women and children.

GEN. RUDENKO: Yes, but it says here "Any kind of measures against women and children."

KEITEL: No, it does not say "any measures". It says "… and not to shrink from taking measures against women and children". That is what it says.
No German soldier or German officer ever thought of killing women and children.

GEN. RUDENKO: And in reality…?

KEITEL: I cannot say in every individual case, since I do not know and I could not be everywhere and since I received no reports about it.

GEN. RUDENKO: But there were millions of such cases?

KEITEL: I have no knowledge of that and I do not believe that it happened in millions of cases.

GEN. RUDENKO: You do not believe it?

KEITEL: No.

GEN. RUDENKO: I shall proceed to another question. I shall now refer to one question, the question of the treatment of Soviet prisoners of war. I do not intend to examine you in regard to the branding of Soviet prisoners of war and other facts; they are sufficiently well known to the Tribunal. I want to examine you in regard to one document, the report of Admiral Canaris, which was presented to you yesterday. You remember yesterday your counsel submitted to you the Canaris report;

it is dated 15 September 1941 and registered under Document Number EC-338. As you will remember, even a German officer drew attention to the exceptional arbitrariness and lawlessness admitted in connection with the Soviet prisoners of war. Canaris in this report pointed to the mass murders of Soviet prisoners of war and spoke of the necessity of definitely eliminating this arbitrariness. Did you agree with the statements advanced by Canaris in his report, with reference to yourself?

KEITEL: I did not understand the last statement. With reference to myself?

GEN. RUDENKO: The last question amounts to this: Were you, Keitel, personally in agreement with the proposals made by Canaris in his report, that the arbitrary treatment permitted should be done away with where Soviet prisoners of war were concerned?

KEITEL: I answered my counsel yesterday...

GEN. RUDENKO: You can answer my question briefly; were you in agreement with it?

KEITEL: Yes, I will be brief – on receiving that letter, I immediately submitted it to the *Führer*, Adolf Hitler, especially on account of the enclosed publication by the Peoples' Commissars, which was dated the beginning of July, and I asked for a new decision. On the whole I shared the objections raised by Canaris, but I must supplement that...

GEN. RUDENKO: You shared them? Very well. I shall now present you with the original copy of Canaris' report, containing your decision.

Mr. President, I shall now present to the defendant the document containing his decision. This decision was not read into the record in court and I shall also present the text of his final decision to the Tribunal.

THE PRESIDENT: Do you have the original?

GEN. RUDENKO: Yes, I gave it to the defendant.
And now, Witness Keitel, will you please follow?

KEITEL: I know the document with the marginal notes.

GEN. RUDENKO: Listen to me and follow the text of the decision. This is Canaris' document, which you consider, a just one. The following are the contents of your decision:

> "These objections arise from the military conception of chivalrous warfare. We are dealing here with the destruction of an ideology and, therefore, I approve such measures and I sanction them." Signed: "Keitel".

Is this your resolution?

KEITEL: Yes, I wrote that after it had been submitted to the *Führer* for decision. I wrote it then.

GEN. RUDENKO: It is not written there that the *Führer* said so; it is said "I sanction them" – meaning Keitel.

KEITEL: And I state this on oath; and I said it even before I read it.

GEN. RUDENKO: This means that you acknowledge the decision. I will now draw your attention to another passage of this document. I draw your attention to Page 2. Please observe that the text of Canaris' report mentions the following:

> "The separation of civilians and prisoners of war who are politically undesirable, and decision to be made in regard to their fate, is to be effected by task forces (*Einsatzkommando*) belonging to the Security Police and the SD in accordance with directives not known to the Wehrmacht establishments and whose execution cannot be checked by the latter."

Canaris writes this; your decision, Defendant Keitel, is written in the margin. It says, "Highly expedient". Is that correct?

KEITEL: Please repeat the last question. The last words I heard were "Canaris writes".

GEN. RUDENKO: Yes, and I am now mentioning the fact that your decision "Highly expedient" appears in the margin, opposite that paragraph, and written by your own hand. Have you found this?

KEITEL: Yes. The word "expedient" refers to the fact that the army offices had nothing to do with these *Einsatzkommandos* and know nothing about them. It states that they are not known to the Wehrmacht.

GEN. RUDENKO: And furthermore it refers to the fact that the Security Police and the SD should wreak vengeance on civilians and prisoners of war? You consider that expedient?

KEITEL: No, I thought it expedient that the activities of these *Kommandos* be unknown to the Armed Forces. That is what I meant. That appears here and I underlined "unknown".

GEN. RUDENKO: I am asking you, Defendant Keitel, known as Field Marshal and one who, before this Tribunal, has repeatedly referred to yourself as a soldier, whether you, in your own bloodthirsty decision of September 1941, confirmed and sanctioned the murder of the unarmed soldiers whom you had captured? Is that right?

KEITEL: I signed both decrees and I, therefore, bear the responsibility within the sphere of my office; I assume the responsibility.

GEN. RUDENKO: That is quite clear. In this connection I would like to ask you, since you have repeatedly mentioned it before the Tribunal, about the duty of a soldier. I want to ask you: Is it in accordance with the concept of a "soldier's duty" and the "honour of an officer" to promulgate such orders for reprisals on prisoners of war and on peaceful citizens?

KEITEL: Yes, as far as the reprisals of August and September are concerned, in view of what happened to German prisoners of war whom we found in the field of battle, and in Lvov where we found them murdered by the hundreds.

GEN. RUDENKO: Defendant Keitel, do you again wish to follow the path to which you resorted once before, and revive the question of the alleged butchery of German prisoners of war? You and I agreed yesterday that as far back as May 1941, prior to the beginning of the war, you had signed a directive on the shooting of political and military workers in the Red Army. I have some…

KEITEL: Yes, I also signed the orders before the war but they did not contain the word "murder".

GEN. RUDENKO: I am not going to argue with you since this means arguing against documents; and documents speak for themselves.
I have a few last questions to ask you: You informed the Tribunal that the generals of the German Army were only blindly carrying out Hitler's orders?

KEITEL: I have stated that I do not know if any generals raised objections or who they were, and I said that it did not happen in my presence when Hitler proclaimed the principles of the ideological war and ordered them to be put into practice.

GEN. RUDENKO: And do you know that the generals, on their own initiative, promulgated orders on atrocities and on the violation of the laws and customs of war, and that these orders were approved by Hitler?

KEITEL: I know that high authorities in the Army issued orders altering, modifying, and even cancelling in part; for instance, as regards jurisdiction, the March decree and other measures, because they also discussed it with me.

GEN. RUDENKO: You do not understand me. I did not ask about modifications, but whether the generals, on their own initiative, ever promulgated orders inciting to the violation of the laws and customs of war.

KEITEL: I do not know of that. I do not know what order you are referring to, General. At the moment I cannot say that I know that.

GEN. RUDENKO: I shall refer to one order only. What I have in mind is General Field Marshal Reichenau's order governing the conduct of troops in the East.

This document, Mr. President, was presented by the Soviet Prosecution as Exhibit Number USSR-12 (Document Number USSR-12). The passages to which I refer are underlined in this document, and I shall read into the record one quotation from this order governing the conduct of troops in the East:

> "Feeding the inhabitants and prisoners of war... is... a mistaken humanity..."

KEITEL: I know the order. It was shown to me during a preliminary interrogation.

GEN. RUDENKO: This order, issued on Reichenau's initiative and approved by Hitler, was distributed as a model order among all the army commanders.

KEITEL: I did not know that; I heard about it here for the first time. To my knowledge I never saw the order either.

GEN. RUDENKO: Of course you would, quite obviously, consider such orders as entirely insignificant. After all, could the fate of Soviet prisoners of war and of the civilian population be of any possible interest to the Chief of the OKW, since their lives were of no value whatsoever?

KEITEL: I had no contact with the commanders at the front and had no official connection with them. The Commander-in-Chief of the Army was the only one who had.

GEN. RUDENKO: I am finishing your cross-examination. When testifying before the Tribunal you very often referred, as did your accomplices, the Defendants Göring and Ribbentrop, to the Treaty of Versailles, and I am asking you, were Vienna, Prague, Belgrade and the Crimea part of Germany before the Treaty of Versailles?

KEITEL: No.

GEN. RUDENKO: You stated here that in 1944, after the law had been amended, you received an offer to join the Nazi Party.

You accepted this offer, presented your personal credentials to the leadership of the Party, and paid your membership fees. Tell us, did not your acceptance to join the membership of the Nazi Party signify that you were in agreement with the programme, objectives, and methods of the Party?

KEITEL: As I had already been in possession of the Golden Party Badge for three or four years, I thought that this request for my personal particulars was only a formal registration; and I paid the required Party membership subscription. I did both these things and have admitted doing them.

GEN. RUDENKO: In other words, before this formal offer was ever made, you already, *de facto*, considered yourself a member of the Nazi Party?

KEITEL: I have always thought of myself as a soldier; not as a political soldier or politician.

GEN. RUDENKO: Should we not conclude, after all that has been said here, that you were a Hitler General, not because duty called you but on account of your own convictions?

KEITEL: I have stated here that I was a loyal and obedient soldier of my *Führer*. And I do not think that there are generals in Russia who do not give Marshal Stalin implicit obedience.

GEN. RUDENKO: I have exhausted all my questions.

SIR DAVID MAXWELL-FYFE: Defendant, do you remember on 2 October 1945 writing a letter to Colonel Amen, explaining your position? It was after your interrogations, and in your own time you wrote a letter explaining your point of view. Do you remember that?

KEITEL: Yes, I think I did write a letter; but I no longer remember the contents. It referred to the interrogations, however.

SIR DAVID MAXWELL-FYFE: Yes.

KEITEL: And I think it contained a request that I be given a further opportunity of thinking things over, as the questions put to me took me by surprise and I was often unable to remember the answers.

SIR DAVID MAXWELL-FYFE: I want to remind you of one passage and ask you whether it correctly expresses your view:
> "In carrying out these thankless and difficult tasks, I had to fulfil my duty under the hardest exigencies of war, often acting against the inner voice of my conscience and against my own convictions. The fulfilment of urgent tasks assigned by Hitler, to whom I was directly responsible, demanded complete self-abnegation."

Do you remember that?

KEITEL: Yes.

SIR DAVID MAXWELL-FYFE: Well, now, I just want you to tell the Tribunal, what were the worst matters in your view in which you often acted against the inner voice of your conscience? Just tell us some of the worst matters in which you acted against the inner voice of your conscience.

KEITEL: I found myself in such a situation quite frequently, but the decisive questions which conflicted most violently with my conscience and my convictions were those which were contrary to the training which I had undergone during my 37 years as an officer in the German Army. That was a blow at my most intimate personal principles.

SIR DAVID MAXWELL-FYFE: I wanted it to come from you, Defendant. Can you tell the Tribunal the three worst things you had to do which were against the inner voice of your conscience? What do you pick out as the three worst things you had to do?

KEITEL: Perhaps, to start with the last, the orders given for the conduct of the war in the East, insofar as they were contrary to the acknowledged usage of war; then something which particularly concerns the British Delegation, the question of the 50 R.A.F. officers, the question which weighed particularly heavy on my mind, that of the terror-fliers and, worst of all, the *Nacht und Nebel* Decree and the actual consequences it entailed at a later stage and about which I did not know. Those were the worst struggles which I had with myself.

SIR DAVID MAXWELL-FYFE: We will take the *Nacht und Nebel*.
My Lord, this document and a good many to which I shall refer are in the British Document Book Number 7, Wilhelm Keitel and Alfred Jodl, and it occurs on Page 279. It is L-90, Exhibit USA-503.
[Turning to the defendant.] Defendant, I will give you the German document book. It is 279 of the British document book, and 289…

KEITEL: Number 731?

SIR DAVID MAXWELL-FYFE: It is Page 289, I do not know which volume it is; Part 2, I think it is.

You see, the purpose of the decree is set out a few lines from the start, where they say that in all cases where the death penalty is not pronounced and not carried out within a week,

"... the accused are in the future to be deported to Germany secretly, and further proceedings in connection with the offences will take place here. The deterrent effect of these measures lies in: (a) the complete disappearance of the accused; (b) the fact that no information may be given as to their whereabouts or their fate."

Both these purposes, you will agree, were extremely cruel and brutal, were they not?

KEITEL: I said both at the time and yesterday, that I personally thought that to deport individuals secretly was very much more cruel than to impose a sentence of death. I have...

SIR DAVID MAXWELL-FYFE: Would you turn to Page 281-291 of yours – 281 of the English Book?

KEITEL: Yes, I have it.

SIR DAVID MAXWELL-FYFE: You say that this is your covering letter:

"The *Führer* is of the opinion:" – Line 4 – "In the case of offences such as these, punishment by imprisonment, or even penal servitude for life, will be considered a sign of weakness. Effective and lasting intimidation can only be achieved either by capital punishment or by measures which keep the culprit's relatives and the population generally uncertain as to his fate."

You will agree that there again these sentences of the *Führer* which you are here transmitting were cruel and brutal, were they not?

KEITEL: Yes.

SIR DAVID MAXWELL-FYFE: Now, what I...

KEITEL: May I add something?

SIR DAVID MAXWELL-FYFE: Certainly, as shortly as you can.

KEITEL: I made a statement yesterday on this subject and I drew your attention particularly to the words: "It is the *Führer's* long considered will", which were intended to convey to the generals who were receiving these orders what was written between the lines.

SIR DAVID MAXWELL-FYFE: But, you know, Defendant, that that was by no means the end of this series of orders, was it? This order was unsuccessful despite its cruelty and brutality in achieving its purpose, was it not? This order, the *Nacht und Nebel* Order, in that form was unsuccessful in achieving its purpose; it did not stop what it was designed to stop? Is that right?

KEITEL: No, it did not cease.

SIR DAVID MAXWELL-FYFE: So that in 1944 you had to make a still more severe order. Would you look at Document D-762? My Lord, that will become Exhibit GB-298.
 [Turning to the defendant:] It says:
 "The constant increase in acts of terror and sabotage in the occupied territories, committed more and more by bands under unified leadership, compels us to take the sternest countermeasures in a degree corresponding to the ferocity of the war which is forced upon us. Those who attack us from the rear at the crisis of our fight for existence deserve no consideration.
 "I therefore order:
 "All acts of violence committed by non-German civilians in the occupied territories against the German Wehrmacht, the SS, or the Police, or against installations used by them, are to be combated in

the following manner as acts of terrorism and sabotage:" – (1) – "The troops," – the SS and so on – "are to fight down on the spot… all terrorists and saboteurs." – (2) – "Those who are apprehended later are to be handed over to the nearest local Security Police and the SD office." – (3) – "Accomplices, especially women, who take no active part in the fighting, are to be employed on labour. Children are to be spared."

Now, would you look at Paragraph II:

"The Chief of the OKW will issue the necessary executive instructions. He is entitled to make alterations and additions as far as required by the exigencies of war operations."

Did you think that was a cruel and severe order or not?

KEITEL: Yes, I do think so, but may I make one small correction? It must have been incorrectly translated. The actual wording is: "Women are to be employed on labour. Children are to be spared." So it says in the original version which I have before me.

SIR DAVID MAXWELL-FYFE: I said "spared". "Spared" meant that they were not to be treated thus. I was careful to mention that.

KEITEL: Yes.

SIR DAVID MAXWELL-FYFE: Now, you had authority to make alterations and additions. Did you, by your alterations and additions, attempt to mitigate the severity of that order in any way?

KEITEL: I have no recollection of having issued any additional orders to mitigate its severity. I may also say that I never would have issued anything without first presenting it to the *Führer*.

SIR DAVID MAXWELL-FYFE: Just let us see what you did issue. Would you look at Document D-764, which will be Exhibit GB-299?

Now, that is your executive order, countersigned I think by the Senior Military Judge, putting forward your order based on that decree; and would you look at Paragraphs 4 and 5:

"All legal proceedings now going on in connection with acts of terrorism, sabotage, or other crimes committed by non-German civilians in the occupied territories which imperil the security or readiness for action of the occupying power are to be suspended. Indictments are to be dropped. Sentences already pronounced are not to be carried out. The culprits are to be handed over with a report on the proceedings to the nearest local Security Police and SD office. In the case of death sentences which have already become final, the regulations now in force will continue to apply.

"Crimes affecting German interests but which do not imperil the security or readiness for action of the occupying power do not justify the retention of jurisdiction over non-German civilians in the occupied territories. I authorize the commanders of the occupied territories to draw up new regulations in agreement with the Higher SS and the Police Leader."

And then you ask them to consider among the first, one handing them over to the SD for forced labour.

That was certainly not mitigation of the order, was it? You were not making it any easier.

KEITEL: There are a few sentences to be added here. This arose out of the daily discussion of these matters which I dealt with later on the same lines as the first decree. I made suitable annotations, and signed them.

SIR DAVID MAXWELL-FYFE: Well, now, that is what you called terrorism and sabotage. Let us look at what happened to people who were guilty of something less than terrorism or sabotage. Look at Document D-763. That will be GB-300. "Non-German civilians..."

KEITEL: Yes.

SIR DAVID MAXWELL-FYFE: "Non-German civilians in the occupied territories who endanger the security or tactical preparedness of the occupying power otherwise than through acts of terrorism and sabotage, are to be handed over to the SD. Section I, Number 3…"
"– that is the part that says women will be employed on labour and children will be spared – "of the *Führer's* order also applies to them."
Well, you knew perfectly well what would happen to anyone who was handed over to the SD, that he would probably be killed, certainly be put into a concentration camp, did you not?

KEITEL: I did not interpret it that way; the words "to be allocated on labour" were always used; but it has become clear to me from what I have learned that they frequently ended in the concentration camp. However, it was always described to us, to me, as a labour camp. That was the description, "labour camps of the Secret State Police".

SIR DAVID MAXWELL-FYFE: But this is August 1944. You will agree that that is a most severe course to take with people who have been guilty of something less than terrorism or sabotage, do you not?

KEITEL: Yes.

SIR DAVID MAXWELL-FYFE: Now, let us…

KEITEL: I assume that you do not wish me to discuss this origin and development here. Otherwise I could explain them; but I will merely answer the question. The answer is, yes, it was a very severe measure. The explanation, if I may state it very briefly, is that, as is known, during the interminable daily situation reports on the incidents in all the occupied territories, I received from the *Führer* instructions and orders which were afterwards crystallized in a form similar to this document; and I think I have already described in detail the way in which I discussed these things with him and how I worked, that on principle I never issued or signed anything which did not agree in principle with his wishes.

SIR DAVID MAXWELL-FYFE: That was severe enough for you for only 3 weeks, was it not, because on 4 September, which is barely 3 weeks later, you issued another order, Document D-766, Exhibit GB-301. Now, this was issued, as it shows, as an agreement with Himmler, Kaltenbrunner, the Reich Minister of Justice and Dr. Lammers. Now look at I:

"Non-German civilians in occupied territories who have been sentenced by German courts for a criminal act against the security or tactical preparedness of the occupying power, the sentence having become final, and who are in custody in the occupied territories or in the home front area, are to be handed over, together with a report on the facts, to the nearest local Security Police and SD office. An exception is made only in the case of those sentenced to death for whom the execution of the penalty has been ordered.

"II. Persons convicted of criminal acts against the Reich or the occupying power and prohibited, in accordance with the directives... issued by the *Führer* for the prosecution of such acts, from intercourse with the outside world, are to be given a distinguishing mark."

Now, had you any idea how many people would be affected by that order?

KEITEL: No, I cannot say anything about that. I know only that it was made necessary by the increasing tension in the occupied territories, due to lack of troops to keep order.

SIR DAVID MAXWELL-FYFE: Well, let me remind you. You called a conference to consider this matter. That is shown in Document D-765, and I also show you D-767, the report of the conference. You need not worry about 765, which just says that there is to be a conference but in Document D-767, which will be Exhibit GB-303, there is a report of the conference. The second paragraph says:

"The *Reichsführer-SS*" – Himmler – "demands in his letter the immediate surrender to the SD of approximately 24,000 non-

German civilians who are under arrest or held for interrogation." – Now listen to this: "No answer was given to the question raised during the discussion as to why they must be surrendered to the SD at the present moment, in spite of the considerable amount of administrative work involved."

Can you give any answer now as to why 24,000 people who had been sentenced should be transferred to the tender mercies of the SD?

KEITEL: May I read this note? I do not know it; may I read it now, please?

SIR DAVID MAXWELL-FYFE: Certainly. You will see that I did not trouble you with it all, but it says what I had already put to you earlier, that the *Nacht und Nebel* Decree had become superfluous as a result of the terror and sabotage decree, and that the Wehrmacht Legal Department had presented these things for discussion.

Now, can you give us any answer as to why these 24,000 unfortunate persons who had been sentenced should be handed over to the tender mercies of the SD?

KEITEL: I must say that I am surprised by the whole incident. I did not attend the conference, and apparently I did not read the note since, as a matter of principle, I always marked every document which had been presented to me with my initials. I am not acquainted with the figures quoted; this is the first time I have seen them; I am not acquainted with them and I do not remember them, unless another order was…

SIR DAVID MAXWELL-FYFE: I will give you something which you have read.

KEITEL: As regards the facts about which you ask, I must answer in the affirmative. I do not know the figures, only the facts.

SIR DAVID MAXWELL-FYFE: And you cannot answer my

question. You cannot give us any reason as to why the Wehrmacht and these other offices were sending the 24,000 people, who had been sentenced by ordinary courts, over to the SD? You cannot give us any reason for that?

KEITEL: No; I may say that up to a point I can. I think "SD" is a misinterpretation. I think police custody was meant. That does not mean the same thing.

SIR DAVID MAXWELL-FYFE: Certainly not.

KEITEL: I do not know if it might have been the same thing.

SIR DAVID MAXWELL-FYFE: Surely you have been at this Trial too long to think that handing people over to the SD means police custody. It means a concentration camp and a gas chamber usually, does it not? That is what it meant in fact, whether you knew it or not.

KEITEL: I did not know it, but it obviously led to the concentration camp in the end. I consider it possible; in any case, I cannot say that it was not.

THE PRESIDENT: Sir David, the last paragraph but one refers to the OKW.

SIR DAVID MAXWELL-FYFE: Yes, My Lord, I am just coming to that.
[Turning to the defendant.] If you will notice that, Defendant, two paragraphs below the one I put to you it states:

"As the OKW is not particularly interested in trying the minor matters still remaining for the military tribunals, they are to be settled by decrees to be agreed upon by local authorities."

It is quite clear that your office was deeply concerned in this business, was it not, Defendant?

KEITEL: I do not know exactly what it means, but it was obviously mentioned at that conference.

SIR DAVID MAXWELL-FYFE: Now, before I put the next document, I want you to realize how we have been going. We started with the *Nacht und Nebel* Decree, which disappeared, and we went on to the Terror and Sabotage Decree. We then proceeded to acts which were less than terror and sabotage, but were criminal acts under the rules of the occupying power.

I now want you to consider what was done to people who simply refused to work. Would you look at Document D-769? That is Exhibit GB-304. That is a telegram from Luftwaffe General Christiansen, who was in the Netherlands, Commander of the Air Forces in the Netherlands, through his Chief of Staff.

Now listen to this:

"Owing to railway strike, all communications in Holland at standstill. Railway personnel does not respond to appeals to resume work. Demands for motor vehicles and other means of transport for moving troops and maintaining supplies are no longer obeyed by the civil population. According to the *Führer's* decree of 18 August 1944" – that is the Terror and Sabotage Decree, which you have already had – "and the supplementary executive instructions of the Chief of the OKW" – which we have already seen – "troops may use weapons only against persons who commit acts of violence as terrorists or saboteurs, whereas persons who endanger the security or tactical preparedness of the occupying power in any other way than by terrorism or acts of sabotage, are to be handed over to the SD."

Then General Christiansen comes in with this:

"This regulation has proved too complicated, and therefore ineffective. Above all, we do not possess the necessary police forces. The troops must again receive authority to shoot also, with or without summary court-martial, persons who are not terrorists or saboteurs in the sense of the *Führer's* decree, but who endanger the fighting forces by passive resistance. It is requested that the *Führer's* decree be altered accordingly, as the troops cannot otherwise assert themselves effectively against the population, which in its turn, appears to endanger the conduct of operations."

Now, Defendant, will you agree that shooting, with or even without trial, railway men who will not work, is about as brutal and cruel a measure as could well be imagined by the mind of man? Do you agree?

KEITEL: That is a cruel measure, yes.

SIR DAVID MAXWELL-FYFE: What was your answer to that cruel measure?

KEITEL: I cannot say. I do not recollect the incident at all, but perhaps the answer is there.

SIR DAVID MAXWELL-FYFE: Well, look at the Document D-770, which is, I think, your answer; it is Exhibit GB-305. You will notice on the distribution list that that goes to the Commander of the Armed Forces in the Netherlands, and further to the signal which we have just been looking at. Now, you say:

"According to the *Führer's* order of 30 July 1944, non-German civilians in the occupied territories who attack us in the rear in the crisis of our battle for existence deserve no consideration. This must be our guiding principle in the interpretation and application of the *Führer's* decree itself and the Chief of the OKW's executive decree of 18 August 1944.

"If the military situation and the state of communications make it impossible to hand them over to the SD, other effective measures are to be taken ruthlessly and independently. There is, naturally" – and I ask you to note the word "naturally" – "no objection to passing and executing death sentences by summary court-martial under such circumstances."

I can not remember, Defendant, whether you have ever had an independent command yourself or not. Have you? Have you had an independent command, apart from your division? I think that was the last independent command you had. You have not had an independent command yourself, have you? Don't I make myself clear?

KEITEL: I did not understand. What do you mean by "independent"?

SIR DAVID MAXWELL-FYFE: I mean that you have not been a commander or chief of an army or army group yourself, if I remember rightly, or of an area, have you?

KEITEL: No, I have not.

SIR DAVID MAXWELL-FYFE: I ask you to put yourself in General Christiansen's position. That answer of yours was a direct encouragement, practically amounting to an order, to shoot these railway men out of hand, was it not? "To take other effective measures ruthlessly and independently."

KEITEL: That is explained by the form of summary court-martial. It is not left to the discretion of the individual; jurisdiction of summary court-martial was provided.

SIR DAVID MAXWELL-FYFE: Just look at the way it is put, Defendant. I suggest to you that it is quite clear. One sentence states: "If handing over to the SD is impossible, owing to the military situation and the state of communications, other effective measures are to be taken ruthlessly and independently."
Then, the next sentence: "There are, naturally" – look at the word "naturally". I suppose that it was *"naturlich"*, in German. Is that correct?

KEITEL: I have not the word *"naturlich"* here. Two words, so far as I can make out, have been inserted.

SIR DAVID MAXWELL-FYFE: But it says: "There are, naturally, no objections to passing and executing death sentences by summary court-martial procedure." What you are saying is that, of course, there is no objection to a summary court, but you are telling him, in addition to that, that he is to take effective measures ruthlessly and independently. If General Christiansen had shot these railway men out of hand, after getting that letter from you, neither you nor any other superior could have blamed him for it, could you?

KEITEL: According to the last sentence, he was obliged to carry out summary court-martial procedure. It says: "There are no objections to the executing of this sentence by summary court-martial under such circumstances." That is how I meant it.

SIR DAVID MAXWELL-FYFE: But what did you mean by "effective measures to be taken ruthlessly and independently"? What did you mean by that, if it was only an ordinary summary court procedure?

KEITEL: Not apart from summary court procedure, but by means of the same. That is what the last sentence means. It is already unusual to appoint a summary court-martial in such cases.

SIR DAVID MAXWELL-FYFE: Yes, even on your basis, to use a military summary court to shoot railway men who will not work is going rather far even for you, is it not? It is going rather far, isn't it?

KEITEL: That was a very severe measure, yes.

SIR DAVID MAXWELL-FYFE: Do you tell the Tribunal that when you make all these additions, taking you through the chain of additions that you make to the order replacing the *Nacht und Nebel* Order, of which you disapproved, do you say that you went to Hitler for every one of these executive orders and answers that you made?

KEITEL: Yes. I went to him on the occasion of every one of these orders. I must emphasize the fact that I did not issue any of these orders without previously submitting it to the *Führer*. I must expressly point out that that was so.

DR. NELTE: Mr. President, I think a misunderstanding has crept into the translation. The translation interprets *"Standgericht"* as summary court. I do not believe that the words "summary court" reflect accurately what we understand in the German language by *"Standgericht"*. I do not know just what you understand in the English or American language by "summary court", but I can imagine that this means some summary procedure.

SIR DAVID MAXWELL-FYFE: I was taking it in favour of the Defendant that it meant the court he referred to yesterday, one officer and two soldiers. I was taking that. If I am wrong, the Defendant will correct me. Is that right, Defendant?

KEITEL: I described this *Standgericht* (summary court-martial procedure) briefly yesterday, and the criterion of a summary court-martial was that it was not always necessary for a fully trained legal expert to be present, although it was desirable.

THE PRESIDENT: While you are on the subject of translation, the Defendant seemed to suggest that there was no word in the German which is translated by the English word "naturally". Is that true?

SIR DAVID MAXWELL-FYFE: I had it checked and I am told that the translation is right.

THE PRESIDENT: There is a German word which is translated by "naturally"? I should like to know that from Dr. Nelte.

DR. NELTE: I am told that a false conception or false judgment might be produced in this connection since in British and American law a summary court has no right to pass sentences of death. I am told that a summary court...

THE PRESIDENT: Excuse me, Dr. Nelte, I did not ask that question. The question I asked you was whether there was any German word which is translated into English by the word "naturally". Is that not a clear question?

DR. NELTE: In the German text it says "under such circumstances, of course". I think the English translation is incorrect in using the word "naturally" and in putting it after "in these circumstances" instead of at the beginning, so that one is led to conclude that it means, "there are naturally no objections (*es gibt naturlich keine Einwendungen*)", whereas the German text says, "Against the passing and executing of death sentences by summary court procedure there are – under such circumstances, of course – no objections (*Gegen die Verhangung und Vollstreckung von Todesurteilen im standgerichtlichen Verfahren bestehen unter solchen Verhaltnissen selbstverstandlich keine Bedenken*)."

THE PRESIDENT: Then the answer to my question is "yes". There is a word in the German which is translated "naturally".

DR. NELTE: Yes, but the words "naturally" and "under such circumstances" are separated in the English version, while in the German version they belong together. "Naturally" refers to "under such circumstances".

SIR DAVID MAXWELL-FYFE: Now I want to come to another point. You told us yesterday that with regard to forced labour you were concerned in it because there was a shortage of manpower and you had to take men out of industry for the Wehrmacht. Your office was concerned with using military forces in order to try and round-up people for forced labour, was it not?

KEITEL: I do not think that is quite the correct conception. The Replacement Office in the High Command of the Wehrmacht...

SIR DAVID MAXWELL-FYFE: If you are going to deny it, I put the document to you: I put General Warlimont's views to you and see if you agree. I think it saves time in the end. If you look at Document 3819-PS, which will be Exhibit GB-306, Page 9 of the English version. It is the report of a meeting at Berlin on 12 July 1944. You have to look on through the document after the letters from the Defendant Sauckel and the Defendant Speer, the account of a meeting in Berlin. I think it is Page 10 of the German version. It starts with a speech by Dr. Lammers and goes on with a speech from the Defendant Sauckel, then a speech from the witness Von Steengracht, then a speech from General Warlimont: "The Deputy of the head of the OKW, General Warlimont, referred to a recently issued *Führer* order." Have you found the portion? I will read it if you have.

KEITEL: Yes, I have found the paragraph "The Representative of the Chief of the OKW..."

SIR DAVID MAXWELL-FYFE: "The Representative of the Chief of the OKW, General Warlimont, referred to a recently issued *Führer* order, according to which all German forces had to participate in the task of raising manpower. Wherever the Wehrmacht was stationed, if it was not employed exclusively in pressing military duties (as, for example, in the construction of coastal defences), it would be available, but it could not be assigned expressly for the purpose of the GBA. General Warlimont made the following practical suggestions:

"a) The troops employed in fighting the partisans are to take over, in addition, the task of raising manpower in the partisan areas. Everyone who cannot give a satisfactory reason for his presence in these areas is to be recruited by force.

"b) When large cities are wholly or partly evacuated on account of the difficulty of providing food, those members of the population suitable for labour are to be utilized for labour with the assistance of the Wehrmacht.

"c) The refugees from the areas near the front should be rounded up with special vigour with the assistance of the Wehrmacht."

After reading this report of General Warlimont's words, do you still say that the Wehrmacht…

KEITEL: I am not aware that the Armed Forces have ever received an order mentioning the rounding-up of workers. I would like to say that I know of no such demand and I have not found any confirmation of it. The conference as such is unknown to me and so are the proposals you mentioned. It is new as far as I am concerned.

SIR DAVID MAXWELL-FYFE: It is quite clear that General Warlimont is suggesting that the Wehrmacht should help in the rounding up of forced labour, isn't it?

KEITEL: But as far as I know it has never happened. I do not know that such an order was given. According to the record, this is a proposal made by General Warlimont, yes.

THE PRESIDENT: Sir David, perhaps in those circumstances you should read the three lines after the passage you have read.

SIR DAVID MAXWELL-FYFE: My Lord, I should. The next line:
"*Gauleiter* Sauckel accepted these suggestions with thanks and expressed the expectation that a certain amount of success could be achieved by this means."

KEITEL: May I say something about that? May I ask that *Gauleiter* Sauckel be asked at a given time whether and to what extent troops of the Armed Forces did actually participate in such matters. It is not known to me.

SIR DAVID MAXWELL-FYFE: No doubt the Defendant Sauckel, will be asked a number of questions in due time. At the moment I am asking you. You say that you do not know anything about it?

KEITEL: No, I do not recollect that any order was given in this connection. I gather from the statement by Warlimont that discussions took place.

SIR DAVID MAXWELL-FYFE: Now I want to ask you a few questions about the murder of various prisoners of war. I want to get it quite clear. Did you mean yesterday to justify the order for the shooting of Commandos, dated 18 October 1942? Did you wish to say that it was right and justified, or not?

KEITEL: I stated yesterday that neither General Jodl nor I thought that we were in a position, or considered it possible, to draft or submit such a written order. We did not do it because we could not justify it or give reasons for it.

SIR DAVID MAXWELL-FYFE: The next question that I put to you is this: Did you approve and think right the order that was made that Commandos should be shot?

KEITEL: I no longer opposed it, firstly on account of the punishment threatened, and secondly because I could no longer alter the order without personal orders from Hitler.

SIR DAVID MAXWELL-FYFE: Did you think that that order was right?

KEITEL: According to my inner convictions I did not consider it right, but after it had been given I did not oppose it or take a stand against it in any way.

SIR DAVID MAXWELL-FYFE: You know that your orders had contained provisions for the use of parachutists being dropped, for sabotage purposes, don't you? Your own orders have contained that provision of parachutists being dropped for sabotage purposes. Don't you remember in the *Fall Grün* against Czechoslovakia? I would put it to you if you like, but I would so much prefer that you try to remember it yourself. Don't you remember that your own orders contained a provision for parachutists being dropped for sabotage purposes in Czechoslovakia?

KEITEL: No.

SIR DAVID MAXWELL-FYFE: You don't?

KEITEL: No, I do not remember the order.

SIR DAVID MAXWELL-FYFE: I refer you to it. My Lord, it is Page 21 and 22 of the document book.

KEITEL: Which document book, please?

SIR DAVID MAXWELL-FYFE: Yes. It ought to be your first document book, and quite early on. It is part of the *Fall Grün*, which is Document 388-PS, and it is Item 11. I think it is somewhere about Page 15 or 16 or 20. You remember the Schmundt minutes and then it is divided into items.

The Tribunal will find it at the foot of Page 21:
[Turning to the defendant.]
"For the success of this operation, cooperation with the Sudeten German frontier population, with deserters from the Czechoslovakian Army, with parachutists or airborne troops, and with units of the sabotage service will be of importance."

KEITEL: May I read the paragraph that I think you mean?

SIR DAVID MAXWELL-FYFE: Yes; it is headed "Missions for the Branches of the Armed Forces…"

KEITEL: "Missions for the Branches of the Armed Forces." It states:
"For success, cooperation with the Sudeten German frontier population and the deserters from the Czechoslovakian Army, with parachutists or airborne troops and with units of the sabotage service can be of importance."
These parachutists and airborne troops were in fact to be set to work on frontier fortifications, as I explained yesterday, since army authorities believed that the artillery resources at our command were insufficient to permit our combating them with artillery.
This does not mean parachutists or saboteurs, but actual members of the German Air Force, and the sabotage service is mentioned at the end.

SIR DAVID MAXWELL-FYFE: The sabotage service must be people who are going to do sabotage if they are going to be of any use, must they not? They do sabotage, don't they?

KEITEL: Undoubtedly; but not by means of airborne troops and parachutists, but through saboteurs in the frontier areas who offer their services for this kind of work. Yes, that is what they are thinking of. We had many such people in the Sudeten region.

SIR DAVID MAXWELL-FYFE: I am not going to argue with you, but I want to have it clear. I now want to come to the way in which this order of the *Führer* was announced. You will find the order – the Tribunal will find it on Page 64 – but what I want him to look at if he would be so kind, is Page 66 of the book, Page 25, Defendant, of your book. The second sentence of the Defendant Jodl's "To the Commanders" about this order. That is on Page 25, and Defendant Jodl says: "This order is for the commanders only and must not under any circumstances fall into enemy hands." Was that because you and the Defendant Jodl were ashamed of the order, that you had this secrecy provision put on it?

KEITEL: I have not found it yet, and I would like to know the connection. Page 25 is a teletype letter.

SIR DAVID MAXWELL-FYFE: From the *Oberkommando* Wehrmacht, dated 19 October. Now have you got it, the second sentence?

KEITEL: Dated 18 October 1942?

SIR DAVID MAXWELL-FYFE: 19 October, issuing order of the 18th. "This order is for commanders only and must not under any circumstances fall into enemy hands." Was that because you were ashamed of the order, that it was put like that?

KEITEL: I have not seen the letter and I think General Jodl should be asked about it. I do not know the contents, but I have already stated the opinion of both of us. I cannot give you the reason.

SIR DAVID MAXWELL-FYFE: You can't give me the reason for this secrecy?

KEITEL: I do not know the motives behind it and I would ask you to put this question to General Jodl. I have not seen it. But I have already stated my own views and those of General Jodl.

SIR DAVID MAXWELL-FYFE: Well, now, I want you to look at the way that even Hitler expresses it with regard to this. If you look – I guess it is Page 31 in our book. It is a report from Hitler wherein he says:
> "The report which should appear on this subject in the Armed Forces communiqué will state briefly and laconically that a sabotage, terror, or destruction unit has been encountered and exterminated to the last man." (Document Number 503-PS)

You were doing your best – and when I say "you", I mean you

collectively, Hitler, yourself, and Jodl and everyone else concerned. You were doing your best to keep quiet about this, about anything being known about this order, weren't you?

KEITEL: That was not my impression; on the contrary, in every case we subsequently published the facts in the Wehrmacht orders, the Wehrmacht report. It is my recollection, namely, that in the Wehrmacht report we stated that such and such an incident had occurred, followed by such and such consequences. That is my recollection.

SIR DAVID MAXWELL-FYFE: I am now only going to ask you to look at one document further on, because in that regard, you remember, after the Soviet Union tried certain people at Kharkov, when you were trying to get up some counter-propaganda – now, look at this document, about these executions, it is Page 308, Document UK-57. You have got a copy of it. I am going to ask you about only two incidents. You see it is a memorandum and the passage that I want you to look at is Number 2, the fourth memorandum, Paragraph 2, which is headed "Attempted Attacks on the Battleship Tirpitz". Do you see that?

KEITEL: Just one moment, I have not found it yet. Battleship Tirpitz, oh, yes.

SIR DAVID MAXWELL-FYFE: Have you got it? Just listen, now:
"At the end of October 1942 a British Commando that had come to Norway in a cutter, had orders to carry out an attack on the Battleship Tirpitz in Drontheim Fjord, by means of a two-man torpedo. The action failed since both torpedoes, which were attached to the cutter, were lost in the stormy sea. From among the crew, consisting of six Englishmen and four Norwegians, a party of three Englishmen and two Norwegians were challenged on the Swedish border; however, only the British seaman in civilian clothes, Robert Paul Evans, born 14 January 1922, in London, could be arrested and the others escaped into Sweden.

"Evans had a pistol pouch in his possession, such as are used to carry weapons under the armpit, and also a knuckle duster."

And now the next page:

"Violence representing a breach of international law could not be proved."

Did incidents such as that, under this order, come to your attention?

KEITEL: I do not remember the actual incident, but I can see that it has been reported by the department.

SIR DAVID MAXWELL-FYFE: Well, now you have told us that you have been a soldier for 41 years; that emphasizes your military position. What, in the name of all military tradition, has that boy done wrong by coming from a two-man torpedo to make an attack on a battleship; what had he done wrong?

KEITEL: No, this is an attack against a weapon of war, if carried out by soldiers in their capacity of members of the armed forces, it is an attack made with the object of eliminating a battleship by means of sabotage.

SIR DAVID MAXWELL-FYFE: But why, why should you not if you were prepared to go on a two-man torpedo for an attack against a battleship, what is wrong with a sailor doing that? I want to understand what is in your mind. What do you, as a man who has been a soldier for 40 years, what do you see wrong for a man doing that, towing out a torpedo against a battleship? Tell us. I cannot understand what is wrong.

KEITEL: This is no more wrong than an attack with an aerial bomb if it is successful. I recognize that it is right, that it is a perfectly permissible attack.

SIR DAVID MAXWELL-FYFE: Well now, if you did not see that incident I will not go through putting the others in, as they are all just the same, men in uniform coming up to the Gironde to attack German ships.

What I want to understand is this. You were a Field Marshal, standing in the boots of Blucher, Gneisenau, and Moltke. How did you tolerate all these young men being murdered, one after the other without making any protests?

KEITEL: I have stated here in detail my reasons for not making any further resistance or objection; and I cannot alter any statement now. I know that these incidents occurred and I know the consequences.

SIR DAVID MAXWELL-FYFE: But, Field Marshal, I want you to understand this. As far as I know, in the German military code, as in every military code, there is no obligation on the part of a soldier to obey an order which he knows is wrong, which he knows is contrary to the laws of war and law. It is the same in your army, and our army, and I think in every army, isn't that so?

KEITEL: I did not personally carry out the orders of 18 October 1942. I was not present either at the mouth of the Gironde or at the attack on the battleship Tirpitz. I knew only that the order was issued, together with all the threats of punishment which made it so difficult for the commanders to alter or deviate from the order on their own initiative. You, Sir David, asked me yourself whether I considered this order to be right or to serve any useful purpose and I have given you a definite answer: that I could not have prevented the action taken at the mouth of the Gironde or in the case of Tirpitz if I had wanted to.

SIR DAVID MAXWELL-FYFE: You see my difficulty. I have given you only two cases; there are plenty more. There are others which occurred in Italy which we have heard. The point I am putting to you is this: You were the representative; that you have told us a hundred times, of the military tradition. You had behind you an officers corps with all its…

KEITEL: No, Sir David, I must deny that. I was not responsible either for the Navy or for the Army or for the Air Force. I was not a commander; I was a Chief of Staff and I had no authority to intervene in the execution of orders in the various branches of the Armed Forces, each of which had its own Commander-in-Chief.

SIR DAVID MAXWELL-FYFE: We have heard about your staff rank, but I want to make this point perfectly clear. You were a Field Marshal, Kesselring was a Field Marshal, Milch was a Field Marshal, all, I gather, with military training behind them and all having their influence if not their command, among the Armed Forces of Germany. How was it that there was not one man of your rank, of your military tradition, with the courage to stand up and oppose cold-blooded murder? That is what I want to know.

KEITEL: I did not do it; I made no further objection to these things. I can say no more and I cannot speak for others.

SIR DAVID MAXWELL-FYFE: Now, let us pass if you can say no more than that. I want to see what you did with regard to our French allies because I have been asked to deal with some matters for the French Delegation.

You remember that on the Eastern Front you captured some Frenchmen who were fighting with the Russians. Do you remember making an order about that? You captured some De Gaullists, as you called them, that is Free French people who were fighting for the Russians. Do you remember your action with regard to that?

KEITEL: I recollect the transmission of a *Führer* order in regard to the surrender of these Frenchmen to their lawful government, which was recognized by us.

SIR DAVID MAXWELL-FYFE: That is not, of course, the part of the order I want to put to you.

"Detailed investigations are to be made in appropriate cases with regard to relatives of Frenchmen fighting for the Russians. If the investigation reveals that relatives have given assistance to facilitate escape from France, then severe measures are to be taken.

"OKW/Wi. Rü is to make the necessary preparations with the respective military commander or the Higher SS and Police Leader in France. – Signed – Keitel."

Can you imagine anything more dreadful than taking severe measures against the mother of a young man who has helped him to go and fight with the allies of his country? Can you imagine anything more despicable?

KEITEL: I can think of many things since I have lost sons of my own in the war. I am not the inventor of this idea; it did not originate with me; I only transmitted it.

SIR DAVID MAXWELL-FYFE: You appreciate the difference, Defendant, between the point which you made and the point which I make. Losing sons in a war is a terrible tragedy. Taking severe measures against a mother of a boy who wants to go and fight for his country's allies, I am suggesting to you, is despicable. The one is a tragedy; the other is the height of brutality. Do you not agree?

KEITEL: I can only say that it does not state the consequences of the investigations and findings. I do not know.

SIR DAVID MAXWELL-FYFE: Well, if that is all the answer you can make I will ask you to look at something else.

KEITEL: No, I should like to add that I regret that any families were held responsible for the misdeeds of their sons.

SIR DAVID MAXWELL-FYFE: Well, I will not waste the time by taking up the word "misdeed". If you think that is a misdeed it is not worth our discussing it further. I just want to protest against your word.

Now, let us see; that was not an isolated case. Just look at Page 110 (a) of the document book which you have, Page 122. This is an order quite early on 1 October 1941.

"Attacks committed on members of the Armed Forces lately in the occupied territories give reason to point out that it is advisable that military commanders always have at their disposal a number of hostages of different political tendencies, namely:

"(1) Nationalists,

"(2) Democratic-bourgeois, and

"(3) Communists.

"It is important that these should include well-known leading personalities, or members of their families whose names are to be made public.

"Hostages belonging to the same group as the culprit are to be shot in case of attacks.

"It is asked that commanders be instructed accordingly. – Signed – Keitel." (Document 1590-PS).

Why were you so particular that, if you happened to arrest a democratic-bourgeois, your commanders should have a sufficient bag of democratic-bourgeois to shoot as hostages? I thought you were not a politician.

KEITEL: I was not at all particular and the idea did not originate with me; but it is in accordance with the instructions, the official regulations, regarding hostages which I discussed yesterday or on the day before and which state that those held as hostages must come from the circles responsible for the attacks. That is the explanation, or confirmation, of that as far as my memory goes.

SIR DAVID MAXWELL-FYFE: Did you agree with that as a course of action, that if you found a member of a democratic-bourgeois family who had been taking part in, say, sabotage or resistance, that you should shoot a number of democratic-bourgeois on his behalf? Did you approve of that?

KEITEL: I have already explained how orders for shooting hostages, which were also given, were to be applied and how they were to be carried out in the case of those deserving of death and who had already been sentenced.

SIR DAVID MAXWELL-FYFE: I am asking you a perfectly simple question, Defendant. Did you or did you not approve of a number of democratic-bourgeois to be taken as hostages, for one democratic-bourgeois who happened to be…

KEITEL: It does not say so in the document; it says only that hostages must be taken; but it says nothing about shooting them.

SIR DAVID MAXWELL-FYFE: Would you mind looking at it since you corrected me so emphatically? Depending upon the membership of the culprit, that is, whether he is a nationalist, or a democratic-bourgeois or Communist, "hostages of the corresponding group are to be shot in case of attacks".

KEITEL: If that is in the document then I must have signed it that way. The document referring to the conference with the commanders shows clearly how it was carried out in practice.

SIR DAVID MAXWELL-FYFE: Now answer my question. Did you approve of that?

KEITEL: I personally had different views on the hostage system, but I signed it, because I had been ordered to do so.

SIR DAVID MAXWELL-FYFE: You say you had a different view. Will you just look at a letter from Herr Terboven, who was in charge in

Norway, Document 870-PS, and it is Page 85, 71 (a), RF-281. This is a report from Terboven for the information of the *Führer* and I want you to look at Paragraph 2, "Countermeasures", Subparagraph 4. Do you see it? Have you got it, Defendant? I am sorry, I did give you the number; probably you did not hear it, 71 (a), Page 71 (a) of the document book. So sorry I did not make it clear. My. Lord, I am told that this has been put in by the French Prosecution as Exhibit RF-281. I gave it a GB number, as I recall.

THE PRESIDENT: What number is it?

SIR DAVID MAXWELL-FYFE: RF-281.
[Turning to the defendant.] Do you find Section 2, Paragraph 4? That is:

"Now I have just received a teleprint from Field Marshal Keitel, asking for a regulation to be issued, making members of the personnel, and, if necessary their relatives, collectively responsible for cases of sabotage occurring in their establishments (joint responsibility of relatives). This demand serves a purpose and promises success only if I am actually allowed to perform executions by firing squads. If this is not possible, such a decree would have exactly the opposite effect."

Opposite the word "if I am actually allowed to perform executions by firing squads" there is the pencil note from you, "Yes, that is best". So that is a third example where I suggest that you, yourself, are approving and encouraging the shooting of next of kin for the act of some member of their family. What do you say to that, your own pencil mark?

KEITEL: I did make that marginal note. An order given in this matter was different. A reply was given which was different. I wrote that note.

SIR DAVID MAXWELL-FYFE: That is what I wanted to know. Why did you write this remark, "Yes, that is best", approving of a firing squad for relatives of people who had committed some occupation offence in Norway? Why did you think it was best that there should be a firing squad for the relations? Why?

KEITEL: It was not done and no order to that effect was given. A different order was given.

SIR DAVID MAXWELL-FYFE: That is not what I am asking, and I shall give you one more chance of answering it. Why did you put your pencil on that document, "Yes, that is best"?

KEITEL: I am no longer in a position to explain that today, in view of the fact that I see hundreds of documents daily. I wrote it and I admit it now.

SIR DAVID MAXWELL-FYFE: Of course, unless it means something entirely different from what you have written, it meant that you approved it yourself and thought the best course was that the relations should be shot by a firing squad.
I think Your Lordship said that you wished to adjourn.

THE PRESIDENT: Yes.

SIR DAVID MAXWELL-FYFE: I am not finished, My Lord. I have a few matters for Monday morning.

THE PRESIDENT: Well, the defendant can return to the dock, and we will proceed with the other applications.

[The defendant left the stand.]

Sir David, shall we deal with these applications in the same way as we have done before?

SIR DAVID MAXWELL-FYFE: Yes, My Lord. The first one that I have is an application on behalf of the Defendant Kaltenbrunner for a witness called Hoess, who was former Commander of the Auschwitz Concentration Camp. My Lord, there is no objection on the part of the Prosecution to that.

THE PRESIDENT: So that is the application which has to be made by a great number of the defendants' counsel.

SIR DAVID MAXWELL-FYFE: Oh, yes, Your Lordship is quite right.

My Lord, as Commandant of the Auschwitz Concentration Camp, the Prosecution feel that he could contribute to the information of the Tribunal, if no objection is forthcoming;

THE PRESIDENT: Dr. Stahmer, I see that you are among the counsel who applied for him. Is there anything you wish to add about that?

DR. STAHMER: I have nothing to add to my written application.

THE PRESIDENT: Thank you. Then the Tribunal will consider this, you see, after you have dealt with them.

SIR DAVID MAXWELL-FYFE: My Lord, the next one is Dr. Naville. Dr. Naville was allowed as witness to the Defendant Göring, provided he can be located. He has been located in Switzerland and I understand he has informed the Tribunal that he sees no use in his coming here as a witness for Göring, and he is now asked for by Dr. Nelte, Counsel for Keitel, to prove that prisoners of war had been treated according to the rules of the Geneva Convention, Dr. Naville having been a representative of the Red Cross. Dr. Nelte, I am told, will be satisfied with an interrogatory, and the Prosecution have no objection to an interrogatory.

THE PRESIDENT: Dr. Nelte?

DR. NELTE: That is correct; I agree, providing that I am allowed to put my questions to Dr. Naville in writing.

But may I add something here, not to this application to present evidence, but with reference to another application, which I already submitted to the Prosecution through the Translation Division yesterday or the day before. My application to admit Hitler's stenographers as witnesses was rejected by the Tribunal as irrelevant. I have now received a letter and an affidavit from one of these stenographers, and in that affidavit I find a passage which refers to Keitel's attitude towards Hitler at interviews and conferences with him.

Public opinion has criticized the defendants as being in the habit of quoting dead men whenever they want to say anything in their favour; and similar statements have been made in this Court. The Defendant Keitel requests that the part of the affidavit which I have already submitted and which I intend to submit, be admitted as an affidavit so that the witness can still be rejected and yet it will be possible for me to submit that passage of the affidavit with the agreement of the Prosecution.

SIR DAVID MAXWELL-FYFE: If Dr. Nelte, My Lord, will submit the passage, we will consider it, but I have not had the chance of doing it up until now.

THE PRESIDENT: Well, if you will carry out that course and if you want, there is no objection to it.

SIR DAVID MAXWELL-FYFE: Very well, you will let me have it, a copy of it?

DR. NELTE: Certainly.

SIR DAVID MAXWELL-FYFE: My Lord, the next application is on behalf of the Defendant Von Schirach, a request to submit an affidavit of Dr. Hans Carossa. The gist of the affidavit is that the defendant tried to keep himself independent of Party directives in matters of literature and art and that, while *Gauleiter* in Vienna, he repeatedly intervened on behalf of Jews and concentration camp inmates. My Lord, the Prosecution have no objection to an affidavit being filed.

The next is an application on behalf of the Defendant Funk for interrogatories to be submitted to Mr. Messersmith, dealing with Funk's relation to the Party and his work in the Reich Ministry of Propaganda. My Lord, the Prosecution have no objection, but remind the Tribunal that the Defendant Funk has already, on 15 March, asked permission to submit another affidavit to Mr. Messersmith, dealing with Mr. Messersmith's affidavit. The Prosecution did not raise any objections, but the Tribunal has not, as far as we know, granted that yet. So I wanted the Tribunal to know there was a previous request…

THE PRESIDENT: Do you mean an affidavit or interrogatory on 15 March?

SIR DAVID MAXWELL-FYFE: Interrogatories.

THE PRESIDENT: Interrogatories? Surely we must have dealt with it.

SIR DAVID MAXWELL-FYFE: Well, that is the information that my office had. They have not seen the…

THE PRESIDENT: I see.

SIR DAVID MAXWELL-FYFE: In case the Tribunal had not dealt with it, we want to point out that there is one outstanding. We have no objection to either.

Then the Defendant Rosenberg requests Hitler's decree to Rosenberg of June 1943. There is no objection on the part of the Prosecution. I am told that we can not trace any previous application but the position at the moment is that we haven't any objection to it.

Then, My Lord, the next is Von Neurath, an application for a questionnaire for Professor Kossuth, long a resident of Prague. Really they ask for interrogatories, My Lord, there is no objection to interrogatories.

Then, My Lord, there is an application in reverse, if I may put it so, from Dr. Dix on behalf of the Defendant Schacht, the downgrading of Herr Huelse, who was drafted as a witness, to an affidavit. My Lord, we have no objection to that.

DR. DIX: This is the witness Huelse. He was granted to me as a witness. In order to shorten and simplify the proceedings, I have decided to forfeit the right to hear the witness because there was an affidavit. I have received the affidavit. While my application to dispense with the witness was pending, however, the witness arrived in Nuremberg. He is here now, and I think therefore, that it will be best for him to stay and for me to be allowed to examine him by confronting him with his own affidavit, asking him to confirm it, and then put some additional questions to him. I think that would be much more practical than having the witness here to no purpose, sending him back again and retaining only the affidavit. My purpose, in any case, was partly to avoid the complications connected with getting him here.

SIR DAVID MAXWELL-FYFE: Do you withdraw the application to have the affidavit...

THE PRESIDENT: Is the witness Huelse a prisoner or not, or an internee?

DR. DIX: He is a free witness. He is not in detention and he is free to move about Nuremberg.

THE PRESIDENT: Can he remain here until the Defendant Schacht's case comes on?

DR. DIX: I hope so. He has told me that he can stay and that he is willing to do so.

SIR DAVID MAXWELL-FYFE: My Lord, we have no objection. The Tribunal has already granted him as a witness. If Dr. Dix wants him as a witness, of course we have no objection to it.

The next one is an application on behalf of the Defendant Streicher, for an affidavit from a Dr. Herold. To put it quite shortly, the Prosecution suggest that it should be interrogatories rather than an affidavit and on that basis we would make no objection.

My Lord, there is only one thing I have to say. I had a most useful discussion with Dr. Dix last night, following out the Tribunal's suggestion of going through the documents. Dr. Dix was most helpful in explaining the purpose of his documents and what they were. I do suggest that if any of the Defence Counsel when they are explaining the documents would also care to explain the purport of their witnesses – I do not want to embarrass them in any way – but if they would voluntarily explain the purport of witnesses, either to Mr. Dodd or myself, we might be able to save them a great deal of time, by indicating whether the evidence of that witness would be agreed to or might be the subject of objection.

I only throw it out now, as we are going to meet over the documents, and if they would extend it to witnesses, I am sure we could achieve a most profitable cooperation.

THE PRESIDENT: You are suggesting, Sir David, are you, that they should explain to you the nature of the evidence which the witness was going to give?

SIR DAVID MAXWELL-FYFE: Yes.

THE PRESIDENT: And if the Prosecution were not going to dispute it, that it might be incorporated in an affidavit?

SIR DAVID MAXWELL-FYFE: Yes, that we could probably

dispense with the witness, and probably incorporate that in an affidavit. Of course, I have been told the general purport of the witness, because I attended on the application, but if they could elaborate on it a little more as it often happens when they see the witness and let me know what the scope of the witness' testimony would be, I could probably concede, either in whole or in part, and save them a lot of work and the Tribunal a lot of time.

THE PRESIDENT: Well, I think the Tribunal would like to know whether the defendants' counsel think that is a possible course, whether it might lead to some shortening of the defence. Could Dr. Dix possibly tell us whether he thinks it would be possible?

DR. DIX: Of course, I cannot make any statement on the views of my colleagues, since I cannot read their minds. All I can say at the moment is that I will recommend to my colleagues, as unusually helpful and practical, the kind of conversation which I had the honour of having with Sir David yesterday. Personally, I think that my colleagues too will agree to this procedure unless there is any particular objection to it, which is, of course, always possible. I cannot say any more at the moment.

THE PRESIDENT: You understand what Sir David was suggesting, that such a conversation should apply not only to documents but also to witnesses and if you could indicate rather more fully than you do in your applications what the subject of their evidence was going to be, possibly the Prosecution might be able to say in those circumstances that upon those matters they should not propose to dispute the evidence and therefore it might be incorporated in an affidavit?

SIR DAVID MAXWELL-FYFE: My Lord, if Your Lordship allows me to interject, if they care to bring a statement on a particular witness' testimony, the Prosecution would, I am sure, in many particulars be prepared to say, "Well, you produce that statement on that point and we will admit it, without any formality."

THE PRESIDENT: Perhaps, Dr. Dix, you and the other counsel for the defendants could consider that matter.

DR. DIX: I have understood it to be exactly as Your Lordship has just stated it. I discussed both the witnesses and the documents with Sir David and that was very helpful; and in that sense I will…

THE PRESIDENT: If that is all we need do at the moment, then…

SIR DAVID MAXWELL-FYFE: If Your Lordship pleases, yes.

THE PRESIDENT: Then the Tribunal will adjourn.

[The Tribunal adjourned until 8 April 1946 at 1000 hours.]